Crosses, Christian and Otherwise

Their Form and Meaning

Crosses,
Christian and Otherwise
Their Form and Meaning

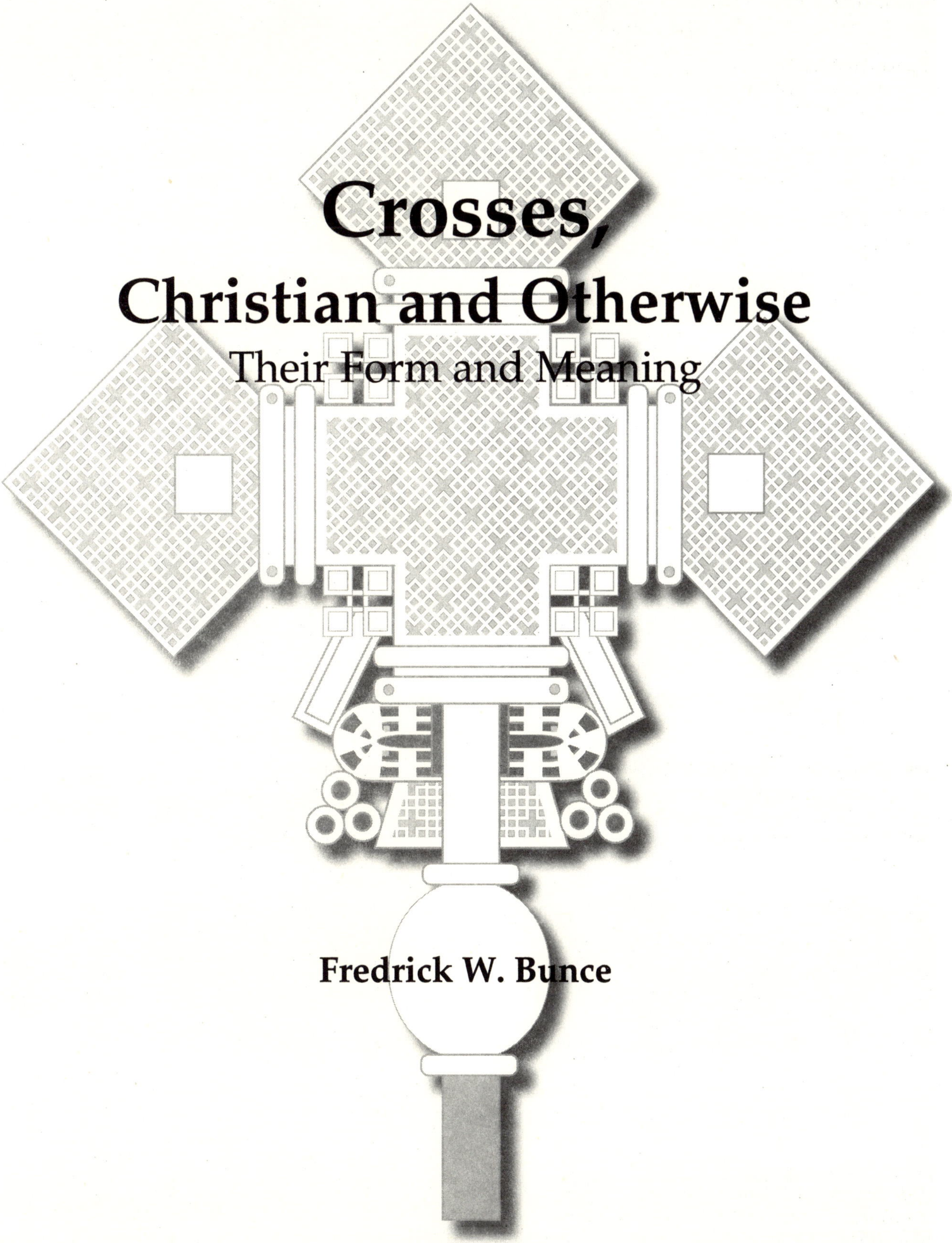

Fredrick W. Bunce

DK PRINTWORLD
Publishers of Indian Traditions

Cataloging in Publication Data — DK

[Courtesy: D.K. Agencies (P) Ltd. <docinfo@dkagencies.com>]

Bunce, Fredrick W.

Crosses, Christian and otherwise : their form and meaning / Fredrick W. Bunce.

p. cm.

Includes bibliographical references (p.) and index.

ISBN 13: 9788124607374

1. Holy Cross. 2. Crosses. 3. Christian art and symbolism. I. Title.

DDC 232.963 23

ISBN 13: 978-81-246-0737-4 **ISBN** 10: 81-246-0737-0

First published in India, 2014

Printed and published by:
D.K. Printworld (P) Ltd.
Regd. office : "Vedaśrī," F-395, Sudarshan Park
(Metro Station: Ramesh Nagar)
New Delhi - 110 015
Phones : (011) 2545 3975, 2546 6019; *Fax* : (011) 2546 5926
e-mail : indology@dkprintworld.com
Web : www.dkprintworld.com

Preface

While doing research for a manuscript entitled *Cruciform, Circular and Apsidal Temple Plans in India: Genesis and Iconography,* I attempted to make certain parallels between obvious cruciform Indian temples and the various cross forms encountered in Christian iconography. In preparing an Appendix, I was faced with a number of sources, primarily on the Internet, which listed and/or illustrated scores of cross forms. Without exception, they stated that there were 200 or 300 different ecclesiastical and heraldic or mundane crosses. But, at best, the various sites, each illustrated separately approximately 100 crosses, give or take a few.

What about the other hundred or so forms? This sent me searching various sites and sources in the attempt to identify the myriad cruciforms just out of interest. Not only was the search, the research one of the most intriguing parts of the project, but also the redrawing of the various crosses using Adobe PageMaker 6.0 offered many challenges. The result was an amassing of over 500 crosses and their variations many of which fell outside the "200 or 300 different ecclesiastical and heraldic or mundane crosses", noted above. The vast majority of the crosses found were used prior to the twentieth century. The possibilities of cruciform designs are endless. Therefore, contemporary cruciforms — i.e. twentieth- and twenty-first-century designs — were, for the most part, not considered with a few exceptions.

Fredrick W. Bunce

Contents

Preface v

List of Figures ix

Introduction 1

- Christian Cross Iconography 2
- Types of Crosses 4
- Christian Cruciform Churches 5
- Hindu and Buddhist Cruciform Temples 6
- Coats of Arms 10
- Shields 12
- Ecclesiastical Implications 14
- Crosses with Militaristic Implications 15
- Crosses with Professional or Trade Implications 15
- Scope 15

Crux Simplex and Tau Crosses 18

- Militaristic Tau Crosses 23

Latin Crosses 24

- Ankh and Chi Rho Variation 30
- Pommée and Botonée Variation 33
- Byzantine, Manx and Coptic Variation 37
- Potent and Crosslet Variation 40
- Moline, Recercelée, Fleurée Variation 41
- Annuleted Variation 44
- Rope Variation 46

Miscellaneous Variation 47

- Processional Variation 56
- Double Crosspiece Variation 60
  - Militaristic Variation 69
- Triple Crosspiece Variation 70
- Militaristic Variation 74
  - Fitchy Variation 77

Greek Crosses 83

- Surface Variation 86

Contents (Continued)

Crosslet/Potence Variation 89

Coptic Variation 92

Interlaced Variation 95

Gammadia Variation 99

Boton/Pommé Variation 101

Annuleted Variation 104

Pattée and Patonce Variation 108

Star/Flame Variation 112

Jerusalem Variation 115

Plant/Animal Variation 118

Anchry, Milrine, Moline, Recercelée Variation 123

Greek Crosses: Militaristic Variation 129

Fleur-de-lys Variation 135

Fitchy Variation 138

Maltese Variation 145

Fylfot/Svastika Variation 150

Miscellaneous Variation 161

Solar Crosses 176

Militaristic Solar Crosses 190

Saltire Crosses 191

Baptismal Variation 201

Miscellaneous Crosses 203

Coloured Crosses 208

Resources 209

Cross Index 213

List of Figures

Figure		Page
1	The fish as symbol	4
2	Basic Cross Types: (left to right) Tau Cross (*crux commissa*), Latin Cross (*crux immissa*), Greek Cross (*crux immissa*), Saltire Cross (*crux decussatta*) and Sun Cross	4
3	Basilica Ulpia, Rome (*c.* CE 112), detail of basilica	5
4	Old St. Peter's, Rome (*c.* CE 333), detail of basilica	5
5	Salisbury Cathedral, England (a. CE 1220)	6
6	Paraśurāmeśvara Temple, Bhubaneswar, (*c.* CE 650)	7
7	Jaina Temple No. 15, Deogaṛh, Uttar Pradesh, (*c.* CE 775)	7
8	Sūrya Temple Ensemble, Sabhāmaṇḍapa, Moḍherā, Gujarat (CE 1026)	8
9	Svarga-Brahma Temple, Ālampur, Andhra Pradesh (*c.* CE 689)	8
10	Kālikā-mātā Temple, Chittorgaṛh, Rajasthan (*c.* CE 700)	9
11	Gupta Temple (Daśāvatāra Temple), Deogaṛh, Uttar Pradesh (*c.* CE 500-525)	9
12	Neak Pean, ensemble (left), Aṅgkor (a. CE 1175) Indicating Widdershin Fylfot Cross (right)	10
13	Stūpa I, Sāñcī (third century BCE)	11
14	Nārāyaṇkannur Temple, Ramantali (CE 928)	11
15	Shield types: European (top two rows) and miscellaneous types (bottom row)	13
16	Latin or Greek and Saltire Cross placed upon shield blasoned on a kite, heater and buckler type shield	13

List of Figures (Continued)

17 Bouttonnée Cross II (far left) & Bouttonnée Cross I (2nd from left) and Maltese Cross I (2nd from right) & Maltese Cross I with foot extended (far right) placed upon a heater type shield 14

18 Heraldic elements on round shield: Latin Cross (left), Greek Cross (2nd left), Slavonic Cross (2nd right), and Escarbouche Cross (right) 14

19 "Potent" or "Potence" as crutch (left) or as gallows (right) 16

20 Proportions of the Latin Cross as derived from a Greek Cross 24

Introduction

Introduction

Christian Cross Iconography

Few symbols, few iconographs in the world are more recognizable than the cross. It is seen primarily as a Christian symbol, and its form is recognized by most of the world's population as a symbol of that faith. However, a number of the types of crosses or cross forms, predate the Common Era, and, therefore, Christianity — e.g. the Ansata Cross, the Fylfot Cross and the Solar Cross. Some cruciforms have developed outside the Christian bounds and have later been adapted by that faith.

In ancient times, the cross was a symbol worn by the Assyrian kings Sansirauman as well as Ashurnasirpal as a sign of their majesty, dominance and supremacy. The Persian tombs of Cyrus, Xerxes and Darius have a cruciform element cut into the exterior. The Greek goddess Artemesia (Diana) was shown with a cross behind her head. Numerous crosses are seen in Meso- and South America prior to the European invasions. The popular Celtic Cross is certainly pre-Christian and many scholars believe that it represented the *axis mundi* and is related to the Norse sun wheel.

The common term "cross" may have come from the Old Norse word *kross* or the Old Irish — i.e. Gaelic/Celtic — *cros*. Both *kross* and *cros* are obviously derived from the Latin word *crux*. However, it is interesting to note that the Old English term for what we now call *cross* was *rod* or *rood* and referred to a crucifix — i.e. a cross upon which hung the body of Jesus Christ. The term *rood* is still applied to that physical division, the visual barrier between the nave and the sanctuary of an English church or cathedral — i.e. the rood-screen — upon which is mounted a cross or crucifix. *Rood* is related to the Dutch word of the same meaning, *roede* as well as the German *rute* which denotes a rod and/or a crucifix. In this sense — i.e. rod, *rood, roede, rute* — may be closer to the act of execution as early forms of crucifixion merely employed a tree trunk or beam or post upon which the hapless victim was hung.

The New Testament states that the Christ was "hung on a tree" (Acts 5:30, 10:39, 13:29; Galatians 3:13 and I Peter 2:24). This may have been an unproductive tree (*arbor infelix*) thought only suitable for execution of criminals. Or the victim may have been tied to a beam (*patibulum*) which was raised and affixed to a tree (*arbor infelix*) or post (*crux composita* or *crux acuta*). The term "cross" also appears often in the New Testament — e.g. I Corinthians 1:17; Galatians 2:19 and Philipians 3:18. The question of "tree" or "cross" is a conundrum not pursued here.

The Latin *crux* is related and applied to the term(s) for torture — i.e. *cruciamentum* or *cruciatus*. The term "crucifixion" is a means of execution or torture upon a *crux*. Indeed the terms for torture and cross were related to crucifixion which was a slow and tortuous means of punishment and ultimately death that was practised in the ancient world. Some see the term "cross" as related to the name "Christ". This is erroneous as it is clearly related to the term *cruciamentum* or *cruciatus*.

Crucifixion is essentially a passive form of torture and/or execution — i.e. the victim is affixed to a cross (*crux immissa* or *crux commissa*) or pole (*crux simplex*) either by ropes or nails and left to die. Other than the attaching the victim to the cross, no other form of punishment or physical violation was generally employed. Frequently, it is believed that only the hands or arms were secured and the feet left free. This would have been the quicker form of execution as the weight of the body would quickly weaken the muscles, particularly of the diaphragm, and ultimately cause suffocation. If, on the other hand, the feet were also secured, they would have provided enough support and the advent of death would have been much slower. This form of crucifixion would have ultimately caused death by dehydration, the subsequent shutting down of vital bodily functions, and/or suffocation.

If nails, rather than ropes or some other tether, were used, it is almost certain that the nails were placed just above the wrist rather than through the palm of the hand as is frequently depicted in paintings of the crucifixion of Jesus Christ. This is particularly true if only the hands or arms were secured. If the nails were placed through the palms of the hand alone, the tendons and muscles are so aligned that weight of the body would cause the victim to ultimately tear loose and fall. However, if the feet, too, were nailed, then the legs would have to be flexed at the knee to allow the nails to pierce the foot, or a canted footrest would have to be affixed to the upright so that the nailing might be accommodated. The use of nails through the feet would have been an extra form of torture and pain and would have extended the agony. In Christian art the crucifixion is depicted with the nails through the palms of the hand and the feet are nailed either separately or together — i.e. a four-nail or a three-nail crucifixion.

This symbol that we now universally recognize — i.e. the cross — was not accepted by the Early Christians as a symbol of their faith. The cross was to them a most odious symbol, a repugnant sign connected with death and torture much in the same way that a gibbet or an electric chair might be considered today. As such the Early Christians were loath to depict the crucifixion on any form. In addition, it was not until after the fifth-century that the divinity, crucifixion and resurrection of the Christ was promulgated and almost universally accepted. The pre-eminent symbol accepted and used by the Early Christians was the fish (**Figure 1**). It was not until the fourth century that Constantine's *Labarum*, the *Chi Rho*, came into use. We may view the *Chi Rho* or *Labarum* as a cruciform, but, its initial use was as a representation of the first letters of Christus (*Chi*) Rex (*Rho*) — Christ King. The appearance of the cross (*crux*) as we know it followed in the next century.

Figure 1: The fish as symbol

Types of Crosses

In general there are considered to be four types of *crux* (cross) — i.e. (1) the *crux simplex* (an upright pole), (2) the *crux commissa* (Tau Cross), (3) the *crux immissa* (Latin Cross), and (4) the *crux decussatta* (Saltire or St. Anthony's Cross). The *crux simplex* is, for the most part, not considered as a "cross" in the traditional sense as it is merely an upright pole upon which a person was hung or nailed, as noted above. But, it was a form employed in *cruciamentum* or *cruciatus*. It was the Phoenicians who added the crosspiece to the *crux simplex* making a *crux immissa*. For this very brief consideration, the author has regrouped the various crosses (**Figure 2**) by general shape or form into:

1. Tau Cross and
2. Latin crosses which are rectangular in form and vertical in alignment,
3. Greek cross which is square in form,
4. Saltire cross which is "X" shaped, and
5. Solar cross which is round or has a major round element.

A large number of the crosses are derived from the Greek Cross — i.e. square crosses — and are heraldic in nature. Of these, there are numerous crosses that are militaristic or have militaristic connotations. Many of the Saltire crosses indicate a primarily heraldic use. This was particularly true during the crusades when battle banners frequently displayed a cross or crosses. It is to be noted that the appearance of these cruciforms — i.e. those derived from the Greek Cross and the Saltire Cross — were subsequent to the crusades. Fewer crosses, numerically, are derived from the Latin Cross. This is doubtless due to its verticality. Furthermore, many of the Latin crosses or those derived from the Latin Cross

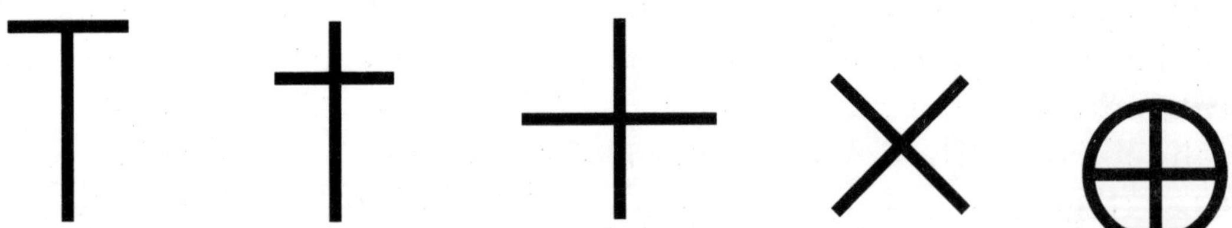

Figure 2: Basic cross types

are exclusively ecclesiastical in nature — e.g. the Latin Cross, the Cruc Humilis, the Calvary Cross and the Lambeau Cross.

Christian Cruciform Churches

It is quite understandable, therefore, that the cruciform assumed iconic significance in the plans of Christian churches. As with any of mans' endeavours these structures were based on pre-existent forms. An early plan is derived from the Roman basilica plan. The design is based upon the Tau Cross or *crux commissa* (**Figure 3**). The Basilica Ulpia is essentially rectangular with an apse at both ends. Rudimentary transepts create a stepped transition between the apse and the main body of the basilica. The basilica was traditionally used as a court of law or for other important public assemblies.

Certainly one of the earliest churches of note that employed the cruciform plan was the basilica of Old St. Peter's of Rome (*c.* CE 333) (**Figure 4**). It possessed the same double colonnade that the Roman basilica employed. The apse is diminished in scale and only one is apparent. It becomes the sanctuary for the Christian church and the locale of the high altar. A distinct transept is seen at the east end forming a Tau Cross plan. Until the

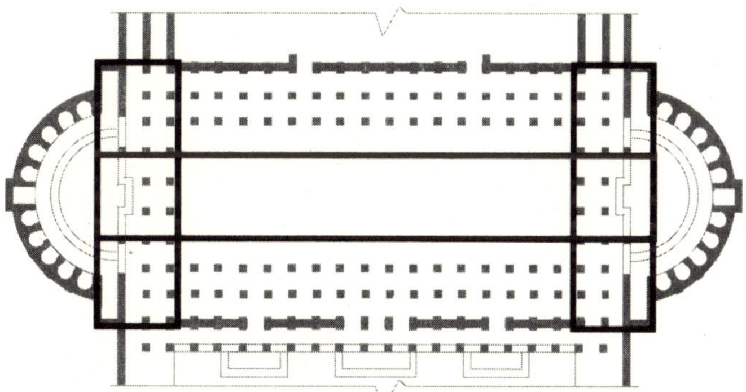

Figure 3: Detail of Basilica Ulpia, Rome (*c.* CE 112)

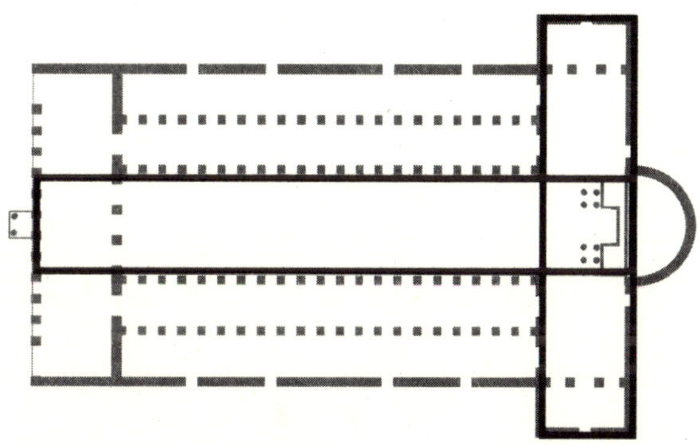

Figure 4: Detail of Old St. Peter's Basilica, Rome (*c.* CE 333)

Renaissance, the cruciform predominated — i.e. a nave with a single transept, or in some cases, a double transept — in the design of Christian churches, small and large, throughout Europe. Medieval architects or master builders of Christian churches experimented with form and design. The basic design form, however, tended to be the Latin Cross. But, there were variations.

Many of the designs were distinctive and often regional in character. The Salisbury Cathedral's plan, clearly cruciform, is based neither on the Tau Cross nor the Latin Cross, but upon the Patriarchal Cross with a double transept and the apse or sanctuary becomes rectilinear rather than hemispherical (**Figure 5**).

The cruciform is not only applicable to ecclesiastical edifices of Christianity alone. Its shape and form are found in examples of sacred buildings of many cultures and faiths.

Hindu and Buddhist Cruciform Temples

Even though the cross is a pre-eminent Christian symbol, there are numerous examples throughout the world in which the cruciform is used. They represent the gamut of religious architecture and the spread of civilizations of every variety. In these instances the cruciform does not possess iconographic connections with the Christian faith. Rather, it appears to reflect other implications, some merely design based.

There are numerous Indian temples — i.e. Buddhist, Hindu and Jaina — which are based on a cruciform plan of one type or another. To state that the genesis of these plans was derived from that Christian icon would be foolhardy and patently erroneous since many of the temples were designed before the advent of the many Christian-cruciform ideals, particularly those temples with two transepts.

The elemental cross — i.e. the *crux simplex* or a simple stake sunk into the earth — finds

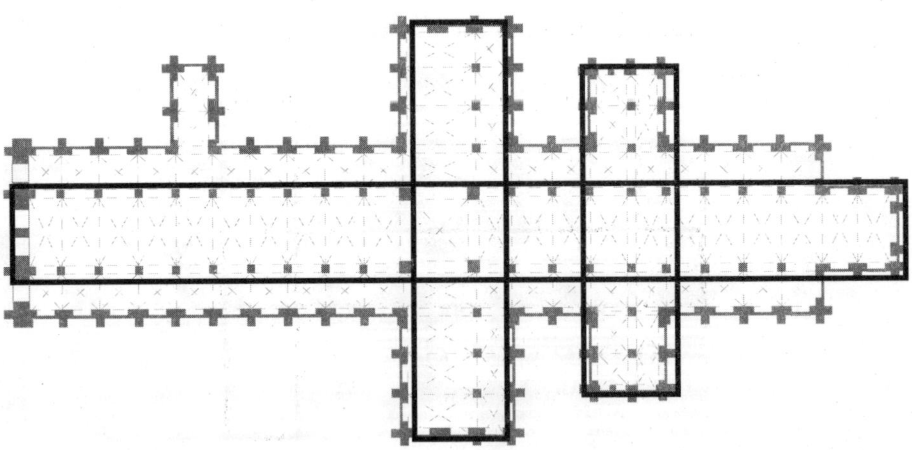

Figure 5: Detail of Salisbury Cathedral, England (a. CE 1220)

a parallel in Bhubaneswar and is exemplified in the Paraśurāmeśvara Temple (**Figure 6**). Here the plan elements of the temple follow each other in a straight line — i.e. strictly axial. Although its *garbhagṛha* and *maṇḍapa* are of different widths, the *crux simplex* is none the less evident, *en plan*.

The Greek Cross, or a square plan, finds few examples among the thousands of temple plans in the vast subcontinent. It is not that the plan was inappropriate. The square was a sacred form to the Hindu faith, whereas the circle was sacred to the Buddhists. Nearly all *garbhagṛhas* of the Hindu temples are square and many are to be found within a larger enclosing architectural element. One salient feature of a square or Greek Cross plan is exemplified in the Jaina Temple No. 15 at Deogaṛh (**Figure 7**). Three shrines and a vestibule comprise the interior of this temple while three shrines and a porch are to be seen on the exterior, creating a Greek Cross plan. Another example of a square or Greek Cross plan is

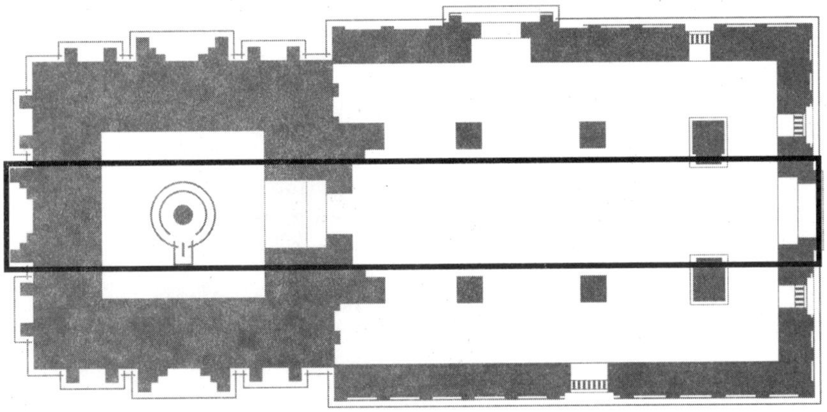

Figure 6: Detail of Paraśurāmeśvara Temple, Bhubaneswar (*c.* CE 650)

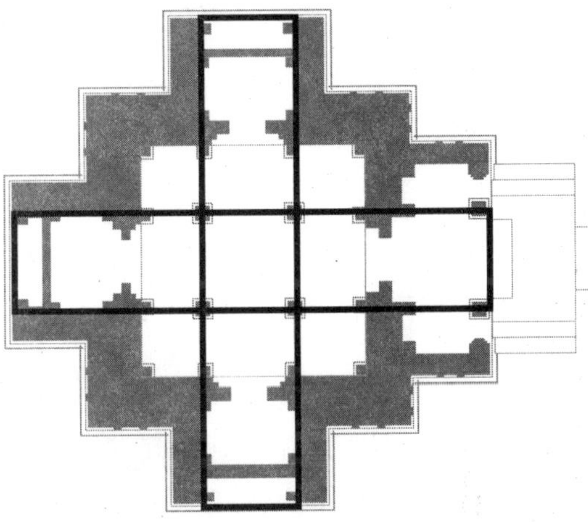

Figure 7: Detail of Jaina Temple No. 15, Deogaṛh, Uttar Pradesh (*c.* CE 775)

seen in the Sabhāmaṇḍapa of the Sūrya Temple Ensemble at Moḍherā. There, the square plan is rotated 45°, however the resultant design is cruciform in alignment (**Figure 8**) and of the Greek Cross variety.

On the other hand, the Latin Cross plan or an axial temple with a prominent transept is seen time and again throughout India. Its numbers attest to this form as being, if not preferred, at least most common. The Svarga-Brahma Temple of Ālampur is a prime example (**Figure 9**) of this cruciform type. The square *garbhagṛha* rests within the surrounding, an enclosing wall creating an ambulatory or *pradakṣiṇāpatha*. Around the exterior are found four porches, one each projecting from each of the exterior façades. They create a Latin Cross, *en plan*.

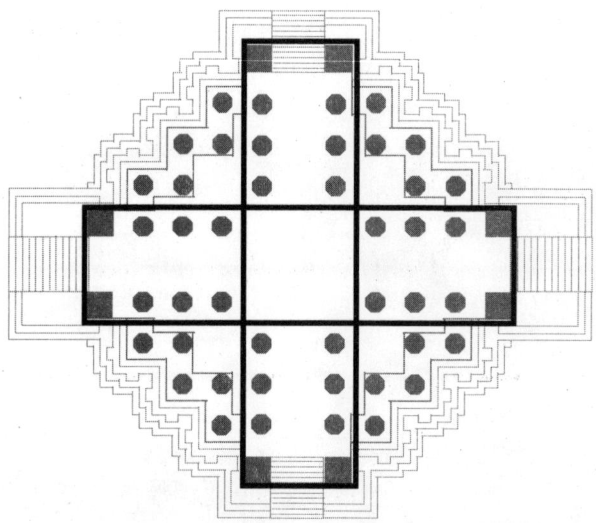

Figure 8: Detail of Sūrya Temple Ensemble, Sabhāmaṇḍapa, Moḍherā, Gujarat (CE 1026)

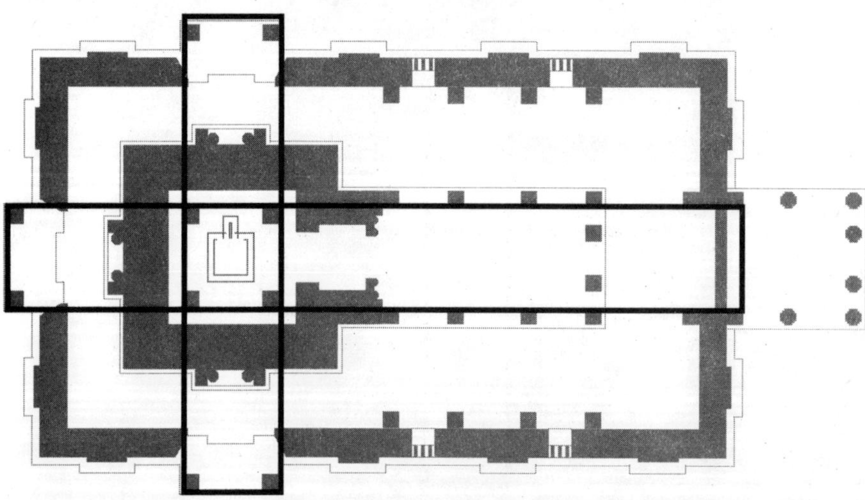

Figure 9: Detail of Svarga-Brahma Temple, Ālampur, Andhra Pradesh (*c.* CE 689)

Numerous temples, particularly in the north of the subcontinent and eastward from Gujarat and Rajasthan, exhibit a plan with a double transept — i.e. recalling the Christo-European Cross of Lorraine, *en forme* (**Figure 10**). They differ from the double transept seen at Salisbury (**Figure 5**), in that the double transepts of India tend to be of equal length. This particular plan found great popularity in the famed and larger temples of Khajurāho — e.g. the Lakṣmaṇa Temple and the Kandarīya Mahādeo Temple. It is to be noted that these porches tended to appear to be more aesthetic in nature than practical as the amount of light that these porches or transepts provided was minimal. On the other hand, they did allow for a freer circulation of air within the interior of the individual temples.

An interesting cruciform temple plan is encountered in the Gupta Temple (Daśāvatāra Temple) of Deogaṛh. Eight extensions — i.e. four at each corner and four centred on each side — create a plan that mimics a Baptismal Cross (**Figure 11**). This plan, like the square or Greek Cross plan, is rarely found.

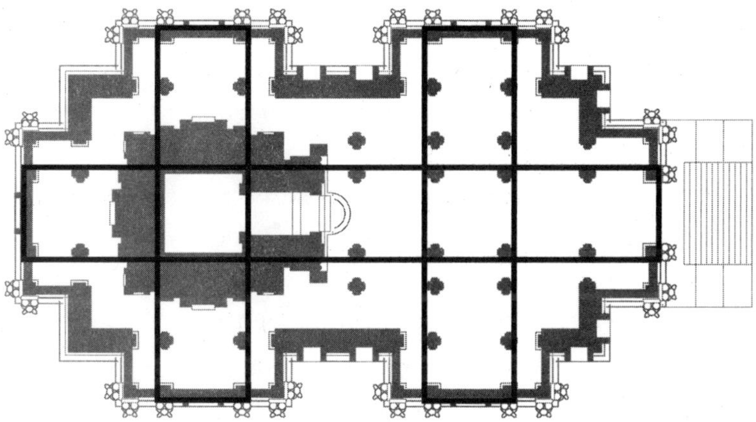

Figure 10: Kālikā-mātā Temple, Chittorgaṛh, Rajasthan (*c*. CE 700)

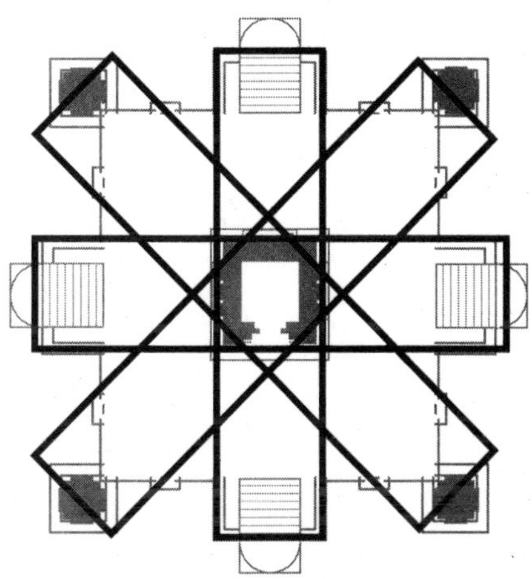

Figure 11: Gupta Temple (Daśāvatāra Temple), Deogaṛh, Uttar Pradesh (*c*. CE 500-25)

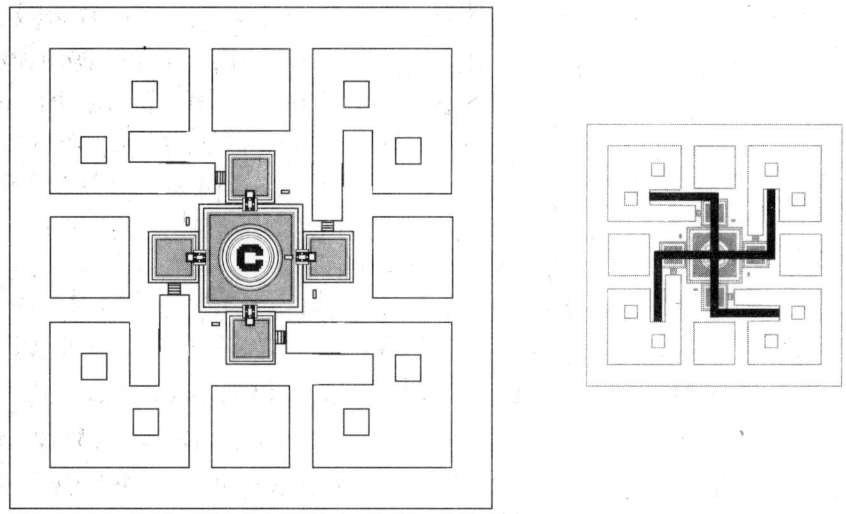

Figure 12: Neak Pean, ensemble (left), Aṅgkor (a. CE 1175), indicating Widdershins Fylfot Cross (right)

Mention must be made of a cruciform monument that is rarely encountered, en plan, and almost never in the plans of a Christian monument — i.e. the Fylfot Cross (*see* Greek Cross: Fylfot/*svastika* Variations). However, within the complex of temples and monuments of the Khmer civilization at Aṅgkor is the small, but important Hindu temple — i.e. Neak Pean (**Figure 12**). Here a Widdershins Fylfot Cross is incorporated into the layout of the gardens surrounding the temple proper. It is seen to be a complex which to that culture is associated with the importance of water. It is of interest that it is the female form of the fylfot which is incorporated into the plan of Neak Pean.

An earlier Indian Buddhist monument makes use also of the Widdershins Fylfot Cross but in a much less obvious manner, and that is the famed Stūpa I of Sāñcī. The immediate ensemble is composed of *stūpa*, its enclosure and four gates oriented to the points of the compass. Here the fylfot is encountered not in the architectural design, but in the ceremonial path, the *pradakṣiṇāpatha*. As a devotee enters any one of the gates and proceeds to accomplish the ritual circumambulation, the path that they trod is roughly in the form of a Widdershins Fylfot Cross (see the dark line in **Figure 13**). It is interesting to note that the circumambulation is clockwise, sunwise, masculine with the right side towards the monument. This would seem to suggest a Sunwise Fylfot Cross.

A ninth cruciform that appears with some frequency particularly in Kerala and Karnataka is related to a form known as the Sun Cross or Solar Cross. Essentially, this cruciform is based upon a circle and generally possesses a vertical and horizontal element or crosspiece. The Nārāyaṇkannur Temple at Ramantali exemplifies this form (**Figure 14**).

Coats of Arms

As noted above, the crusades spawned a proliferation of crosses that were heraldic in

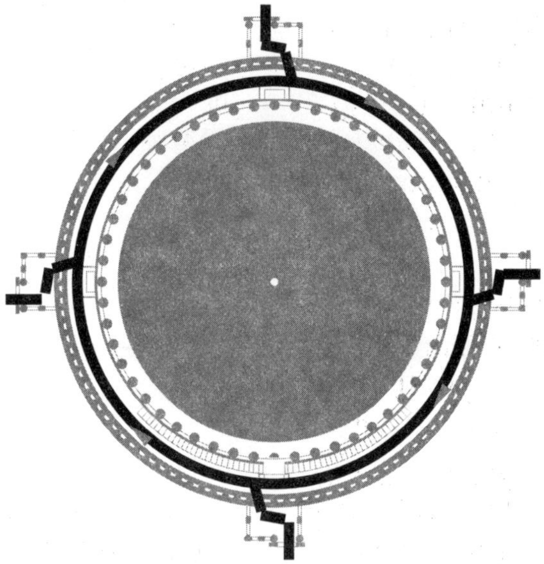

Figure 13: Stūpa I, Sāñcī, India, third century BCE

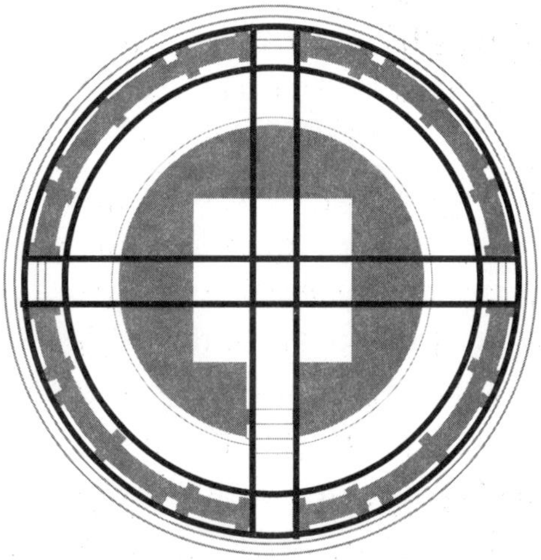

Figure 14: Nārāyaṇkannur Temple, Ramantali, India (CE 928)

nature. They were incorporated into coats of arms — i.e. a symbol of identification, a badge, an emblem or a medieval logo. These were individualized and meant to impart certain information of the bearer to those who observed it. Not only were coats of arms considered symbolic of a particular individual and/or family, they often identified those who were directly employed and/or allied with that person. This became particularly important on the field of battle during this period where the only thing that differentiated one combatant from another was a coat of arms. In the pitch of battle, symbols from the coat of arms were used to identify one's allies as well as enemies. Frequently a salient element of the coat of arms would be attached to the shield as a badge of recognition. Again this was convenient when in the confusion of a melée — i.e. close, personal, hand-to-hand combat — where no clear lines were evident. During the crusades, the cross became the badge-of-the-day, a mark emblazoned upon a shield for quick identification, particularly for the Christians when they were opposing the Muslims. For the Muslims, their badge was either a crescent or a multi-pointed star.

Shields

Shields were generally carried by those who were involved in the close, man-to-man, hand-to-hand combat. These combatants, these knights generally bore one of the following weapons: a sword, a mace, a short spear, a battle axe, flail or a combination of these weapons. Usually a dagger for extremely close combat or when their primary weapon was no longer available was tucked in their belt. In nearly every case a shield was carried as a means of defence. Its employment was to ward off missiles or the blows of an enemy's sword or other weapon. They were neither unwieldy nor excessively heavy as that would impinge on the combatants mobility and drain his physical reserves. Normally, the shields would have been constructed of wood or layers of leather and, at times, covered with a thin sheet of metal. If a shield was hit directly by a forceful blow of a sword, battle axe or even a metal-tipped arrow, their defensive integrity could well have been breached or compromised.

The shield, therefore, was a defensive device, a means of protection rather than an offensive weapon. The shield was to the knight a badge of identity and its forms varied (**Figure 15**). Other combatants, such as archers, usually did not carry a small, easily held shield as they were placed some distance from the melée, or if they did bear a shield it would have been less portable and of a size not easily carried. For the common foot-soldier who possessed weapons of offence, a shield was not always in their repertoire of battle.

The size and shapes of shields employed to display the heraldic symbol were of some importance. The application of either a simple Latin or Greek or Saltire Cross upon a shield whether of the kite, heater or buckler type presented no major design problems whatsoever (**Figure 16**). Other cross forms which are inherently square or cross-axial — e.g. a Bouttonnée Cross or Maltese Cross — when placed upon the field of a rectilinear shield, may have appeared less than satisfactory from a visual standpoint (**Figure 17**). A Bouttonnée Cross II and/or a Maltese Cross I fit upon the shield's field, but the square proportions of the two crosses upon an essentially vertical field may offend some sensitive eye (**Figure 17** [left and second from right, respectively]). The extension of the foot of the Bouttonnée Cross II forming a Bouttonnée Cross I presents no problems (**Figure 17** [second from left]). On the other hand the extension of the foot of the Maltese Cross I presents an ungainly and less than satisfactory solution (**Figure 17** [right]). Clearly, certain cross forms — i.e. the Greek Cross and the Solar Cross types — simply do not lend themselves

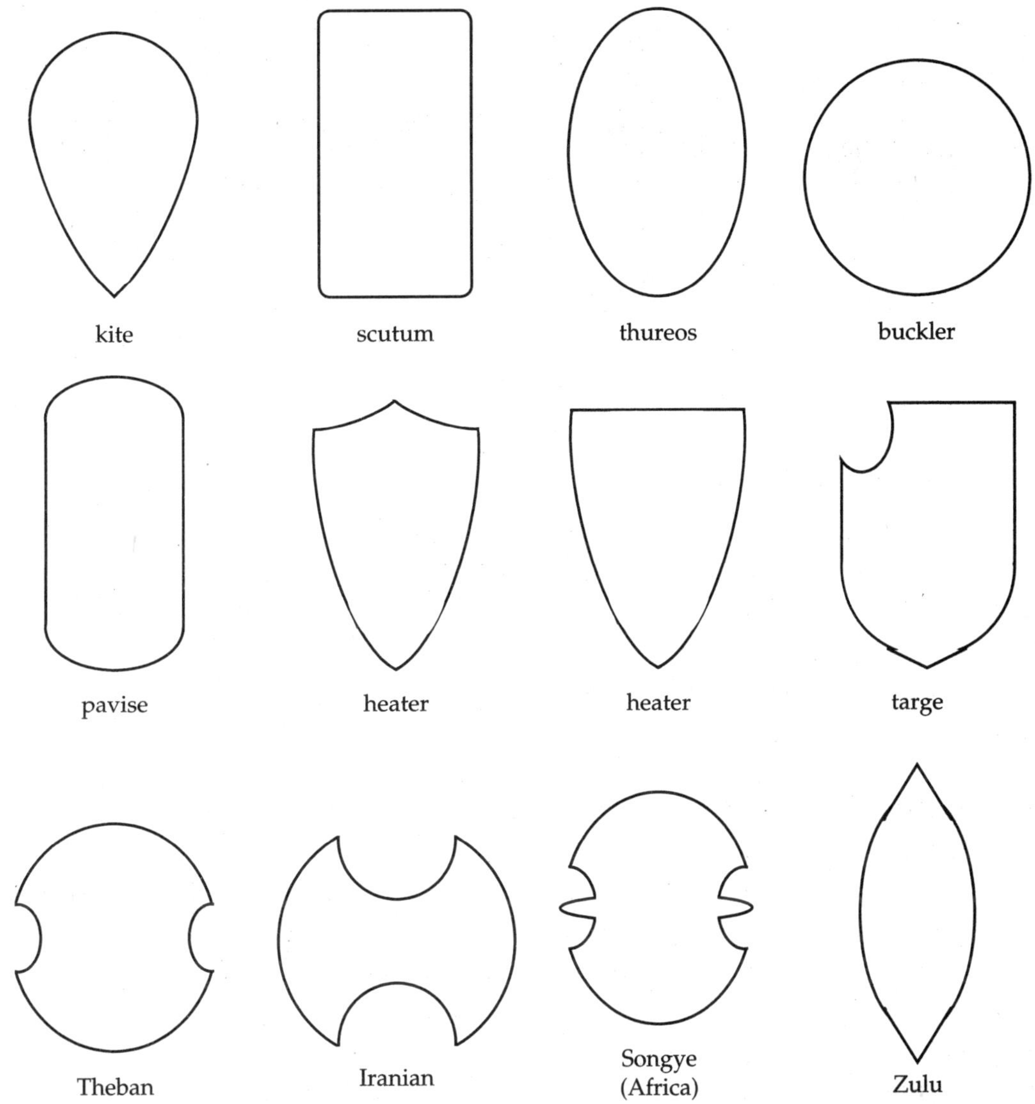

Figure 15: Shield types: European (top two rows) and miscellaneous types (bottom row)

Figure 16: A Latin or Greek and Saltire Cross placed upon shield blasoned on a kite-, heater- and buckler-type shield

Figure 17: Bouttonnée Cross II (far left) and Bouttonnée Cross I (second from left), and Maltese Cross I (second from right) and Maltese Cross I with foot extended (far right) placed upon a heater-type shield

to a rectilinear format — e.g. the kite, scutum, thureos, pavise and heater types. This became important as the art and application of heraldry developed over the centuries. Conversely, if a round shield is employed the opposite becomes applicable as essentially rectilinear crosses when compressed to fit within a round format loose their impact and identity — e.g. the Slavonic Cross and the St. Nicholas's Cross. Various cruciform shapes were altered and adapted to conform to their needs and mode of display (**Figure 18**).

Ecclesiastical Implications

A number of crosses illustrated herein are purely ecclesiastical in origin and use — e.g. Latin Cross (aka *crux immissa, crux capitata, crux ordinaria*), Patriarchal Cross I, II and III, Eastern Orthodox Cross, Papal Cross I and II, Slavonic Cross, St. Nicholas's Cross, Byzantine Cross, Coptic Cross, Ethiopian Cross, Celtic Cross and Basque Cross Rosary. At times any cruciform may be employed outside of its ecclesiastical origin and found emblazoned upon a coat of arms. Only a few are formally associated with the crucifixion of the Christ — e.g. Tau Cross, Latin Cross (aka *crux immissa, crux capitata, crux ordinaria*), *crux humilis*, Thieves' Cross I and II, and Calvary Cross. They may be seen as crosses which are ecclesiastically in common use. On the other hand, there are those which are connected with the disciples or apostles of Jesus Christ — i.e. St. Peter's Cross, St. James's

Figure 18: Heraldic elements on round shield: Latin Cross (left), Greek Cross (second left), Slavonic Cross (second right) and Escarbouche Cross (right)

Cross, St. John's Cross, and St. Andrew's Cross I and II. A large number of crosses are associated with Christian Saints — e.g. St. Boniface's Cross, St. Brendon's Cross, St. Bride's Cross, St. Bridgit's Cross, St. Chad's Cross, St. Clement's Cross, St. Columba's Cross, St. Cuthbert's Cross, St. George's Cross, St. Gilbert's Cross, St. John of Jerusalem's Cross, St. Julian's Cross, St. Lazarus's Cross, St. Nicholas's Cross and St. Olga's Cross — of these many are militaristic.

In addition, there are also a smaller number of cruciforms which were conceived outside of Christianity and which may be seen to have certain magical/spiritual significance. They may be dated to BCE, or have been produced within the CE and not Christian in intent. Often times these forms were assumed by the Christian faith. These other cruciforms, too, are included herein.

Crosses with Militaristic Implications

Within heraldic or mundane crosses, many are found to bear militaristic or weapon's design origins — e.g. the Damascus Cross — or derived from weapon forms — e.g. Cross of the Order of St. James I and II, Cross Crosslet Fitchy, the Crux Pattée Fitchée, Cross Fichée, the Cross Double Fitch, Pheon Cross, Damascus Cross and Crux Pattée Fitchée Base. A number of crosses are associated with militaristic endeavours or Christian militaristic orders which grew out of the Crusades — e.g. Cross of Lorraine, the Crosslet Crossed, Teutonic Cross, Jerusalem Cross I and II, Knight's Templar Cross, Maltese Cross I and II, Cross of the Order of Avis, Cross of the Order of Calatrava I and II, Cross of the Order of Santo Domingo, Barbée Cross, Cross of the Knights of Christ and Sunwise Fylfot Cross. Still others bear designs that were taken from fortifications of the period — e.g. Bretesse Cross, Cross Demisarcel, Cross Dymock and Cross Urdée.

Crosses with Professional or Trade Implications

There are a number of heraldic crosses that seem to have been derived from professions — e.g. the Moline Cross, Milrine Cross and Dovetail Cross. While others appear to have been patterned on everyday objects — e.g. Shepherd's Cross, Chain Cross, Anchor Cross, Knotted Cross, St. Brighid's Cross and Croix Cablée. A few find their origins in animal forms — e.g. St. Brendon's Cross or Dolphin Cross and Ermine Cross — or plant forms — e.g. Order of St. James Cross II, Fleur-de-lys Cross, Fleury Cross, Fleurette Cross, St. Brighid's Cross, Avellane Cross, Ragulée Cross, Order of Calatrava's Cross, Cleves' Cross and Burgundy Cross.

Scope

Within the Christian world the symbol of the cross is so potent that virtually any object, natural or man-made, can be employed in its design. The variations appear *ad nauseam* and only those which appear before the twentieth century are included herein, with very few exceptions. Therefore, this study is essentially restricted to those cruciform symbols that appear prior to the twentieth century and those which find their common usage in either ecclesiastical realms and/or the heraldry of the medieval period through the nineteenth century. In addition, cruciforms will be included which essentially fall outside of the Christian connotation — e.g. Norse crosses, pre-Christian Swiss solar crosses and numerous fylfot crosses. As noted above, this study will be divided into six major sections — i.e. Tau Crosses, Latin Crosses, Greek Crosses, Solar Crosses, Saltire Crosses and Miscellaneous Crosses. Further, where applicable, there will be a number of subdivisions within each section for clarity as well as a section specifically indicating those crosses within the group which are militaristic in content or intent. In addition, within the Greek Cross section, there is a rather extended sub-section dealing with the Fylfot/*Svastika* variations. Finally, there are a number of "crosses" included herein which do not possess Christian applications — e.g. Norse Solar crosses as well as Swiss Solar crosses.

There are a number of terms which appear problematical. One is the heraldic term "potent" or "potence". The term does not apply the definition that is equated to power or powerful or virile, but to a "crutch" or crutch-shaped extension in the form of a Tau or Latin Cross. The term "potent" or "potence" finds its origins in Medieval English where it refers to a "crutch" (**Figure 19** [left]) and to Old French where it refers to a "crutch", but also as "gallows" (**Figure 19** [right]) or "bracket". The Latin "potentia" is power, but in Medieval Latin it meant "crutch". "Potent", "crutch", "gallows" present problems. Whether related to Tau Cross as seen in Teutonic Cross or Latin Cross as encountered in the Cross Crosslet Humilis, the symbol — i.e. "potent" or "potence" — is found regularly in cross heraldry. Certainly, its application to a gallows, an implement of execution would relate it to the cross.

In addition, the primary names or titles of each cross is as they are found in the initial sources. In many cases these titles vary considerably — e.g. Fourché Cross I, Forked Cross and Miller Rebated Cross and Pall Cross. The term of the initial source is used and followed by the other term-names after "aka" — e.g. Fourché Cross I, aka Forked Cross, Miller Rebated Cross and Pall Cross.

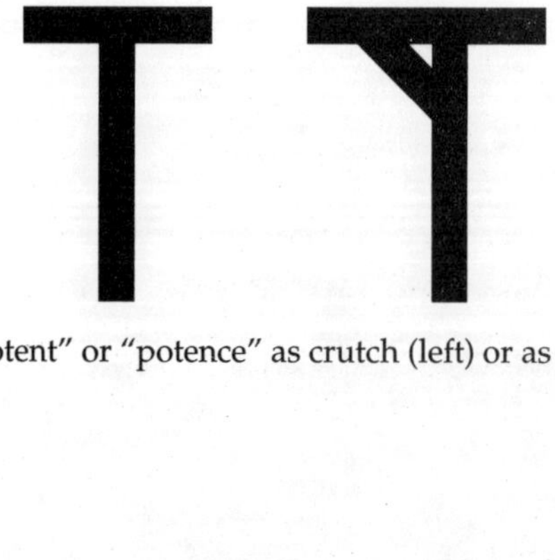

Figure 19: "Potent" or "potence" as crutch (left) or as gallows (right)

Crosses

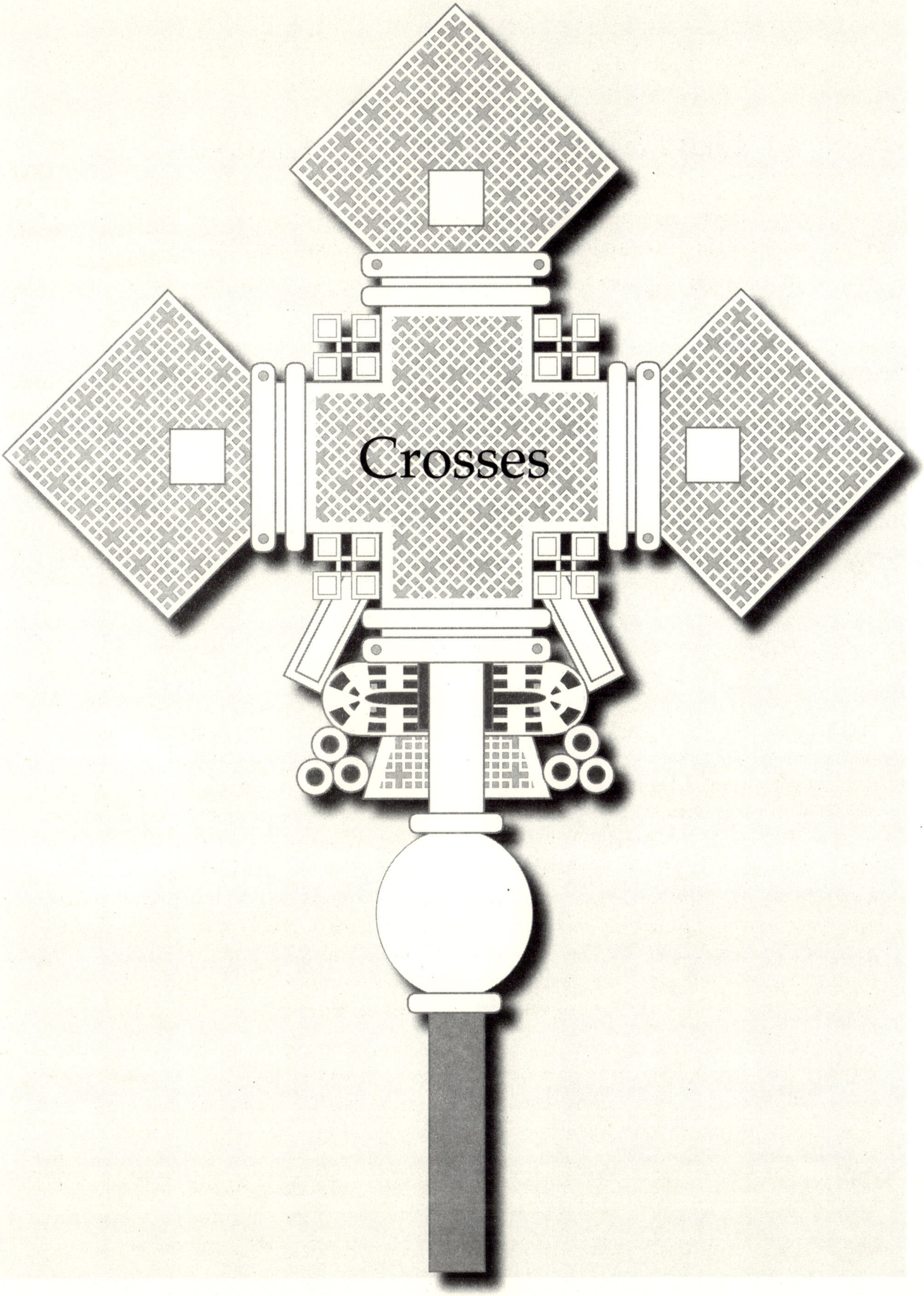

Crux Simplex and Tau Crosses

The *crux simplex* is, by its name, the simplest of all forms for crucifixion. It is merely a stake sunk into the ground or the trunk of a tree, generally a dead tree.

The Tau Cross is an ancient symbol and is identified by many names — i.e. St. Anthony's Cross, Old Testament Cross, Anticipatory Cross, Advent Cross, Egyptian Cross, *crux commissa* and / or *croix commissée*. This cross is truly universal in its ancient use. It is found in the Anasazi (ancient Hopi) culture as well as the Maya civilization. It appears prominently in many Mediterranean cultures. In Egyptian civilization Tau Cross was a symbol to mark jars of sacred water. The Tau Cross was an icon for the Sumerian deity Tammuz, god of the sun and consort of Ishtar. As such, through its association, it symbolized death and resurrection as well as spring rituals which revolved around Tammuz. Part of the ritual involving this rite is the marking of the forehead with a Tau Cross. Moses encountered the Medianites in the Sinai who wore a Tau Cross mark on their foreheads. Later, it was called the "Yahweh Mark". In Greece it symbolized Attis, the deity of life, death and rebirth.

The Attis myth is confusing at best. Zeus, the philandering Magnus Pater, became enamored with Cybele, known as the Mater Deum Magna (the great mother goddess), who rejected him. While she slept he masturbated and spilled his seed on her. In time Cybele gave birth to the androgynous — some myths say hermaphrodite — Agdistis. This deity was demonic and terrorized the gods. In fear, the gods banned together and completely castrated him, cutting away his aggressive male parts — some myths say Dionysus tricked Agdistis into emasculating himself. From the earth where his blood spilled sprang an almond tree (*Prunus dulcis*) — some myths say that beautiful flowers sprang from the torrents of blood flowing from Agdistis wound. Later, Nana, a young, virginal, earthly maid — some myths state that Nana is Cybele in disguise — ate the fruit of this tree on 25 March during the Vernal equinox festival and gave birth nine months later (25 December) to Attis — some myths say Nana saw these flowers and held them to her breast, whereupon Cybele caused her to become pregnant. In either account this is a case of virgin birth. The child, Attis, was placed in the reeds of the river to die, but was rescued by shepherds — an obvious parallel to the Moses story. He grew healthy and handsome and was later referred to as the "good shepherd".

Cybele saw the youth — some myths say he was her grandson while others state that he was her son — and was totally enamored of him. He rejected her advances, whereupon she caused him to go mad. Sitting at the base of a pine tree, he castrated himself and died — some myths state it was Cybele herself who castrated him. Other myths state that Attis returns his mother's advances causing the jealousy of his half-brother / sister Agdistis, who now in the form of a woman also falls in love with Attis and seduces him. Cybele tells Attis of her sadness caused by his union with Agdistis. He, then in great remorse, sits beneath a pine tree and castrates himself and dies. From his blood springs the pomegranate (*Punica granatum*). The grief stricken Cybele takes Attis to the sacred cave where, after three days she revives him — now her — and reintroduces her — formerly him — as her risen daughter.

The pomegranate becomes the symbol of Attis, she. Therefore, a symbol of the mystic female much in the same way that the almond is a feminine symbol associated with Agdistis, she.[1]

In Rome the Tau Cross represented Mithras the mediator between the supreme deity and earth. In Christianity, the Tau Cross is a mark for life, resurrection, reincarnation and blood sacrifice.

The earliest crux (Lat. crucifigere) or means of putting one to death was to tie or nail the one being punished to a simple post set in the ground, the *crux simplex*. A dead tree devoid of branches may also be used. Then the Phoenicians added the cross piece, creating the *crux immissa*.

Crux simplex

The Tau Cross, one of the simplest of the cross forms, is an ecclesiatical cross in common use. It predates Christianity and its earliest manifestation is found in Egyptian tombs. Its name recalls the Greek letter "tau" sign of tau (τ). With a "handle" (circle on top) it becomes the Ankh or *crux ansalata*. The Tau Cross I is a cross found in ecclesiastical situations and also appears in heraldry. It is also referred to as the St. Anthony's Cross, Old Testament Cross, Anticipatory Cross, Advent Cross, Egyptian Cross, *crux commissa*, *croix commissée* and *crux taumata*.

Tau Cross I
aka St. Anthony's Cross, Old Testament Cross, Anticipatory Cross, Advent Cross, Egyptian Cross, *crux commissa, croix commissée, crux taumata*

1 Fredrick W. Bunce, *The Sacred Dichotomy: Thoughts and Comments on the Duality of Female and Male Iconography in South Asia and the Mediterranean*, New Delhi, 2005, pp. 7-8.

Crux Simplex and Tau Crosses (Continued)

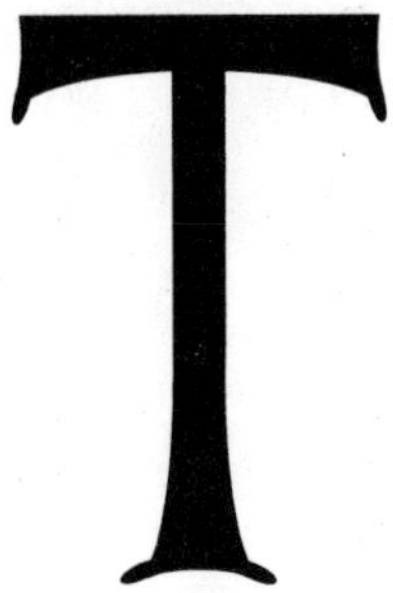

Tau Cross II
aka *crux commissa*, St. Anthony's Cross, Egyptian Cross, Advent Cross

A variation of Tau Cross I. A cross that is frequently employed in heraldry. It is in the form of the capital letter "T". This Tau Cross, which is found in ecclesiastical situations, appears in heraldry and also referred to as the *crux commissa*, St. Anthony's Cross, Egyptian Cross and Advent Cross.

Thieves' Cross I
aka Bent Cross, Dismas Cross

The Theives' Cross I is a variation of the Tau Cross. This form of the Tau Cross is frequently seen in the paintings of the Northern (German) Renaissance, and is the cross form for the thieves flanking the cross of the Christ. In this form, the extremities crosspiece slope downwards. It is as though the weight of the body pulls the ends down via the attached arms. It is usually made of rough wood or branches. It is also referred to as the Bent Cross and Dismas Cross.

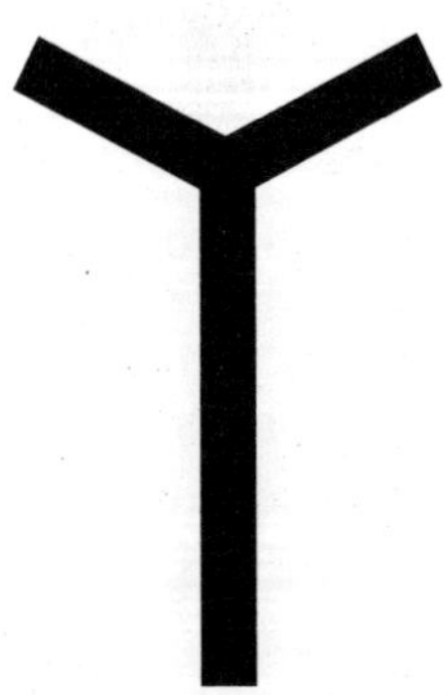

Thieves' Cross II
aka Furka Cross, "Y" Cross, Dismas Cross

A variation of the Tau Cross. This cross is associated with the thieves who were crucified with Jesus Christ. This particular form of a Tau Cross was popular in German art during the sixteenth century. Essentially it set the thieves apart from Christ's Latin cross when depicting the crucifixion. The Thieves' Cross II is a cross that is found neither in ecclesiastical situations nor does it appear in heraldry. It is also referred to as the Furka Cross, "Y" Cross and the Dismas Cross.

Crux Simplex and Tau Crosses (Continued)

A variation of the Tau Cross and Thieves' Cross II. This particular form is seen in Northern Renaissance paintings in the sixteenth century. The Thieves' Cross III is a cross that is not seen in ecclesiastical situations or does it appear in heraldry. It is also referred to as the Dismas Cross.

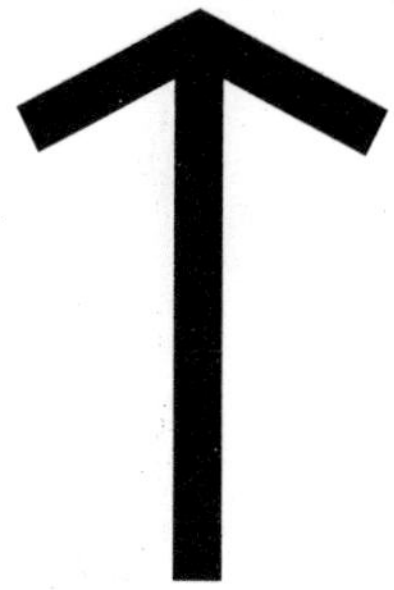

Thieves' Cross III
aka Dismas Cross

The Hammer Cross first appeared in ancient Egypt where it was a sign attached to jars of sacred water. In the eighteenth century, the Hammer Cross became a symbol in the arms of the Company of Plasterers. It is shown in the form of a double-headed hammer used by plasterers and masons. In its more complex form it is related to the Norse deity Thor, as the hammer of Thor. Iconographically it denotes honour and uprightness. The Hammer Cross is exclusively found in heraldry. It is a variation of the Tau Cross.

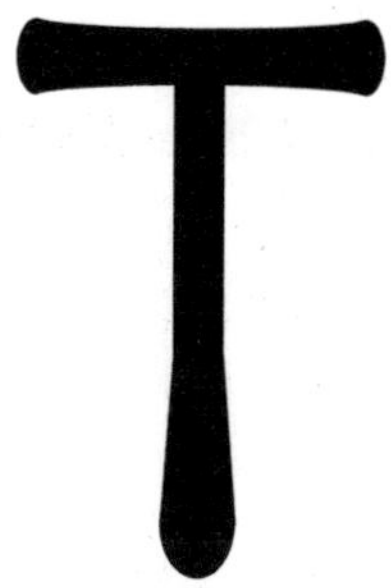

Hammer Cross

The Rogacina Cross is a variation of the Tau Cross. It, along with the Osmorog Cross, the Rogacina Dwukrotnie Przekrzyzowana and the Rogacina Przekrzyzowana crosses, is singularly Polish in character and design. It is related to the Thieves' Cross II and is a cross that is exclusively employed in Polish heraldry. Polish heraldry is unique in Europe as attested to by the Rogacina, and the Rogacina Dwukrotnie Przekrzyzowana crosses. Having been part of the Grand Duchy of Lithuania, the kingdoms of Prussia and Austria, Poland developed an individualistic set of heraldic-cruciform icons.

Rogacina Cross

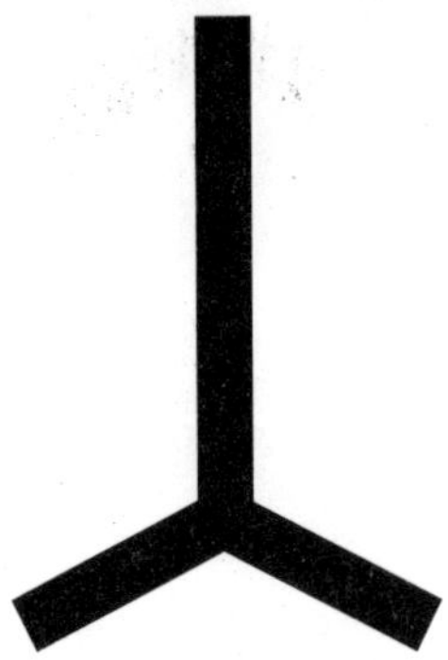

Pall Cross

The Pall Cross is symbolic of the ornamentation and/or the pall worn by clerics. Here it is shown inverted and thus may be seen to be the Tau variation of the Latin St. Peter's Cross. The Pall Cross is a variation of the Thieves' Cross II, the Tau Cross, and is a cross that is employed in heraldry.

Irminsu Cross
aka Asatru Cross

The Irminsu Cross is a symbol associated initially with Norse religions and Odin. As a cruciform, the Irminsu Cross is often, erroneously, applied to Christianity. It is also known as an Asatru Cross and is a form solely found in heraldry of Scandinavia.

Raguly Tau Cross
aka Ragged Tau Cross, Ragulated Tau Cross

The Raguly Tau Cross is a symbol rarely encountered. As a cruciform, the Raguly Tau Cross, erroneously, is sometimes referred to as a form of a Portate Cross. It is a form solely encountered in heraldry. It is also known as a Ragged Tau Cross and Ragulated Tau Cross.

Militaristic Tau Crosses

Whereas there are numerous Latin crosses and myriad Greek crosses that bear militaristic applications. There are, on the other hand, a dearth of Tau Cross forms that have such applications.

A rare example of a variation of the Tau Cross, which has militaristic applications, is the Tau Cross Fitchy. In this example, the lower member is in the form of a knife or dagger while the crosspiece is double fitchy. The term fitchy or *fitchée* refers to the end or foot which is pointed. It is thought by some that the fitchy foot allowed the victims to more easily place the cross in the ground before they were executed! This seems unlikely. The fitchy foot is a variation that appears, primarily, during the crusades and is more likely a referent to a dagger or sword blade. It is also referred to as the *crux commissa*, St. Anthony's Cross, Egyptian Cross, Advent Cross and *croix tau fitchée*.

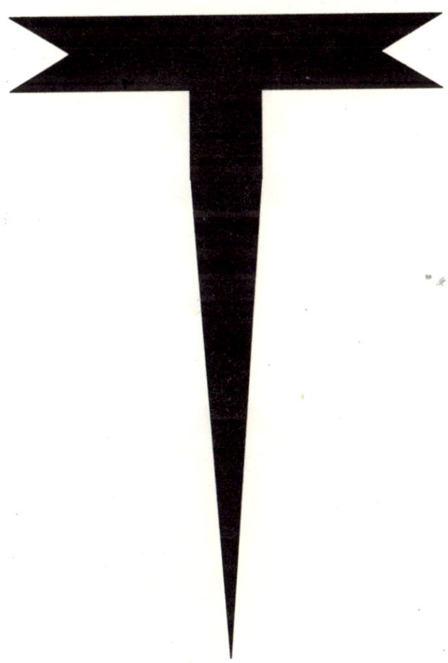

Tau Cross Fitchy
aka *crux commissa*, St. Anthony's Cross, Egyptian Cross, Advent Cross, *croix tau fitchée*

Latin Crosses

The Latin Cross is a later symbol adopted by Christianity. It replaced the fish (**Figure 1**), lamb, alpha and omega and phoenix, among others, as the pre-eminent symbol of the faith. Originally, the Latin Cross was considered a pagan symbol causing many Early Church Fathers to object to its use as a Christian icon as being onerous. The true Latin Cross, when folded top to bottom, creates a cube and/or a Greek Cross (**Figure 20**). The terms which refer to the Latin Cross, proper, are: *crux immissa, crux capitata, crux ordinaria, crux sublimis,* Holy Rood, Western Cross and Protestant Cross. The latter term — i.e. Protestant Cross — is a referent to the depiction of the empty cross, Christ resurrected, rather than the crucifix — i.e. the depiction of the crucified Christ. A common variation of the true Latin Cross is seen in *crux humilis* in which the lower extension is shorter, bring the crosspiece nearer to the ground. The Latin Cross became the source of numerous variations — e.g. Shrouded Cross, Double-span Cross, the Armenian Cross I, etc.

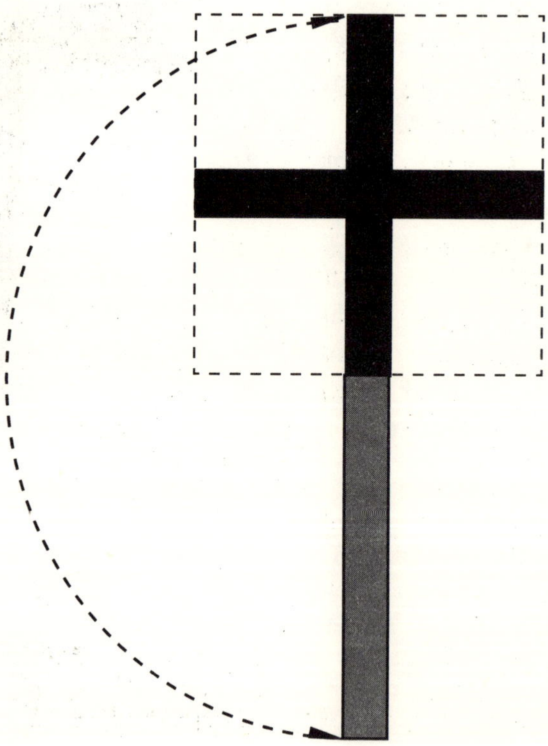

Figure 20: Proportions of the Latin Cross as derived from a Greek Cross

Latin Crosses (Continued)

The Latin Cross is an ancient pagan symbol. It was used by the Persians, Greeks and Romans as a means of execution. However, as a device of execution, the Tau Cross was more popular as it required simpler assembly. This form of the cross — i.e. the Latin Cross — is found in Neolithic Scandinavia as well as China and Africa. It is an ecclesiastical cross in common use. It is a form that is frequently employed in heraldry but is more prevalent in ecclesiastical situations. The Latin Cross is also referred to as the *crux immissa, crux capitata, crux ordinaria, crux Sublimis,* Holy Rood, Protestant Cross and the Western Cross.

Latin Cross
aka *crux immissa, crux capitata, crux ordinaria, crux sublimis,* Holy Rood, Protestant Cross, Western Cross

The *crux humilis* is a variation of the Latin Cross. As opposed to Latin Cross (*crux sublimis*) with the crosspiece placed higher on the upright, this cross brings the victims feet closer to the ground and to the attacks of the mob. It is also seen as a more economical use of the wooden element. The *crux humilis* is a cross that is frequently employed in heraldry but is more prevalent in ecclesiastical situations and is in common use. It is also referred to as the *crux immissa,* Holy Rood, *crux capita, crux ordinaria* and the Latin Cross.

Crux Humilis
aka Crux Immissa, Holy Rood, Crux Capita, Crux Ordinaria, Latin Cross

The Latin Cross Voided is a variation of the Latin Cross. It is a cross that is frequently employed in heraldry but is more prevalent in ecclesiastical situations but is also in common use. It is also referred to as the Fimbriated Cross and White Cross.

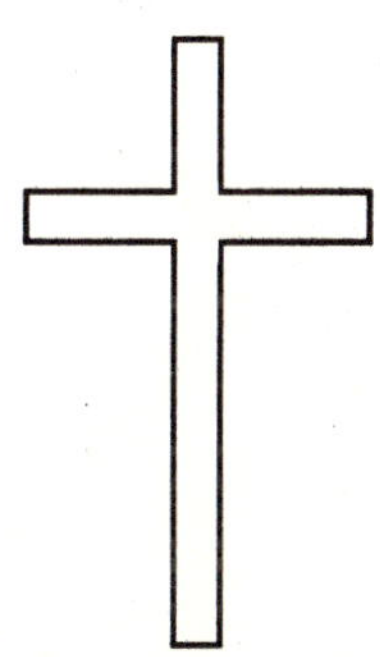

Latin Cross Voided
aka Fimbriated Cross, White Cross

Latin Crosses (Continued)

Moussué Cross I
aka Emousée Cross, Blunted Cross

The Moussué Cross is one of the numerous variations of the Latin Cross. It is a cross with blunted or rounded ends. The Moussué Cross is a symbol found in ecclesiastical situations and occasionally appears in heraldry. It is also referred to as the Emousée Cross and Blunted Cross.

St. Peter's Cross
aka *crux invertere*

Legend states that St. Peter was crucified upside down, not wanting to be crucified in the same manner as the Christ, as such the St. Peter's Cross is symbolic of humility. The inverted cross is also associated with devil worship since the main element points downwards, towards Hell. In this case it is an anti-Christian symbol. The St. Peter's Cross is a variation of the Latin Cross and is a cross that is employed in heraldry and also appears in paintings where St. Peter's crucifixion is the subject. It is also referred to as *crux invertere*.

St. Gilbert's Cross I
aka Portate Cross, Portale Cross

The St. Gilbert's Cross I refers to the cross of that is carried (portated). The Christian tradition states that the Christ carried his cross to the place of execution as part of his sentence. There is no reference anywhere else that those who were crucified were forced to carry their crosses to the site of execution. The St. Gilbert's Cross I is a variation of the Latin Cross and a cross that is employed in heraldry. It is also referred to as the Portate Cross and Portale Cross.

The Calvary Cross I is set upon three steps which refer to the trinity and/or "faith, hope and love". The three steps also represent Mt. Golgatha. The cross is also seen as a cross that is placed upon a table, hence: Altar Cross. The Calvary Cross is a variation of the Latin Cross and *crux humilis*. It is a cross that is sometimes employed in heraldry but is more prevalent in ecclesiastical situations. It is also referred to as the Holy Cross, Stepped Cross Altar Cross and Graded Cross.

Calvary Cross I
aka Holy Cross, Stepped Cross, Altar Cross, Graded Cross

The Lambeau Cross is essentially a Latin Cross surmounting a dovetail base element. The three "feet" or lambeau or label or lambel which are described as ragged (raguly) pendants. The lambeau may refer to the Trinity. It is a mark of cadency that is often employed by the eldest son, often a prince and as such would refer to the Christ. The central lambel represents the son and the outer ones represent the parents. This interpretation may be applied to the Christ, Virgin Mary and God, the Father. The Lambeau Cross is a cross that is frequently employed in heraldry.

Lambeau Cross

The St. Nino Cross is a variation of the Latin Cross and is related to the Thieves' Cross III. St. Nino or St. Nina was responsible for introducing Christianity in Georgia. Her icon is the cross shown to the right. Its form is no dissimilar to Rogacina Cross of Poland. The St. Nino Cross is a cross found in heraldry and also appears in ecclesiastical situations.

St. Nino Cross

Thieves' Cross IV

The Thieves' Cross IV is a variation of the Latin Cross and related to Thieves' Cross I and III. It is almost exclusively found in heraldry and appears in painting as well.

Pope's Cross

The Pope's Cross is a variation of the Latin Cross and is allied to Thieves' Cross I. It is a simple, relatively modern form, and is a cross that is employed in ecclesiastical situations.

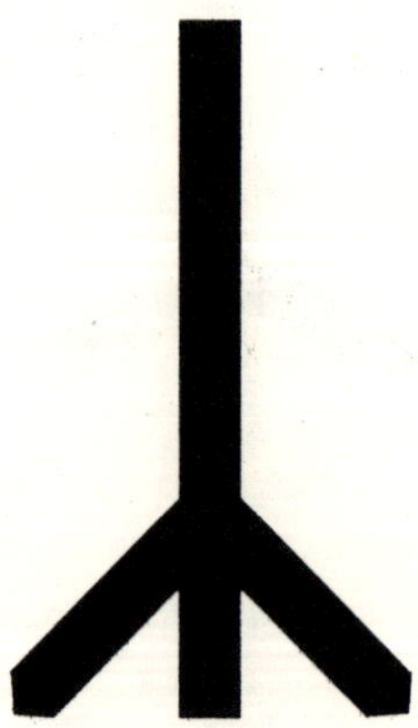

Broken Cross
aka Neronic Cross, Nero's Cross

The Broken Cross is symbolic of the dominance of the Christ over physical death since the crosspiece has been broken and has fallen to the ground. It is related to Pall Cross and Thieves' Cross II as well as St. Peter's Cross. The Broken Cross is a variation of Latin Cross, and is a cross that is employed in heraldry. It is also referred to as Neronic Cross as Emperor Nero attempted to subdue Christianity, unsuccessfully.

The Double-span Cross is allied to Voided Cross but with crossing filled. It is related to Gamma Cross and/or Gammadia Cross as well as a variation of Latin Cross, and is a cross that is employed in heraldry.

Double-span Cross

The Lithuanian Cross is allied to Armenian Cross II. It is an open cross — i.e. composed of wrought bars, topped with a Paté Cross and including a crescent. It is a variation of Latin Cross, and is a cross that is seldom employed in heraldry, but frequently encountered in ecclesiastical situations. It is also referred to as Lietuvis Kryzius.

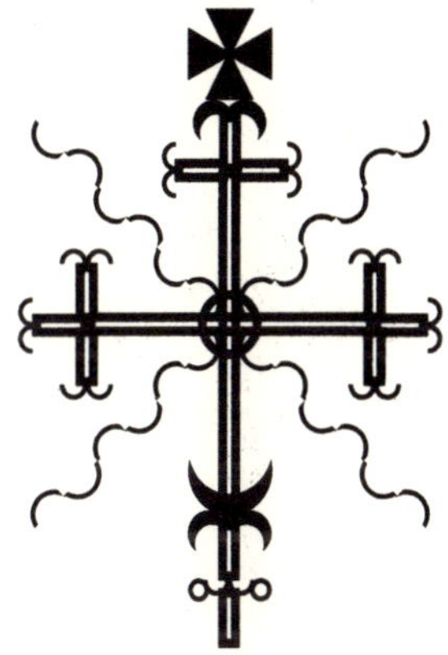

Lithuanian Cross
aka Lietuvis Kryzius

Latin Crosses: Ankh and Chi Rho Variation

The Ankh and the Chi Rho are two important cruciform symbols employed in Christian iconography. The Ankh, the use of which predates Christianity, is an ancient Egyptian symbol. It is a referent to life, life-giving forces and the soul. It appears held by both priests and the Pharaoh in tombs of that ancient civilization. As such it is an apt adaptation to Christian symbols. It was depicted by the Copts as early as the fourth century and may have been a reference to the "Tree of Life". Essentially, the Ankh is a Tau Cross with a circular ring on top.

The Chi Rho is an acronym for Christ the King. It also known as the Constantine's Cross or the Labarum or Chrismon and consists of the Greek letters chi (χ) and rho (ρ). These two letters allude to Christus Rex or Christ the King. The Chi Rho was popular long before the cross became the pre-eminent Christian symbol.

Ansata Cross I
aka Looped Tau Cross, Handled Cross, Ankh

The Ankh or Ansata Cross I is an ancient Egyptian symbol initially. The Ankh of immortality was first adopted by the Copts. In its simplest form as seen to the right, it consists of a Tau Cross with a ring at the top, above the upright member. The Ankh or Ansata Cross I is a variation of Tau Cross, and is a symbol that is employed in heraldry. It is also referred to as the Looped Tau Cross, Handled Cross and Ankh.

Ansata Cross II
aka Looped Tau Cross, Ankh Cross, Coptic Cross

The Ansata Cross II is related to the Ansata Cross I and Solar Cross. In this variation, the ring holds a simple Greek Cross and is similar to the Saxon Cross IV. The cross within a ring symbolizes the dominance of Christianity over the world and ancient non-Christian beliefs — i.e. the ring referring to the world. It is a variation of the Tau Cross and a sign that is frequently employed in heraldry. It is also referred to as the Looped Tau Cross, Coptic Cross and Ankh Cross.

The Ansata Cross III is related to the Ansata Cross I and Solar Cross. It is a variation of Tau Cross. The Ansata Cross III is often seen in heraldry but seldom in ecclesiastical situations. It is also referred to as the Looped Tau Cross and Ankh Cross.

Ansata Cross III
aka Looped Tau Cross, Ankh Cross

The Ansata Cross IV is related to the Ansata Cross I and Chi Rho Cross III. It is a variation of the Tau Cross. The Ansata Cross IV is often seen in ecclesiastical situations but seldom in heraldry. It is also referred to as Coptic Cross.

Ansata Cross IV
aka Coptic Cross

The Chi Rho Cross I is one of the simplest of this form. Here rho (ρ) is clear. Chi (χ) is abbreviated and part of its crosspiece is hidden in the uprightness of the rho. There are numerous variations of this cross (Chi Rho Cross IV, V and VI) which may be seen as a variation of Saltire Cross. Here, Chi Rho Cross I is a variation of Latin Cross. The Chi Rho Cross I is a cross found in ecclesiastical situations and also appears in heraldry, particularly ecclesiastical heraldry. It is also referred to as the Labarum, Constantine's Cross and Chrismon.

Chi Rho Cross I
aka Labarum, Constantine's Cross, Chrismon

Chi Rho Cross II
aka Labarum, Constantine's Cross, Chrismon

The Chi Rho Cross II is a more formal variation of the Chi Rho Cross I. As with the Chi Rho Cross I, rho (ρ) is clear, but chi (χ) is abbreviated. The Chi Rho Cross II is a variation of Latin Cross. The Chi Rho Cross II is a symbol found in ecclesiastical situations and occasionally appears in heraldry. It is also referred to as the Labarum, Constantine's Cross and Chrismon.

Shepherd's Cross

The Shepherd's Cross is related to the Chi Rho Cross, but rho (ρ) resembles a shepherd's crook and, therefore, refers to the Christ as the Good Shepherd. The Shepherd's Cross is a variation of the Latin Cross. It is found in ecclesiastical situations and also appears in heraldry.

Latin Crosses: Pommée and Bottonée Variation

A number of crosses have a circular termination — i.e. at the end of the crosspiece and vertical member. These appear as circular knobs, either singly — e.g. Saxon Cross or Pomy Cross I — doubled or more often tripled — e.g. the Bottonée Cross, Blessing Cross or Slavonic Cross. These terminations are referred to as either "botton" or "pommée". The "pommée" also refers to a knob as found on the pommel of a sword. Whereas, the "botton" (Fr.: *bouton*) refers to a bud or button or knob. Within the section of Greek crosses, there is a number of additional variations on the botton/pommée.

The Pommée Cross I possess four pommels at the terminations of the cross arms and upright member. The term "pommel" — i.e. pommée — refers to the knobs or pommels that are found on the hilt of a sword and its guard piece. Since the pommel is also found at the foot of this cross, a militaristic application is not entirely applicable. The Pommée Cross I is a variation of the Latin Cross and is a cross that is employed in heraldry. It is also referred to as the Pomy Cross and Croix Pommée.

Pommée Cross I
aka Pomy Cross, Croix Pommée

The Pommée Cross II is one of a number of distinctive early cross forms found in Great Britain. This particular example was incised into a stone slab. With its three bottons at the top, it recalls the hilt and guard portions of a sword, although it is not intrinsically a militaristic cross as a whole. The Pommée Cross II is a variation of the Latin Cross. It is related to the Saxon Cross II, III, IV and V.

Pommée Cross II
aka Saxon Cross

Rood Cross I

The Rood Cross I is purely ecclesiastical in origin and a variation of Pommée Cross I and Rood Cross II. It possesses a distinctive form with large circular terminations (pommée) and a long rectangular form behind the cross. Generally, a painted crucifix would appear upon this cross and sometimes a sculptural representation of the crucified Christ. The Rood Cross I is a variation of the Latin Cross and a form that has purely ecclesiastical implications and use. It is rarely seen in heraldry.

Sarcellee Cross
aka Croix Sarcellée, Sarcelly Cross

The Sarcellee Cross is ostensibly related to the Recercelée Cross, but its form and name are disputed. It possesses a double pommel and is a variation of the Latin Cross. The Sarcellee Cross is only encountered in heraldry. It is also known as the Croix Sarcellée and Sarcelly Cross.

Bouttonnée Cross I
aka Botonny Cross, Budded Cross, Croix Tréfflée, Croix Botonnée

The Bouttonnée Cross I cross is related to the Gothic Cross. The "botton" or "boutton" here refers to buds. The appearance of a cluster of three buds (trefoil) alludes to the Trinity and/or dominance over the three spheres — i.e. heaven, earth and hell. It also possesses references to the twelve months of the year as well as to the twelve daylight hours. The Bouttonnée Cross I is a variation of Latin Cross and is a symbol that is frequently employed in heraldry. It is also referred to as the Botonny Cross, Budded Cross, Croix Tréfflée and Croix Bottonée.

Latin Crosses: Pommée and Botonée Variation (Continued)

The Blessing Cross represents a hand-held cross, one that is carried, usually by a cleric and employed in offering a blessing to the assembled. The Blessing Cross is a variation of Latin Cross and is a cross form that is employed in heraldry but more frequently encountered in ecclesiastical situations.

Blessing Cross
aka Hand-held Cross

The Slavonic Cross combination of Bouttonnée Cross and Cyrilic Cross with the Christogram "ICXC" — i.e. the first and last letters of Jesus (IC) and the first and last letters of Christ (XC). The upper crosspiece refers to the inscription nailed to the top of the cross and the angled lower crosspiece alludes to the footrest — i.e. the *suppedaneum*. This cross is associated with Russian Orthodox Church. The Slavonic Cross is a variation of the Latin Cross, and is a cross that is employed in heraldry, particularly in ecclesiastical heraldry. It is also referred to as the Russian Orthodox Cross.

Slavonic Cross
aka Russian Orthodox Cross

The Rosicrucian Cross I is a hermetic symbol of an ancient society. The rose is symbolic of the power of the Blood of Christ to redeem. In this instance there are four variations of the rose, one upon the other. The glory rays that extend at the crossing contain the INRI, normally referring to "Jesus of Nazareth, King of the Jews". However, another possibility exists, and that is, "nature is renewed by fire". The Rosicrucian Cross I is a variation of the Latin Cross and the Botoné Cross, and is a cross that is employed in heraldry, particularly as it applies to Rosicrucian Society. It is also referred to as the Rose Cross.

Rosicrucian Cross I
aka Rose Cross

Latin Potent Pomelled Cross

The Latin Potent Pommelled Cross is a Potent Cross in which the ends of all the cross pieces except the base possess pommels. The Latin Potent Pommelled Cross is a variation of the Latin Cross, and is a cross that is employed in heraldry.

Latin Crosses: Byzantine, Manx and Coptic Variation

Many cross forms are strongly influenced by the various major denominations and the cultures from which they sprang. They are often highly individualistic — e.g. Celtic, Orthodox (both Greek and Russian) and Byzantine. They all possess the basic elements of Latin Cross — i.e. an upright post with a crosspiece at a distance significantly closer to the top than the bottom. However, the Coptic crosses provide the most varied forms which all possess elaborate surface treatment and are multi-pierced. Their numbers are such that only the smallest numbers are illustrated and described herein.

The Byzantine Cross I form is frequently seen in Greek Orthodox Church. It is considerably simpler than either Patriarchal Cross III or Eastern Orthodox Cross and may predate them, en forme. The Byzantine Cross is a variation of the Latin Cross, and is a cross that is employed in heraldry as well as in ecclesiastical situations. It is also referred to as the Fourchette Cross. Fourchette translates as "fork". However, the terminations do not resemble a fork. Fourchette refers to a forked termination, but with the ends cut off abruptly.

Byzantine Cross I
aka Fourchette Cross

The Byzantine Cross II is frequently seen in the Greek and Eastern Orthodox churches. It is simpler than the Byzantine Cross I, Patriarchal Cross III or Eastern Orthodox Cross and may predate them, en forme. The Byzantine Cross II is a variation of the Latin Cross, and is a cross that is found in ecclesiastical situations and also appears in heraldry.

Byzantine Cross II

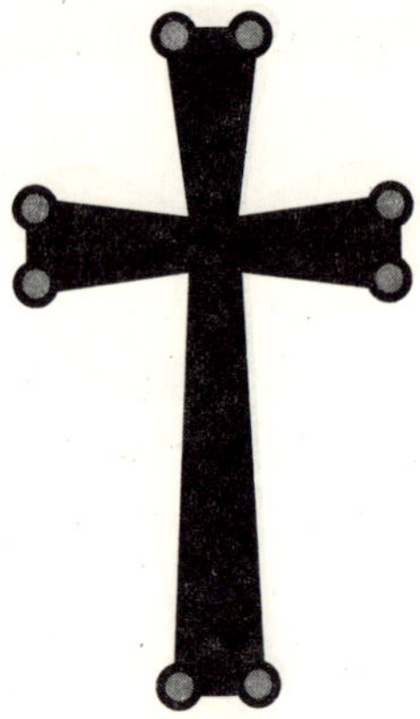

Byzantine Cross III

The Byzantine Cross III is a variation of Byzantine Cross II, but with the addition of gems at the eight corners of the vertical element and the crosspiece. Eight represents regeneration and resurrection. It may also refer to the Beatitudes. The Byzantine Cross III is a variation of the Latin Cross, and is a symbol found in ecclesiastical situations and occasionally appears in heraldry.

Manx Cross I
aka **Sundulf's** Cross

The Manx Cross I is one of a number of variations on a theme. The Isle of Man was an important site for Celtic culture. Its relative isolation from the major Celtic cultures of Great Britain and Ireland created an interesting variation. The Manx Cross I is related to Celtic Cross — i.e. a Latin Cross with circular voids at the crossing. It is a variation of the Latin Cross and a cross that is employed in ecclesiastical situations. It is also referred to as the Sundulf's Cross.

Coptic Cross I
aka Ethipoian Cross

The Coptic Cross I is similar to Coptic Cross V illustrated in Greek Cross section, but with five Bouttonnée crosses (see Greek/Coptic Cross Variations). The Coptic Cross I is one of a number of variations developed by the Copts, an early form of Christianity still practised in north-east Africa. It is a variation of the Latin Cross and a cross that is employed in heraldry. It is also referred to as the Ethiopian Cross.

The Coptic Cross II is similar to Byzantine Cross II and a variation of the Latin Cross. The Coptic Cross II is one of a number of variations developed by the Copts (see Greek crosses). The Coptic Cross II is essentially a cross found in ecclesiastical situations.

Coptic Cross II

The Coptic Cross III is another variation of the Latin Cross. As with a great number of Coptic crosses, the proportions of the width to the height is heavier than many Latin Cross variations and heavier than the Coptic crosses I and II. As one of a number of variations developed by the Copts, it is a cross that is exclusive to ecclesiastical situations.

Coptic Cross III

The Coptic Cross IV is similar to the Coptic Cross I. It is a variation of the Latin Cross and a cross that is essentially found in ecclesiastical situations.

Coptic Cross IV

Latin Crosses: Potent and Crosslet Variation

Many cross forms possess small crosspieces either in the form of a Cross Potent or a Cross Crosslet. These are especially prevalent in Greek crosses and appear less often in Latin cross forms.

Teutonic Cross I
aka Latin Cross Potent

The Teutonic Cross I is an example of a Latin Cross Potent. It is not a cross in common use, but it does appear from time to time. Its name suggests that the Teutonic Cross I is associated with the Teutonic Order, an order of succour rather than an aggressive order of liberation. This cruciform and its Greek Cross varieties were a symbol worn by the Teutonic Knights.

Rood Cross II

The Rood Cross II is purely ecclesiastical in origin. It possesses a distinctive form with large rectangular terminations and a long rectangular form behind the cross. The Rood Cross II is traditionally a painted cross, or more precisely painted crucifix which hung above the rood screen of English churches. The form is Byzantine and also seen in Italian Proto-Renaissance. The Rood Cross II is a variation of the Latin Cross and a form that has purely ecclesiastical implications and use. It is almost never seen in heraldry.

Cross Crosslet Humilis
aka Potent Cross Humilis

The Cross Crosslet Humilis is also known as Potent Cross Humilis. The term "potent" refers to the head of a crutch which may appear to be in the form of a Tau Cross — e.g. Teutonic Cross — or as a Latin Cross (crosslet) as seen here (see "Introduction" reterm "potent"). The Cross Crosslet Humilis is a variation of Latin Cross, and is a cross that is frequently employed in heraldry. It is also referred to as the Potent Cross Humilis.

Latin Crosses: Moline, Recercelée, Fleurée Variation

Common forms are often used as a design basis for Latin Cross. The Moline, Recercelée, Fleurée Cross variations are more prevalent in Greek Cross forms. These variations are derived from items of practical use — e.g. a forged metal brace on wheels or millstones.

The Moline Cross may come from the term "moline" which generally refers to a cross with ends split as in a windmill (*moulin*). It also refers to the reinforcing, iron piece found centred within a mill wheel — i.e. millrind — a wooden wheel and often appears as a bifurcated termination related to the *fleur-de-lys*. It denotes centredness and strength of purpose. It often appears in the form of a Greek cross as a part of heraldry (*see* "Greek Crosses: Anchry, Milrine, Moline, Recercelée Variations"). The Moline Cross is a variation of the Latin Cross. The Moline Cross is frequently encountered in heraldry but rarely in ecclesiastical situations. Also, it is referred to as the Milrine Cross, Croix Fer-de-moline, Croix Molinée, Croix Recercelée, and Croix Anillée.

Moline Cross
aka Milrine Cross, Croix Fer-de-moline, Croix Molinée, Croix Recercelée, Croix Anillée

The Moline Voided Cross is a variation of Cross Moline with the central portion of the upright and crosspiece voided. It often appears in the form of a Greek cross as a part of heraldry (*see* "Greek Crosses: Anchry, Milrine, Moline, Recercelée Variations"). *En forme*, it is related to the Gamadia Cross but with extension of the lower upright element. The Moline Voided Cross is a variation of the Latin Cross and it is always encountered in heraldry.

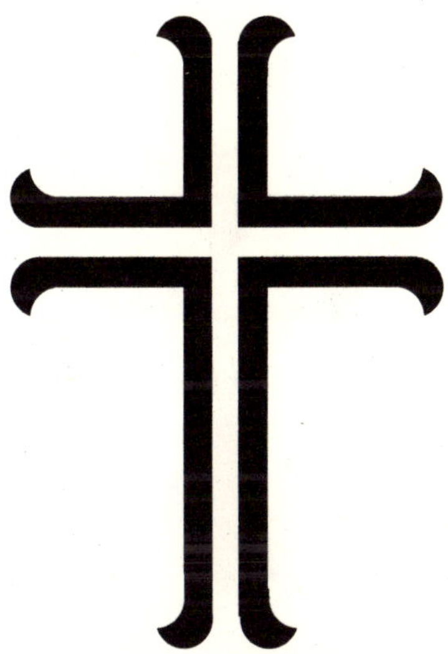

Moline Voided Cross

Latin Crosses: Moline, Recercelée, Fleurée Variation (Continued)

Recercelée Cross I
aka Croix Recercellée, Croix Recercellé, Recercele Cross, Recercely Cross, Croix Rocercellé, Croix Fourché, Forked Cross, Fourchy Cross, Miller's Cross, Miller Rebated Cross

The Recercelée Cross I is with its eight pointed terminations may refer to the Beatitudes. It is related to the Cross Moline and the square Cross Fourché (*see* "Greek Crosses: Anchry, Milrine, Moline, Recercelée Variations"). The Recercelée Cross is a variation of the Latin Cross, and is a cross that is exclusively employed in heraldry. The Recercelée Cross is also referred to as the Croix Recercellée, Croix Recercellé, Recercele Cross, Recercely Cross, Croix Rocercellé, Croix Fourché, Forked Cross, Fourchy Cross, Miller's Cross, and the Miller Rebated Cross.

Recercelée Cross II
aka Croix Recercellée, Croix Recercellé, Recercele Cross, Recercely Cross, Croix Rocercellé, Croix Fourché, Forked Cross, Fourchy Cross, Miller's Cross, Miller Rebated Cross

The Recercelée Cross II is a simpler version of the Recercelée Cross I. It is related to Cross Moline and symbolizes strength. The Recercelée Cross II is a variation of the Latin Cross and is always exclusively in heraldry. It is also known as Croix Recercellée, Croix Recercellé, Recercele Cross, Recercely Cross, Croix Rocercellé, Croix Fourché, Forked Cross, Fourchy Cross, Miller's Cross and Miller Rebated Cross.

Gothic Cross
aka Fleurée Cross, Flory Cross, Floretty Cross

The Gothic Cross is French in origin, hence the Gothic and fleurée connotation. It symbolizes one who has conquered. The Fleurée is a referent to the *fleur-de-lys* which, in turn, signifies the trinity and purity. There are numerous variations of this cross in the Greek Cross section. The Gothic Cross is a variation of the Latin Cross and a form that is frequently employed in heraldry and rarely in ecclesiastical situations. It is also referred to as the Fleurée Cross, Flory Cross and Floretty Cross.

The Calvary Cross II is a variation of the Calvary Cross I with a fleury termination at the top similar to the Gothic Cross and is referred to as either enhendée or potence. The three steps refer to the trinity and/or "faith, hope and love". The three steps also represent Mt. Golgatha. The Calvary Cross II is a variation of the Latin Cross, and is a cross that is frequently encountered in heraldry but rarely in ecclesiastical situations. It is also referred to as the Heytesbury Cross.

Calvary Cross II
aka Heytesbury Cross

The Camargue Cross is a symbol that is found primarily in the Rhone Valley of France. It is the emblem of Saints Maries-des-la-mer Church. The terminations refer to the pikes employed by the mounted herdsmen and the anchor-like bottom alludes to the numerous fisherman of the region. The Camargue Cross is a variation of the Latin Cross and is restricted to both ecclesiastical and heraldry with the Rhone Valley. It is also referred to as the Cowherder's Cross.

Camargue Cross
aka Cowherder's Cross

The St. Thomas Cross is a symbol that is found primarily in South Asia and associated with the Syriac-Orthodox and Syro-Malabar Catholic Churches and the Knanaya Christians. It is an iconic device found from India to Malaysia. The base of the cross recalls a lotus and possesses three levels, revering to the Christian Trinity. The St. Thomas Cross is a variation of the Latin Cross and is restricted to both ecclesiastical and heraldry with the area noted. It is also referred to as the Nazrani Cross, Mar Thoma Cross and Manichean Cross.

St. Thomas Cross I
aka Nazrani Cross, Mar Thoma Cross, Manichean Cross

Latin Crosses: Annuleted Variation

A device that is frequently seen decorating crosses is a small circle or annulet. Normally they are found decorating the terminations of the cross, either singly, in pairs or tripled. It is traditionally a symbol of faithfulness and strength, although it is also seen as a symbol of nobility and jurisdiction gained through royal favour. The annulet is also a mark of cadency and represents the fifth son.

Armenian Cross I
aka Khachkar Cross, Goshavank Cross, Siroun Cross

The Armenian Cross I is viewed as being originally a pagan fertility symbol representing rebirth and spring. It was adapted and transmuted by early Christians in Armenia into this distinctive form. The Armenians are considered to be the first country to convert to Christianity in CE 321. The circle clusters (annulets) are seen here as solar discs which represent the light of Christianity. The term "khachkar" refers to carved stone crosses, while "siroun" is translated as lovely. The Armenian Cross I is a variation of the Latin Cross, and is a cross that is employed in heraldry and also adorns steeples of churches and shrines. It is also referred to as the Khachkar Cross, Goshavank Cross and Siroun Cross.

Armenian Cross II
aka Khachkar Cross

The Armenian Cross II is a variation of Armenian Cross I. The cluster of three solar discs are replaced by one. The Armenian Cross II is also a variation of the Latin Cross, and is a cross that is often encountered in ecclesiastical situations and environs. It is also referred to as the Khachkar Cross.

The Occitan Cross IV is one of a number of variations of the Occitan Cross I. The majority of these variations are related to the Greek Cross, *en forme*, and their employment is almost exclusively found in the Languedoc area of France. The Occitan Cross IV is a variation of the Latin Cross, more specifically the *crux humilis*. It is a symbol that is frequently employed in heraldry and only rarely in ecclesiastical situations or environs. It is also referred to as Toulouse Cross and Languedoc Cross.

Occitan Cross IV
aka Toulouse Cross, Languedoc Cross

Latin Crosses: Rope Variation

There are a few Latin cross forms which are composed entirely of or partially of rope. These crosses merely indicate the wide variety of sources that the cross can be based upon.

Rope Cross I

The Rope Cross I is seen as the representation of a cross that emphasizes the brutality of a crucifixion in that the areas of the hands and feet are obviously intended for nails, rather than secured by ropes. The Rope Cross I is a variation of the Latin Cross, and is a cross that is employed in heraldry.

Rope Cross II

The Rope Cross II is seen as the representation of a cross that de-emphasizes the brutality of a crucifixion. Here, ropes decorate the terminations which were to be employed to secure the victim rather than nails. The Rope Cross II is a variation of Rope Cross I, related to the Latin Cross, and is a cross that is employed in heraldry.

Rope Cross III

The Rope Cross III is an extension of the Rope Cross I. It is a variation of the Latin Cross. The Rope Cross III is almost always encountered in heraldry but only in the rarest circumstances is it found in ecclesiastical situations.

Latin Crosses: Miscellaneous Variation

There are numerous variations found based upon the proportions of the Latin Cross, although the heraldic-based Greek Crosses far outnumber Latin variations. Many of the Latin crosses are heraldic in origin, however, a number of them are ecclesiastically based as well. The Latin Cross and its variations are almost exclusively employed in altar crosses, Crucifixes and Rood Crosses, Greek Cross not being adaptable to these uses.

The Christ referred to himself as "the Alpha and Omega" — i.e. the beginning and the end. As such, this statement is believed to assert the divinity of the Christ, as well as a member of the Trinity. The Alpha and Omega Cross is the principal element in the arms of the Principality of Asturias which sees itself as the only region of Spain to resist Moorish conquest. The Alpha and Omega Cross I is a variation of the Latin Cross, and is a cross that is frequently employed in heraldry.

Alpha and Omega Cross I

The Alpha and Omega Cross II is less often encountered — i.e. the merging of alpha and omega, one over the other. In this case the two Greek letters are set within a sun disc. The Alpha and Omega Cross II is a variation of the Latin Cross as well as the Solar Cross, and is a cross that is almost exclusively found in religious heraldry.

Alpha and Omega Cross II

IHS Cross
aka Neronic Cross

The IHS Cross is normally seen to refer to the acronym of the Latin *Iesus Hominum Salvator* or "Jesus Saviour of the World". Although there are other interpretations: *Iesus Hierosolymae Salvator* or "Jesus the Saviour of Jerusalem", *Iesus Habemus Socium* or "Jesus Is Our Companion", *In Hoc Signo vinces* or "this sign is your hope", *In Hoc Signo spes mea* or "by this sign you shall conquer". The IHS Cross is a variation of the Latin Cross, and is a cross that is frequently employed in ecclesiastical heraldry. It is sometimes referred to as the Neronic Cross.

Marian Cross I

The Marian Cross I is a variation of the Latin Cross. It is essentially a Roman Catholic icon and represents the strong connection between the Christ and the Virgin Mary. It is a cross form that is generally only employed in heraldry or in ecclesiastical literature.

St. Boniface Cross
aka Eternal Cross, Roman Cross

The St. Boniface Cross is a simple Latin Cross with an infinity symbol or lemniscate entwined over the crosspiece and the upright. It symbolizes eternal peace through the crucifixion and resurrection since the cross is empty. In addition, it symbolizes the primacy of the Roman Catholic Church. The St. Boniface Cross is a variation of and related to the Latin Cross and is almost exclusively found in heraldry. It is also referred to as the Eternal Cross and Roman Cross.

The Shrouded Cross is symbolic of the Resurrection of the Christ and victory over death. The cross is empty and the shroud which was normally employed to wrap the body of the victim is draped over the crosspieces. Frequently, during the period of Lent the cross is shrouded as a mark of mourning and anticipation of the crucifixion and resurrection of the Christ. The Shrouded Cross is a variation of and related to the Latin Cross and is employed in heraldry. It is also referred to as Empty Cross.

Shrouded Cross
aka Empty Cross

The Glory Cross is an anticipatory cross in that the radiance at the crossing represents the star of Bethlehem. The Glory Cross symbolizes both the birth and death of the Christ. It is a variation of the Latin Cross, related to the Solar Cross and is a cross that is frequently employed in heraldry. It is also referred to as the Natal Cross, Nativity Cross and Bethlehem Star Cross.

Glory Cross
aka Natal Cross, Nativity Cross, Bethlehem Star Cross

The Crown and Cross is one of a number of variations of the Latin Cross. The iconography applies to the dominance of Christianity, through the cross throughout the world. It also is a referent to the Christ King — i.e. Christus Rex. The Crown and Cross is a variation of the Latin Cross that is normally employed in ecclesiastical heraldry.

Crown and Cross

Crescent Cross
aka Croix Croissant, Moon Cross, Lunate Cross

The Crescent Cross is an interesting variation. The moon is normally not a symbol associated with patristic Christianity, but Islam. Its use here refers to the relationship, both geographically and theologically between Christianity and Islam. The crescent moon is usually shown green in colour. The Crescent Cross is a variation of the Latin Cross, and is a cross that is frequently employed in heraldry. It is also referred to as the Croix Croissant, Moon Cross, and Lunate Cross.

Skull and Crossbones with Cross

The Skull and Crossbones with Cross is a symbol that is found primarily in Christian art, particularly painting. It represents the victory over death through the crucifixion and resurrection. The Skull and Crossbones with Cross is a variation of the Latin Cross and a form that has purely ecclesiastical implications and use. It is rarely seen in heraldry.

Golden Dawn Rose Cross
aka Lamen Cross, Rosicrucian Cross

The Golden Dawn Rose Cross is a symbol of the Hermetic Order of the Golden Dawn and related to the Rosicrucians. It is a variation of the Latin Cross and a form that has purely heraldic in nature. It is also referred to as Lamen Cross and Rosicrucian Cross.

The Aiguisée Cross I is a cross that, due to the sharp terminations of the upright and crosspiece (*fitched*), is associated with the Passion of Christ. The Aiguisée Cross is a variation of the Latin Cross, and is a form that is employed in heraldry almost exclusively. It is also referred to as the Aiguise Cross, Urdée Cross, Cross of Suffering, Passion Cross and Pointed Cross.

Aiguisée Cross I
aka Aiguise Cross, Urdée Cross, Cross of Suffering, Passion Cross, Pointed Cross

The Chain Cross is one of a number of variations on Latin Cross that draws from common articles. The Chain Cross is a variation of the Latin Cross, and is a cross that is exclusively employed in heraldry. It is also referred to as the Annulets Braced Cross.

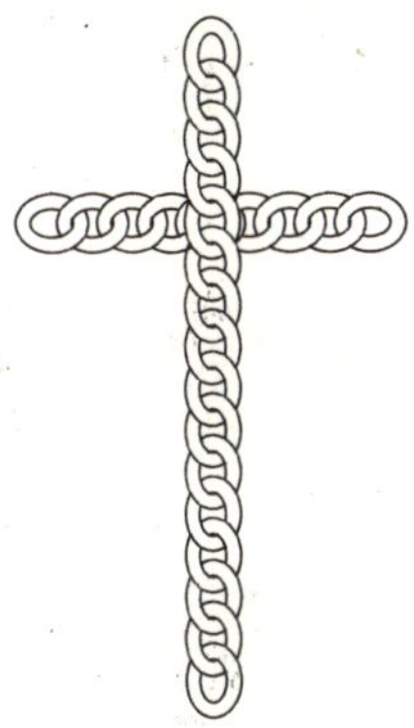

Chain Cross
aka Annulets Braced Cross

The St. Brendon's Cross is composed of two dolphins and an upright. It is a referent to the early Celtic missionary St. Brendon who was shipwrecked while travelling to a far off island and was saved by a whale or dolphin. By this type of salvation he is related to prophet Jonah. The St. Brendon's Cross is a variation of the Latin Cross and a form that is employed in heraldry. It is also referred to as the Dolphin Cross.

St. Brendon's Cross
aka Dolphin Cross

Crux Gemmata I

The Crux Gemmata I is a cross form that appears frequently in the Orthodox traditions. It is composed of thirteen gems set or inlaid upon a cruciform element. The central gem represents the Christ and the twelve other gems are symbolic of the twelve disciples. The Crux Gemmata I is a variation of the Latin Cross, and is a cross that is essentially a cross found in ecclesiastical situations.

Martin Luther Cross

The Martin Luther Cross is composed of a white rose with a heart and a dark cross all set upon a Latin Cross. The white rose became a symbol assumed by Martin Luther and symbolizes joy and peace. The red heart refers to the sacrifice of the Christ, while the black cross is a referent to mortification and pain. The large cross upon which all rests carries a similar intent. The Martin Luther Cross is a variation of the Latin Cross and a form that is almost exclusively found in heraldry.

Rosicrucian Cross II
aka Rose Cross

The Rosicrucian Cross II is a hermetic symbol of an ancient society. The rose is symbolic of the power of the blood of Christ to redeem. The Rosicrucian Cross I is a variation of the Latin Cross and is a cross that is nearly always employed in heraldry. It is also referred to as the Rose Cross.

The Midsommarstang Cross is a symbol that is found primarily in Sweden. The Midsommarstang Cross is a variation of the Latin Cross. It is strictly ecclesiastical and erected out-of-doors for the spring festival. It is rarely seen in heraldry.

Midsommarstang Cross

A cross design found in and around Kiev, consisting of a Latin Cross with eleven smaller Latin crosses, amounting to twelve crosses. This may be a reference to the twelve months of the year. The three small crosses at the top terminus refer to the three crosses of Calvary. The crosses at the end of the crosspiece are symbolic of the outstretched hands of the crucified Christ, while the four extending from the crossing is a referent to the spread of Christianity to the four quarters of the world. A variation of the Latin Cross, it is frequently employed in heraldry and may be seen adorning the steeple of churches or shrines. It is also referred to as the Ukranian Kyiv (Kiev) Cross.

Snowflake Cross I
aka Ukranian Kyiv (Kiev) Cross

The Obelus Cross I is a symbol that is found primarily in typography to indicate a footnote. The term "obelus" is Greek for a roasting spit. It is sometimes referred to as a dagger. It is rarely seen in heraldry.

Obelus Cross I

Obelus Cross II

The Obelus Cross II is a variation of the Obelus Cross I.

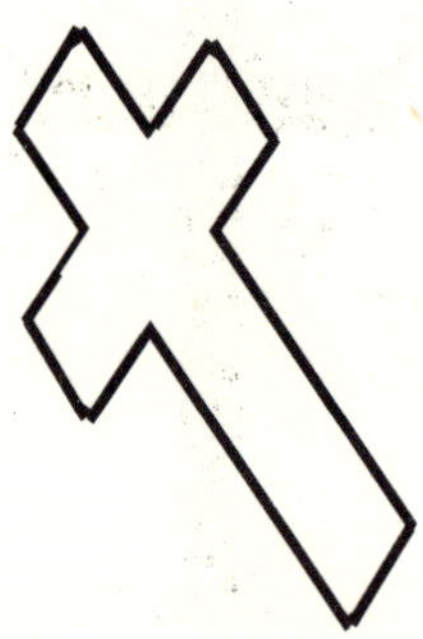

St. Gilbert's Cross II
aka Portate Cross, Portale Cross

The St. Gilbert's Cross II is a variation of the St. Gilbert's Cross I and a variation of the Latin Cross as well as being a cross that is exclusively employed in heraldry. It is also referred to as Portate Cross and Portale Cross.

Penal Cross

The Penal Cross is of seventeenth-century Irish origin. Anglican penal laws forbade the crucifix in Ireland. Small crosses with the crucifix embossed were therefore worn around the neck as a means of circumventing this restricted code. The size of the image and unusual shape was such as to make the icon nearly undetectable. The Penal Cross is a variation of the Latin Cross and a form that has purely ecclesiastical implications and use. It is rarely, if ever, seen in heraldry.

The Achaemenian Persian tombs of Cyrus, Xerxes and Darius have a cruciform element on the exterior within which the entrance and "windows" were carved. This form has no application to Christian iconography whatsoever. It is a form, as noted, that was cut into the rock face over and including the entrance to the tombs of the Persian sovereigns. This form had royal implications and was a symbol that was often associated with royalty of the period.

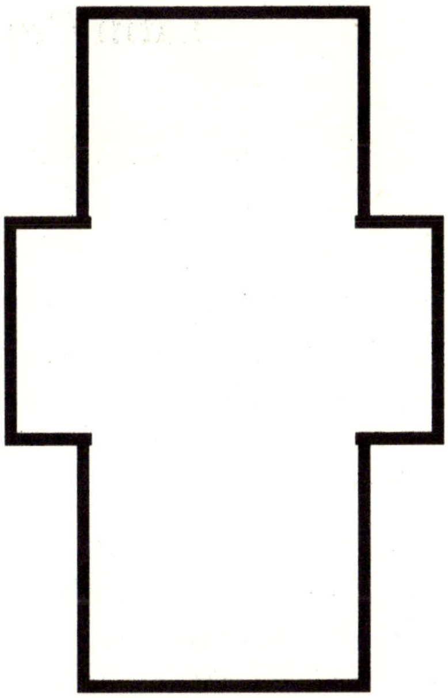

Persian Cross

The Infinity Cross is composed of two infinity symbols. It is a referent to Paradise and the everlasting joys of that place. The Infinity Cross is a variation of the Latin Cross and a form that is employed in heraldry. It is also referred to as the Everlasting Cross.

Infinity Cross
aka Everlasting Cross

Latin Crosses: Processional Variation

There are a number of specialized crosses in common use that are carried or held in ecclesiastical procession. For the most part, any number or variety of pre-existent cruciforms were utilized and affixed atop a staff. The forms were highly varied. Thus formed, the cross could be held high so that the assembled worshippers might view it. Often Processional Crosses are highly elaborate with carved or engraved surfaces, painted images and mounted with numerous jewels. The Coptic Processional Crosses provide some of the most elaborate examples. A few of the hundreds of Processional Crosses are shown below.

At times the term *hasta* is applied to Processional Crosses. *Hasta* is Latin for spear or lance. *Hasta* crosses generally do not carry militaristic implications, but are so named for their extended lower element. *Hasta* or Processional crosses are generally not employed in heraldry, but are in common use, ecclesiastically.

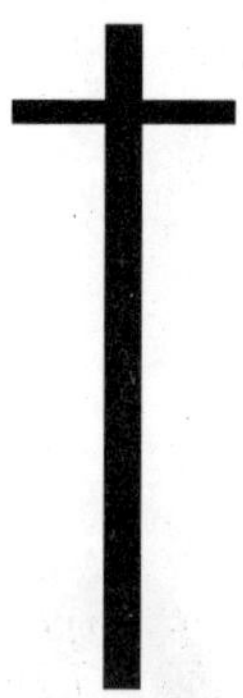

Hasta Cross
aka *crux hasta*

The Hasta Cross is variation of the Latin Cross with an elongated vertical element. It becomes a symbol representing a staff and related to a shepherd's staff, as well as Christ who is often referred to as the "Good Shepherd". The Latin term *hasta* translates a spear. However, in this case it carries no militaristic implications. The Hasta Cross is a cross that is employed in ecclesiastical situations, primarily. It is also referred to as the *crux hasta*.

Coptic Processional Cross

Coptic crosses appear in a variety of form. The Coptic Processional Cross is but one of them.

The Serbian Processional Cross, shown in a painting of Tsar Stefan Dusan, is a Patriarchal Cross adorned with prominent jewels. In this instance the cross is part of the royal regalia.

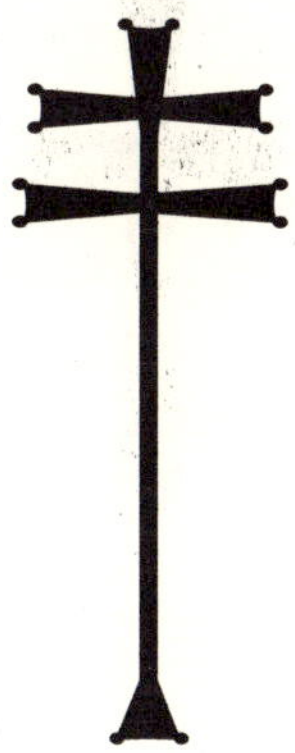

Serbian Processional Cross
(carried by Tsar Stefan Dusan)

The Crux Invincta is an implement or cross form that is associated with the Christ. It symbolizes his victory over death. This cross tops a long staff and is carried by the Christ as a child as well as after his resurrection in numerous visual representations. The Crux Invincta is a variation of Greek Cross, and is a cross that is employed in paintings and infrequently in heraldry.

Crux Invincta
aka Victory Cross

The Bouttonnée Processional Cross from Venice consists, *en forme*, of a Croix Bouttonnée. It is essentially a cross found in ecclesiastical situations.

Bouttonnée Processional Cross
(Venice)

Latin Crosses: Processional Variation (Continued)

Byzantine Processional Cross

The Byzantine Processional Cross is, *en forme*, a variation of Byzantine Cross II. It is a cross found in ecclesiastical situations and rarely appears in heraldry.

Polish Medieval Processional Cross

The Polish Medieval Processional Cross is, *en forme*, a variation of the Latin Cross. It is a cross that was employed in ecclesiastical situations solely.

Leo XIII Processional Cross

The Leo XIII Processional Cross is not unique, but exhibits a highly ornate surface. It is exclusively employed in ecclesiastical situations surrounding the Papacy.

The Coptic and Ethiopean crosses are highly individualistic and ornate, *en forme*. The Ethiopean Processional Cross is composed of a number of geometric elements. It is exclusively found in ecclesiastical situations.

Ethiopean Processional Cross

Latin Crosses: Double Crosspiece Variation

The cross with a double crosspiece is seen in various permutations of forms as well as names. As a symbol it is found in ancient Samaria as an ideogram for the sovereign. The Patriarchal Cross[1] and other ecclesiastical variations usually indicate the upper crosspiece as shorter than the lower one. In Christian iconography the upper crosspiece refers to the plaque traditionally nailed over the head of the crucified Christ bearing the letters "INRI" — i.e. *Isus Nazarenus Rex Iudaeorum* or Jesus of Nazareth King of the Jews — and referred to as the *titulus cruses*. Another important cross with a double crosspiece is the Lorraine Cross. Normally the Lorraine cross possesses two crosspieces of the same width, one close to the top and one close to the bottom. It was first employed by the Duke Godefroy de Boullion of Lorraine during his participation in a Crusade which freed Jerusalem.

Patriarchal Cross I
aka Crux Gemina, Archiepiscopal Cross, Titulus Cross

The Patriarchal Cross I is an adaptation of Latin Cross, particularly *crux humilis*, with an additional, narrower crosspiece equidistant between the top and the main crosspieces. Traditionally this cross was employed in the arms of Patriarchs of the Church, who were considered second to the Pope. Patriarchal Cross I in which the upper cross arm is shorter and symbolizes the placard, the titulus, that was nailed at the top with the Christogram: "INRI". The Patriarchal Cross I is a cross found in ecclesiastical situations and environs, and also appears in heraldry. It is also referred to as Crux Gemina, Archiepiscopal Cross, and Titulus Cross.

[1] The patriarchate is essentially divided into four main groups — i.e. Orthodox Patriarchs of Kiev, Greece, Albania and Poland; Eastern Orthodoxy including the Patriarches of Antioch, Alexandria, Constantinople, Jerusalem, Moscow, Georgia, Romania, Bulgaria and Serbia; the Oriental Orthodoxy including the Malankara Orthodox Sxvian Church, Jacobite Syrian Christian Church, Armenia, Auxum and Asmara; Latin Patriarchs of Venice, Lisbon, East Indies and Jerusalem.

The Patriarchal Cross II is an adaptation of the Patriarchal Cross I as well as being one of the numerous crosses with a double crosspiece. In this variation the extension of one of the arms of the upper crosspiece is the same as that crosspiece's distance from the top. The main crosspiece mimics that distance. It may also be viewed, *en forme*, as a Greek Cross atop a Tau cross. The Patriarchal Cross II is a variation of the Patriarchal Cross I and related to the Latin Cross. It is a cross that is frequently employed in heraldry. It is also, at times, referred to as Cross of Lorraine.

Patriarchal Cross II
aka Cross of Lorraine

The Patriarchal Cross III is a variation of the Patriarchal Cross I with the second additional crosspiece, slanted at the bottom. This is seen as a footrest — i.e. the *suppedaneum*. This cross is a cross in common use. At times it is confused with the Eastern Orthodox Cross or the Russian Cross. The Patriarchal Cross III is related to the Latin Cross, particularly *crux humilis* variation. It is a form that is frequently employed in heraldry particularly of the Eastern Rite churches. It is also referred to as the *crux suppedaneum*.

Patriarchal Cross III
aka *crux suppedaneum*

The Patriarchal Cross IV is derived from Patriarchal Cross I as well as being one of the numerous crosses with a double crosspiece. Here all the terminations are triple budded (trefoil) creating a distinctive variation. The Patriarchal Cross IV is related to the Latin Cross. It is also referred to as the Narbonne Cross.

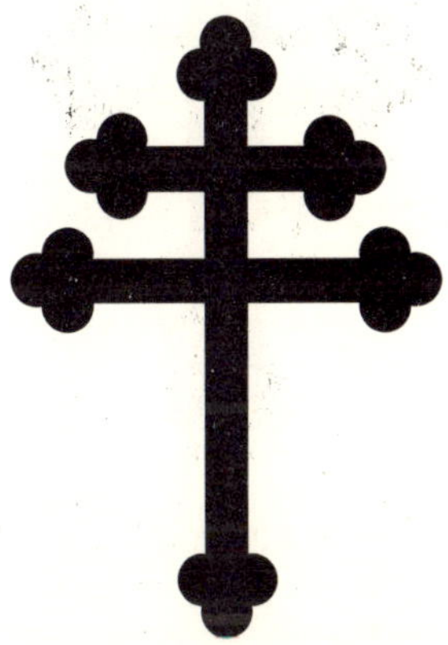

Patriarchal Cross IV
aka Narbonne Cross

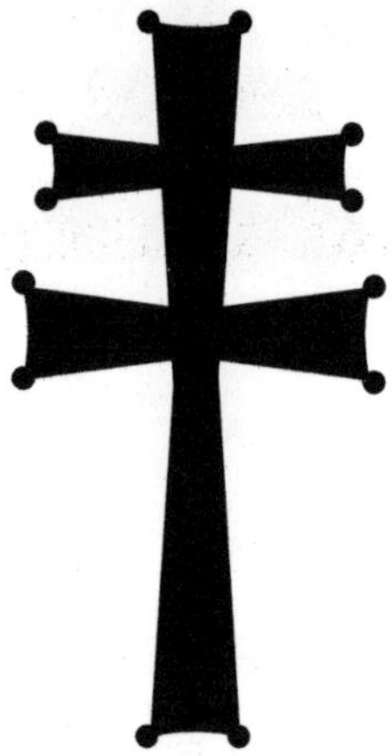

Pattée Patriarch Cross

The Pattée Patriarch Cross is derived from Patriarchal Cross I as well as being one of the numerous crosses with a double crosspiece. Here all the terminations are adorned with gems creating a distinctive variation. The Pattée Patriarch Cross is a variation that is indigenous to Hungary.

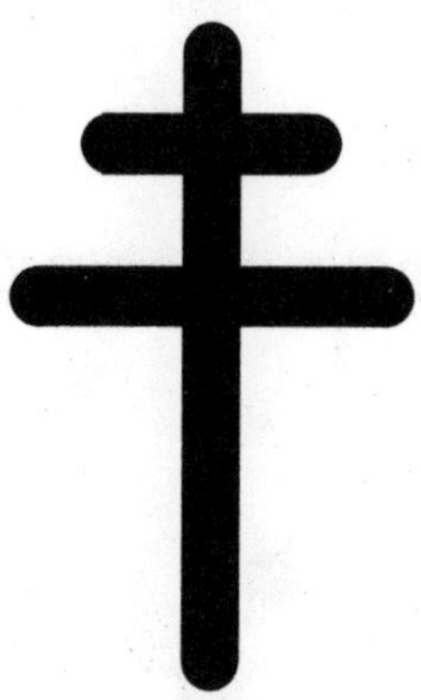

Moussé Patriarchal Cross
aka Cross of Lorraine

The Mousée Patriarchal Cross is a variation of the Patriarchal Cross I as well as being one of the numerous crosses with a double crosspiece. It is also referred to as the Cross of Lorraine.

St. Nicholas Cross
aka St. Olga's Cross

The St. Nicholas Cross is imposed of both a *crux boutonée* and the Patriarchal Cross III as well as being one of the numerous crosses with a double crosspiece. St. Nicholas was the Archbishop of Myrna and was popular among both the Roman Catholics of the eastern Mediterranean and the Orthodox Christians as well. This cross is also associated with St. Olga of Kiev who was Regent of Kiev, grandmother of St. Vladimir and great grandmother of Sts. Boris and Gleb. The St. Nicholas Cross is a variation of the Patriarchal Cross III and related to the Latin Cross. The Cross is a symbol found in ecclesiastical situations and environs, and occasionally appears in heraldry of both the Roman and the Orthodox churches. It is also referred to as the St. Olga's Cross.

Latin Crosses: Double Crosspiece Variation (Continued)

The Lorraine Cross I is the simplest form of that cross as well as being one of the numerous crosses with a double crosspiece. It is a sign found in the tenth century and first encorporated by Godefroy de Boullion into his arms. Later, it was associated with René d'Anjou and the Hermetic revival. This cross is a variation of the Latin Cross with an additional crosspiece. A variation in which the lower cross arm appears in equal relation to the bottom of the vertical as does the top crosspiece. This cross form may be viewed as a Latin Cross with a cross of St. Peter overlaid upon it. The Lorraine Cross I is a variation of the Patriarchal Cross and associated with the Latin Cross. It is a cross that is frequently employed in heraldry. It is also referred to as the *crux gemina*.

Lorraine Cross I
aka *crux gemina*

The Lorraine Cross II is the traditional form employed in the arms of the Dukes of Lorraine as well as being one of the numerous crosses with a double crosspiece. The terminations bear a lozenge with three small botons, or a bezant with three botons similarly placed. The Lorraine Cross II is a variation of the Patriarchal Cross and associated with the Latin Cross. It is a cross that is frequently employed in heraldry. It is also referred to as the *crux gemina*.

Lorraine Cross II
aka *crux gemina*

The Lorraine Cross III is a variation on the Lorraine Cross I, as well as being one of the numerous crosses with a double crosspiece, but with the top crosspiece shorter than the bottom. The Lorraine Cross III is a variation of the Latin Cross, and is a symbol that is frequently employed in heraldry. It is also referred to as the *crux gemina*, Lothringian Cross, Free French Cross, and de Gaulle Cross.

Lorraine Cross III
aka *crux gemina*, Lothringian Cross, Free French Cross, de Gaulle Cross

Lorraine Cross IV
aka *crux gemina,* Free French Cross,
de Gaulle Cross

The Lorraine Cross IV is a variation of the Lorraine Cross I, but with the top crosspiece shorter than the bottom and equidistant from the top and the main crosspiece. The main crosspiece is equidistant between the top and bottom of the upright. The Lorraine Cross IV is a variation of the Latin Cross, and is a cross that is employed in heraldry. It is also referred to as the *crux gemina,* Free French Cross and de Gaulle Cross.

Lorraine Cross V
aka *crux gemina,* Free French Cross,
de Gaulle Cross

The Lorraine Cross V is a variation of the Lorraine Cross IV, as well as being one of the numerous crosses with a double crosspiece, but with the addition of triple botons (trefoil) at the end of each termination. The Lorraine Cross V is a variation of the Latin Cross and is a cross that is seen in heraldry. It is also referred to as the *crux gemina,* Free French Cross and de Gaulle Cross.

Rogacina Przekrzyzowana Cross

The Rogacina Przekrzyzowana Cross is a variation of the Latin Cross with an additional crosspiece. It, along with Osmorog Cross, Rogacina Dwukrotnie Przekrzyzowana Cross and Rogacina Cross are uniquely Polish in character and design. A Polish heraldic cross with a second crosspiece, it is related to the Cross of Lorraine and the Thieves' Cross II.

The Caravaca Cross is a cross form that was popular in Mexico, being brought there by the Franciscan missionaries as well as being one of the numerous crosses with a double crosspiece. Its origin is supposedly from Caravaca, Spain, where the original cross carried a piece of True Cross at the crossing — hence the quatrefoil piercing and the appearance of a reliquary space. The Caravaca Cross is a variation of the Patriarchal Cross I, and is a cross that is employed in heraldry.

Caravaca Cross

The Zurich Cross is a highly unique cruciform found in the colophon of the Zwingli Bible in Zurich. It is a variation of the Latin Cross with a double crosspiece. The upper crosspiece and the foot are moline in character, while the lower crosspiece is emousée. The Zurich Cross is a cross that is employed in religious heraldry.

Zurich Cross

Traditionally the Anchor Cross I is symbolic of hope as well as being one of the numerous crosses with a double crosspiece. It also reflects the Christ as the fisher of men. The Anchor Cross I is also associated with St. Clement, an early Bishop of Rome, who was executed by being tied to an anchor and tossed into the sea. It is a variation of the Latin Cross with an additional crosspiece forming the bottom portion of an anchor. It is also referred to as St. Clement's Cross and Mariner's Cross.

Anchor Cross I
aka St. Clement's Cross, Mariner's Cross

Anchor Cross II
aka St. Clement's Cross, Mariner's Cross

The Anchor Cross II is a variation of Anchor Cross I as well as being one of the numerous crosses with a double crosspiece. The terminations of the upper crosspiece are triangular, *en forme*. It is also referred to as St. Clement's Cross and Mariner's Cross.

Long Cross Felloe

The Long Cross Felloe is a variation of the Patriarchal Cross and the Thieves Cross I as well as being one of the numerous crosses with a double crosspiece. It is often seen in heraldry but seldom in ecclesiastical situations.

Rebated Lambeau Cross
aka Lorraine Cross (with hook)

The Rebated Lambeau Cross is a variation of the Patriarchal Cross and the Lambeau Cross I as well as being one of the numerous crosses with a double crosspiece. It is often seen in heraldry but seldom in ecclesiastical situations. It is also referred to as Lorraine Cross with hook.

The Patriarchal Paté Fleury Cross is a variation of Patté Cross I and the *Fleur-de-lys* Cross as well as being one of the numerous crosses with a double crosspiece. It is often seen in heraldry but seldom in ecclesiastical situations.

Patriarchal Paté Fleury Cross

The Patriarchal Cross V is a seldom encountered variation of the Patriarchal Cross I and related to Potent Cross as well as being one of the numerous crosses with a double crosspiece. It is often seen in heraldry but seldom in ecclesiastical situations.

Patriarchal Cross V
aka *crux gemina*, Portate Patriarchal Cross

The Patriarchal Paté Cross is a variation of the Patriarchal Cross as well as being one of the numerous crosses with a double crosspiece. It is often seen in heraldry but seldom in ecclesiastical situations.

Patriarchal Paté Cross

Patriarchal Pommeté Cross

The Patriarchal Pommeté Cross is a variation of the Patriarchal Cross as well as being one of the numerous crosses with a double crosspiece. It is often seen in heraldry but seldom in ecclesiastical situations.

Patriarchal Charged and Voided Cross

The Patriarchal Charged and Voided Cross is a variation of the Patriarchal Cross as well as being one of the numerous crosses with a double crosspiece. It is often seen in heraldry but seldom in ecclesiastical situations.

Patriarchal Paté Conjoined and Annulated Cross

The Patriarchal Paté Conjoined and Annulated Cross is a rare variation of the Patriarchal Cross as well as being one of the numerous crosses with a double crosspiece. It is often seen in heraldry but seldom in ecclesiastical situations.

Latin Crosses: Double Crosspiece, Militaristic Variation

There are an extremely small number of partriarchal-type crosses than can be considered as militaristic.

The Enhendée Cross I is an adaptation of the Patriarchal Cross I. In this variation the extension of the foot of the cross terminates in either an abbreviated *fleur-de-lys* or in a termination similar to the foot of the Zurich Cross. The Enhendée refers to a termination, the form similar to the Patonce Cross as described by Pierre Palliot in delineating the Bishop of Herchfield's Patriarchal Cross. The Enhendée Cross is a variation of the Latin Cross. It is a cross that is employed in heraldry. It is also referred to as Anserated Cross.

Enhendée Cross I
aka Anserated Cross

The Patriarchal Cross Fitchy is part of the arms of those associated with Knights of the Grand Cross, and particularly those of high ecclesiastical rank in Canada. Any fitchy-footed symbol refers to unshakable faith and the defence thereof. A variation of the Latin Cross with two cross pieces — i.e. the Patriarchal Cross — and a cross that is frequently employed in heraldry. It is also referred to as the *crux gemina fitchée* the and Knights of the Grand Cross.

Patriarchal Cross Fitchy
aka *crux gemina fitchée*, Knights of the Grand Cross

Latin Crosses: Triple Crosspiece Variation

The cross with three crosspieces is one that finds less permutations than the cross with two crosspieces. There are various interpretations regarding the three crosspieces (*see* Papal Cross I, re. ecclesiastical interpretation). Those outside the Roman Catholic Church see the three crosspieces as representing the Trinity, the three crosses of Calvary, and the three principles of faith, hope and love. Outside of the Papal Cross, the triple crosspiece cross is encountered in the Eastern Orthodox Cross, Rogacina Dwukrotnie Przekrzyzowana Cross of Poland and the Cross Crosslet Crossed. The Eastern Orthodox Cross's crosspieces have an entirely different interpretation. However, as one of the two major liturgical and apostolic faiths — i.e. along with Roman Catholicism — the three crosspieces may also be seen as a parallel variation of Papal Cross and a subtle means of establishing its own co-primacy. The Rogacina Dwukrotnie Przekrzyzowana Cross may be viewed as related to the Eastern Orthodox Cross. The Cross Crosslet Crossed is a variation on a theme.

Papal Cross I
aka Patriarchal Cross, Maronite's Cross

The Papal Cross I is a variation of the Latin Cross with two additional crosspieces. This cross is only associated with the papacy and is seen in the coat of arms of the individual popes. The three arms symbolize a number of concepts. Initially it is seen to represent the trinity, the three crosses of Calvary, and religious authority on earth, in the church and heaven. It also symbolizes the Pope as Bishop of Rome, Patriarch of the West and Successor of St. Peter. The addition of the third crosspiece indicates the Pope's supremacy over the Patriarchs who possess but two crosspieces in their crosses. The Papal Cross I is a cross that is only employed in papal heraldry. It is also referred to as Patriarchal Cross, and the Maronite's Cross.

Papal Cross II

The Papal Cross II is seen by many to be the earliest form of the Papal Cross. In this version, the two short arms are placed equidistant from the top and bottom of the upright and the central crosspiece. The Papal Cross II is a cross that is only employed in papal heraldry.

Latin Crosses: Triple Crosspiece Variation (Continued)

The Papal Cross III is a variation of both Papal Cross I and II. In this version the crosspieces are all of the same width. This would seem to imply that the various interpretations as listed in Papal Cross I are all of equal importance. They refer to the equality of the pope as the Bishop of Rome, the Patriarch of the West and the Successor of St. Peter. It is a cross that is only employed in papal heraldry. It is also referred to as the Patriarchal Cross, and the Maronite's Cross.

Papal Cross III
aka Patriarchal Cross, Maronite's Cross

The Eastern Orthodox Cross I is a variation of the Latin Cross with two additional crosspieces. The upper crosspiece is the *titulus cruses* carrying the acronym INRI — i.e. *Isus Nazarenus Rex Iudaeorum* or Jesus of Nazareth King of the Jews — and the angled bottom crosspiece is seen as a footrest — i.e. *suppadaneum*. It is seen as part of the preservation of the Eastern Orthodox tradition from Constantinople (Byzantium) as practised in Russia. It is also referred to as the Russian Cross, Eastern Cross, Slavic Cross, Ukraine Cross, *crux suppadaneum* and Cross of the Fathers.

Eastern Orthodox Cross I
aka Russian Cross, Eastern Cross, Slavic Cross, Ukraine Cross, *crux suppedaneum*, Cross of the Fathers

The Eastern Orthodox Cross II is a variation of the Eastern Orthodox Cross I. It is seen as part of the preservation of the Eastern Orthodox tradition from Constantinople (Byzantium) as practised in Russia. It is also referred to as the Russian Cross, Eastern Cross, Slavic Cross, Ukraine Cross, *crux suppadaneum* and Cross of the Fathers.

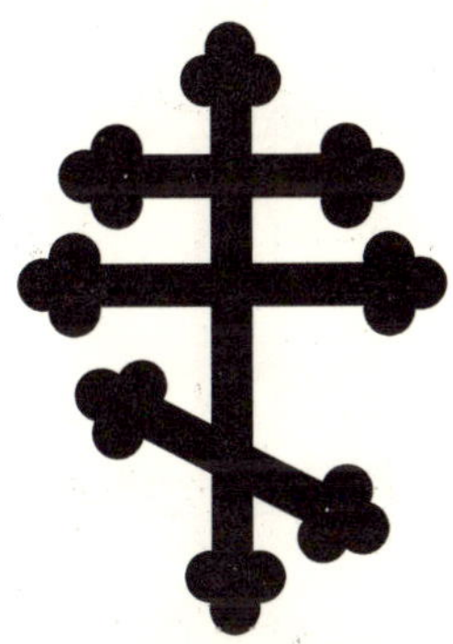

Eastern Orthodox Cross II
aka Russian Cross, Eastern Cross, Slavic Cross, Ukraine Cross, *crux suppedaneum*, Cross of the Fathers

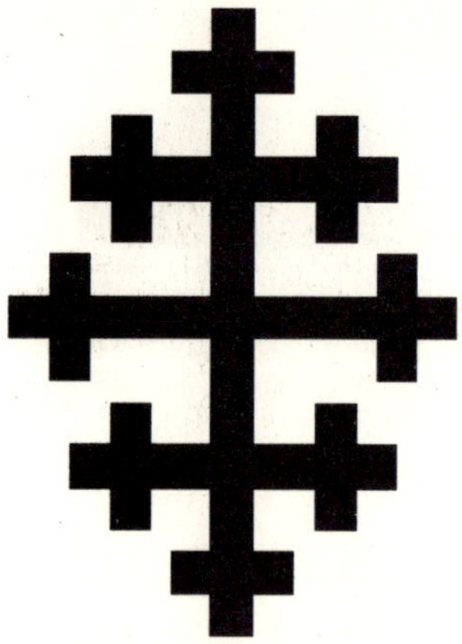

Cross Crosslet Crossed I

The Cross Crosslet Crossed I is a variation of the Papal Cross II. The crosslets proliferate and amount to eight which is a number associated with Paradise and also the day of circumcision and resurrection after the entry into Jerusalem. It is a variation of the Latin Cross with two additional crosspieces.

Rogacina Dwukrotnie Przekrzyzowana Cross

The Rogacina Dwukrotnie Przekrzyzowana Cross is a variation of the Lorraine Cross with an additional crosspiece. It, along with the Osmorog Cross, Rogacina Przekrzyzowana Cross and Rogacina Cross are uniquely Polish in character and design. The Rogacina Dwukrotnie Przekrzyzowana Cross is a Polish heraldic cross with a third crosspiece that is also related to the Papal Cross.

Rogacina Przekrzyzowana i Rozdarta Cross

The Rogacina Przekrzyzowana Rozdarta Cross is a variation of the Papal Cross and Rogacina Dwukrotnie Przekrzyzowana Cross. It, along with the Osmorog Cross, Rogacina Przekrzyzowana Cross and Rogacina Cross, is uniquely Polish in character and design. The Rogacina Przekrzyzowana i Rozdarta Cross is a Polish heraldic cross with three crosspieces.

The Lorraine Cross VI is a variation of the Lorraine Cross IV, but with the addition of the crosspieces to an anchor. The Lorraine Cross VI is a variation of the Anchor Cross I and related to the Latin Cross. It is a form that is seen in heraldry.

Lorraine Cross VI

Latin Crosses: Militaristic Variation

A number of Latin crosses are directly associated with military orders and/or have intrinsic military associations — i.e. weapons. Many of these forms found their genesis during the crusades. *En forme,* the crosspieces and upper portion of the vertical member resemble the hilt of a sword. The aggressive nature of Christianity as epitomized in the crusades, underlines this quality. Most, if not all, of the examples illustrated are connected with war or armed conflict or religious orders that are militaristic. One of the characteristics of militaristic crosses is to be seen with the fitchy foot, or a dagger or sword-like lower part of the vertical element. In other examples, the lower termination is in the form of an Enhende or Patonce Cross or as a *fleur-de-lys* of various and often exaggerated form. These are often referred to and resemble an elaborate spear or lance head.

Cleves Cross I
aka Latin Cross Flory

The Cleves Cross I is related to the Fleury Cross and *Fleur-de-lys* Cross. A variation of the Latin Cross and related to the Cleves Cross III. The Cleves Cross I is solely found in heraldry and its terminations possess a decided militaristic connotation with the exaggerated *fleur-de-lys*. The Cleves Cross I is also referred to as the Latin Cross Flory.

Fleury Cross
aka Croix Fleurée, Flory Cross, Floretty Cross, Fleuronny Cross

A variation of the Latin Cross, which has militaristic applications. Related to *Fleur-de-lys* Cross and as such, its form also recalls a barbed fighting spear. It is frequently employed in heraldry. It is also referred to as the Croix Fleurée, Flory Cross, Floretty Cross and Fleuronny Cross.

Latin Crosses: Militaristic Variation (Continued)

A variation of the Latin Cross which has militaristic applications. Related to *Fleur-de-lys* Cross and as such, its form also recalls a barbed fighting spear. It is frequently employed in heraldry.

Fleurette Cross

Enhendée Cross II is a variation of the Patriarchal Cross which has militaristic applications. Related to the Gothic Cross and Cross Moline. Its form also recalls a barbed fighting spear. It is frequently employed in heraldry.

Enhendée Cross II

The Fleur-de-lys Cross is a variation of Latin Cross which has militaristic applications. It is related to the Gothic Cross and Cross Moline. The *fleur-de-lys* form, which is more developed than the triple elements of the Gothic Cross, also recalls a barbed fighting spear. It is frequently employed in heraldry.

Fleur-de-lys Cross

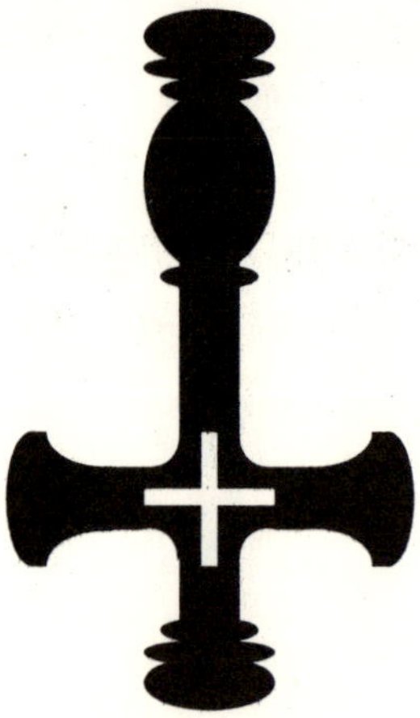

Thor's Cross
aka Thor's Hammer

It is a variation of the St. Peter Cross which has militaristic applications. The Thor's Cross is the hammer of Thor with the application of a Greek Cross at the cross piece. It is frequently employed in heraldry. It is also referred to as the Thor's Hammer.

Sacrifice Cross

Sacrifice Cross is a variation of the Latin Cross which has militaristic applications. In this a sword is superimposed over the cross form. It is often used at war memorial sites.

Latin Crosses: Fitchy Militaristic Variation

Numerous Latin crosses are derived from other Latin or Greek crosses and possess a pointed (fiché) lower extension or foot. This gives the cross a decided dagger-like appearance and emphasizes its military association.

A Dutch cross, the Order of Saint Jacob Cross indicates a fitchy foot.

Order of Saint Jacob Cross

The Fitchy-Footed Cross is one of the simplest of the militaristic variations. It is, at times, seen as a simple marker that is driven into the earth as a sign or as a place of temporary worship. However, the fitchy-foot is unmistakable in its blade-like appearance. Any fitchy-footed symbol refers to unshakable faith and the defence thereof. The Fitchy-Footed Cross is a variation of the Latin Cross and a symbol that is only encountered in heraldry. It is also referred to as the Fixed Cross and Fitchy-foote Cross.

Fitchy-Footed Cross
aka Fixed Cross, Fitchy-foote Cross

Order of St. James Cross I
aka St. James Cross, Orden de Santiago de Espada Cross, Military Order of St. James of the Sword, Flory Fitch Cross

The Order of St. James Cross I is a variation of Latin Cross which has militaristic applications. This cross with blade is dedicated to St. James the Greater who is the patron of the military Orden de Santiago de Compestela (Order of St. James of Compostela), one of the four major religio-militaristic Spanish orders. The lower member is in the form of a knife or dagger. Any fitchy-footed symbol refers to unshakable faith and the defence thereof. The Cross of St. James is red in colour. The Order of St. James Cross I is a variation of the Latin Cross and a cross that is frequently employed in heraldry. It is also referred to as the St. James Cross, Orden de Santiago de Espada Cross, Military Order of St. James of the Sword and Flory Fitch Cross.

Order of St. James Cross II
aka Orden de Santiago de Espada Cross, Military Order of St. James of the Sword

The Order of St. James Cross II is a variation of the simple Order of St. James Cross I in which the *fleur-de-lys* forms have been exaggerated as well as the fitchy foot which refers to unshakable faith and the defence. The Order of St. James Cross II is a variation of the Latin Cross with militaristic applications and is a cross that is employed in heraldry. It is also referred to as the Orden de Santiago de Espada Cross or Military Order of St. James of the Sword.

Order of St. James Cross III
aka St. James Cross, Orden de Santiago de Espada Cross, Military Order of St. James of the Sword, Flory Fitch Cross

The Order of St. James Cross III is a variation of the Order of St. James Cross II in which the crosspiece terminations are exaggerated. The Order of St. James Cross III is a variation of the Latin Cross and a symbol that is employed in heraldry. It is also referred to as the St. James Cross, Orden de Santiago de Espada Cross, Military Order of St. James of the Sword and Flory Fitch Cross.

The Order of St. James Cross IV is a variation of the Order of St. James Cross II in which the crosspiece and the top terminations are similar and spear-head-like. The Order of St. James Cross IV is a variation of the Latin Cross and a symbol that is employed in heraldry. It is also referred to as the St. James Cross, Orden de Santiago de Espada Cross and Flory Fitch Cross or Military Order of St. James of the Sword.

Order of St. James Cross IV
aka Orden de Santiago de Espada Cross, Military Order of St. James of the Sword

The Pattée Fitchée Cross I is essentially a simple pattée cross in which the lower part of the upright is a pointed blade that resembles a dagger. As with any fitchy-footed cross, the symbol refers to unshakable faith and the defence. The Pattée Fitchée Cross I is a variation of the Latin Cross which has militaristic applications. It is a cross that is employed in heraldry. It is also referred to as the Croix Patté Fiché.

Pattée Fitchée Cross I
aka Croix Patté Fiché

The Pattée Fitchée Cross II is a variation of the Latin Cross, and has militaristic applications. The pointed blade has militaristic connotations. Any fitchy-footed symbol refers to unshakable faith and the defence thereof. It is a cross that is frequently employed in heraldry. It is also referred to as Croix Patté Fiché and Fitchy Foot Croos.

Pattée Fitchée Cross II
aka Croix Patté Fiché, Pattée Fitchy Foot Cross

Crosslet Fitchy Cross I
aka Croix Fiché

Crosslet Fitchy Cross I is a variation of the Latin Cross which has militaristic applications. Represents the trinity and the lower member is in the form of a knife or dagger. Any fitchy-footed symbol refers to unshakable faith and the defence thereof. A cross that is frequently employed in heraldry. It is also referred to as the Croix Fiché.

Crosslet Fitchy Cross II
aka Croix Fiché

The Crosslet Fitchy Cross II is a variation of the Crosslet Fitchy Cross I which has militaristic applications. It represents the trinity and the lower member is in the form of a knife or dagger. Any fitchy-footed symbol refers to unshakable faith and the defence thereof. A cross that is frequently employed in heraldry. It is also referred to as the Croix Fiché.

Bouttonnée Fichée Cross
aka Order of the Holy Sepulchre Cross, Botonny Fitchy Cross, Budded Fitchy Cross, Croix Tréfflée Fichée, Trefoil Fitchy Cross

The Bouttonnée Fichée Cross as with other fitchy-foot crosses may be viewed as being forced into the earth and used during temporary religious ceremonies. The Bouttonnée Fichée Cross is a variation of the Latin Cross, specifically Bouttonnée Cross, and a cross that is solely found in heraldry, in particular it is included in the arms of high ecclesiastical rank in Canada. It is also referred to as the Order of the Holy Sepulchre Cross, Botonny Fitchy Cross, Budded Fitchy Cross, Croix Tréfflée Fichée and Trefoil Fitchy Cross.

The Couped Fitchy Fusil Cross is a variation of the Tau Cross Fitchy which has militaristic applications. The addition of the fusil may refer to the original bearer's profession. Any fitchy-footed symbol refers to unshakable faith and the defence thereof. The Couped Fitchy Fusil Cross is frequently employed in heraldry.

Couped Fitchy Fusil Cross

A variation of the Pattée Fitchée Cross II, the Pattée Fitchée Rebated Cross has militaristic applications. The blunted blade has militaristic connotations that may refer to a more peaceful application. It is a cross that is employed in heraldry. It is also referred to as the Paty Fitchy Foot Rebated Cross.

Pattée Fitchée Rebated Cross
aka Paty Fitchy Foot Rebated Cross

A variation of the Pattée Fitchée Cross II, the Pattée Double Fitchée Cross has militaristic applications. It, with a double blade, has militaristic connotation. Any fitchy-footed symbol refers to unshakable faith and the defence thereof. The Pattée Double Fitchée Cross is a cross that is employed in heraldry.

Pattée Double Fitchée Cross

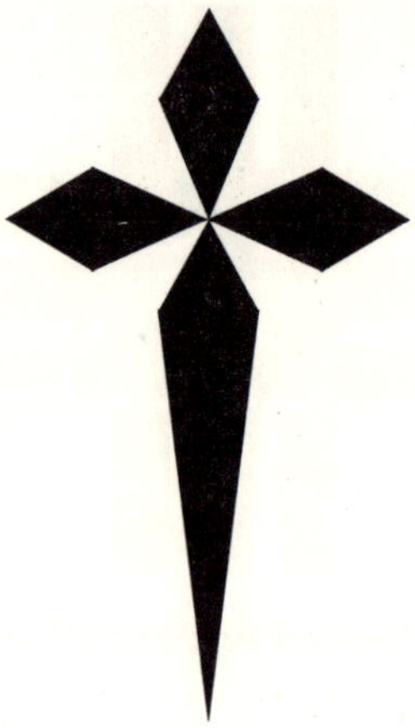

Obelus Fitchy Cross I

The Obelus Fitchy Cross I is a symbol that is found primarily in typography to indicate a footnote. The term "obelus" is Greek for a roasting spit. It is sometimes referred to as a dagger. It is rarely seen in heraldry and is a variation of the Obelus Cross I.

Obelus Fitchy Cross II

The Obelus Fitchy Cross II is a variation of the Obelus Cross I.

Greek Crosses

The Greek Cross, *crux quadrata,* as it applies to Christian iconography, is essentially a design device and the various permutations are usually referred to as "armoury" related — i.e. designed for a circular shield. *En forme,* the Greek Cross was not an implement of execution. This cruciform type appears early in human history and culture; such as it is found in caves and petroglyphs. It is the Chinese character (+) for the numeral ten (10). Its application to Christian iconography immediately follows the acceptance and appearance of Latin Cross. Its appearance in the Common Era (CE) is most often encountered in European heraldry, particularly during and after the crusades. For this type of employment the Greek Cross is eminently applicable to round shields as well as coats of arms. Some surmise that its popularity was due to those who had a preference for symmetry as it is a cross-axial form. It is of interest to note that the variations of the Greek Cross far outnumber those found between Tau and Latin crosses combined. In this section, there are a number of crosses which resemble a Greek Cross only in that they are cross-axial and/or fit within a square.

Along with the Tau Cross, the Greek Cross is one of the simplest of the cross forms and is in common use. It is associated with the square. Early Christian churches tended to be either Tau Cross or Latin Cross in design. When green, it is known as the St. Lazarus Cross I. The origins appear to be early Turkic/Armenian and are referred to as *animal*. The Greek Cross is frequently employed in heraldry as well as in ecclesiastical situations. It is also referred to as *crux immissa quadrata*, St. George's Cross, Earth Cross, Wind Cross and St. Lazarus Cross.

Greek Cross
aka *crux immissa quadrata*, St. George's Cross, Earth Cross, Wind Cross, St. Lazarus Cross

The Fracted Cross is so called because the surface is broken up — i.e. fractured. The result of being "fracted" here provides a cross with a decidedly three-dimensional appearance. The Fracted Cross is a variation of the Greek Cross and a cross-form symbol that is frequently employed in heraldry as well as in ecclesiastical situations. It is also referred to as Gobony Cross.

Fracted Cross
aka Gobony Cross

Quarter Pierced Cross I
aka Quarter-voided Cross, Square-pierced Cross, Croix Equipollée

The Quarter Pierced Cross I is composed of five sections. Normally, the centre section is of the same colour as the field upon which the cross sits. The four "arms" may refer to the four quarters or the four mysteries of the cross. The Quarter Pierced Cross I is a variation of the Greek Cross and a symbol that is only encountered in heraldry. It is also referred to as the Quarter-voided Cross, Square-pierced Cross and Croix Equipollée.

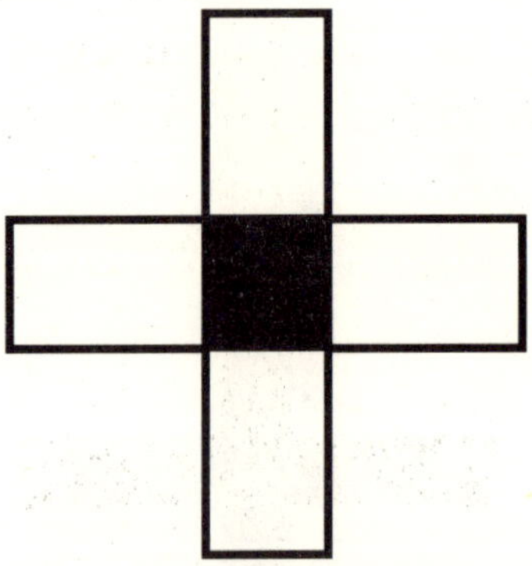

Quarter Pierced Cross II
aka Quarter-voided Cross, Square-pierced Cross, Croix Equipollée

The Quarter Pierced Cross II is a variation of Quarter Pierced Cross I as well as of the Greek Cross, and a symbol that is solely employed in heraldry (*see* Quarter Pierced Cross I). It is also referred to as Quarter-voided Cross, Square-pierced Cross and Croix Equipollée.

Tronçonnée Cross
aka Croix Demembré, Dismembered Cross

The Tronçonnée Cross is a variation of the quarter Pierced crosses as well as of the Greek Cross. The name refers to the separation into five parts of the cross. The term *tronçonnée* means "dismembered". It is a cross that is employed in heraldry but not in ecclesiastical situations. It is also referred to as the Croix Demembré and the Dismembered Cross.

The Saltired Cross is not to be confused with Saltire Cross. In this instance the "Saltire" refers to the "X" formed at the crossing. This is a cross denoted polarity. The Saltired Cross is a variation of the Greek Cross and a symbol that is employed in heraldry.

Saltired Cross

The Conqueror's Cross displays the first and last letters of Jesus (IC) and the first and last letters of Christ (XC) above the crosspiece. Below is the Greek word for conqueror (NIKA). It is a variation of the Greek Cross, and is a cross that is found in ecclesiastical situations and environs, and also appears in heraldry. It is also referred to as the Victor's Cross.

Conqueror's Cross
aka Victor's Cross

The Peronnée Cross is based upon both the Teutonic Cross and Calvary Cross I. The steps can differ in number, as many as eight may be seen. It is a variation of Greek Cross and is frequently employed in heraldry. It is also referred to as the Conjoined Cross, Gradey Cross, Graded Cross, Stepped Cross and Altar Cross.

Peronnée Cross
aka Conjoined Cross, Gradey Cross, Graded Cross, Stepped Cross, Altar Cross

Greek Crosses: Surface Variation

The surface of the Greek Cross provides a canvas upon which a number of variations are displayed. In nearly every case these crosses are heraldic in nature.

Quarter Cross

The Quarter Cross refers to the fact that there are four divisions, quarters. Frequently, they are coloured as shown to the right. The Quarter Cross also resembles the Gammadia Cross I. The Quarter Cross is a variation of the Greek Cross and a form that is employed in heraldry.

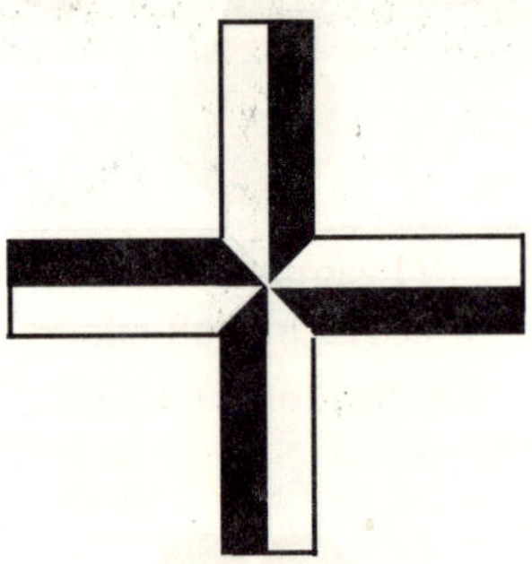

Gyronny Cross
aka Croix Gyronnée

The Gyronny Cross is a variation of the Quarter Cross. Gyroné refers to the alternated eight divisions and is symbolic of unity. The term is employed in tailoring in which eight alternate parts are joined as seen in the illustration to the right forming a pin-wheel design. The Gyronny Cross is also a variation of the Greek Cross and is employed in heraldry. It is also referred to as the Croix Gyronnée.

Compony Cross
aka Gobony Cross

The Compony Cross is one of a number of crosses with a surface consisting of a repeat design. In this case a positive–negative square pattern would seem to suggest polarity, but in the case of the "compony" design, the pattern refers to constancy. The compony variation is frequently encountered as a border pattern on shields. The Compony Cross is a variation of the Greek Cross and a symbol that is always employed in heraldry and never in ecclesiastical situations. It is also referred to as the Gobony Cross.

The Potenty Cross is one of a number of crosses with a surface consisting of a repeat design. In this case a positive–negative potent or crutch pattern which again suggests polarity as well as strength. The Potenty Cross is a variation of the Greek Cross and a symbol that is frequently employed in heraldry but never seen in ecclesiastical situations. It is also referred to the Potent Cross and Potency Cross.

Potenty Cross
aka Potent Cross, Potency Cross

The Vairy Cross is one of a number of crosses with a surface consisting of a repeat design. In this case there is a positive–negative bell-like pattern, which again suggests polarity. The "vair" variation is derived from a pattern employed in the fur lining of cloaks. The fur employed was from small animals which necessitated this type of repeat. Many refer to the "vair" element as a bell. The Vairy Cross is a variation of the Greek Cross and a symbol that is frequently employed in heraldry. It is also referred to as the Very Cross and Croix Vairé.

Vairy Cross
aka Very Cross, Croix Vairé

The Checky Cross is a cross with a surface consisting of a repeat design. In this case a checkerboard pattern which suggests polarity as well as constancy. The Checky Cross is a variation of the Greek Cross. It is only encountered in heraldry. It is also referred to as the Croix Echequetée.

Checky Cross
aka Croix Echequetée

Point in Point Cross

The Point in Point Cross is one of a number of crosses with a surface consisting of a repeat design. In this case, there is a positive–negative triangular pattern which again suggests polarity as well as being somewhat aggressive in appearance. The Point in Point Cross is a variation of the Greek Cross and a symbol that is only employed in heraldry and never in ecclesiastical situations.

Greek Crosses: Crosslet/Potence Variation

The Cross Crosslet Cross derives one of its names from "potent" referring to a crutch from the Old French "potence". "Potent" is also derived from the Latin "potentia" meaning powerful. It is a cross that along with the Teutonic Cross is sometimes associated with crusading knights. It represents the four writers of the Gospels as well as taking the message to the four quarters of the earth. The Cross Crosslet Cross is a variation of the Greek Cross and is frequently employed in heraldry as well as in restricted ecclesiastical situations. It is also referred to as the Potent Cross and Croix Croisée.

Cross Crosslet Cross
aka Potent Cross, Croix Croisée

The Teutonic Cross II is related to the Cross Crosslet Cross above. It is a cross that, along with the Cross Crosslet, is often associated with crusading knights, particularly the "Knights of the Teutonic Order", and the "Knights Templar". The "Teutonic Order" was a militaristic order of Baltic and northern Germanic knights. The Teutonic Cross is a variation of the Greek Cross and a cross that is frequently employed in heraldry. It is also referred to as the Potent Cross and Marian Cross.

Teutonic Cross II
aka Potent Cross, Marian Cross

The Teutonic Cross III derives its name from its form being adapted by the Teutonic knights of northern Europe. It is one of the numerous variations of the Greek Cross and a cross that is frequently employed in heraldry as well as in ecclesiastical situations. It is also referred to as the Cross Potent and sometimes as Marian Cross.

Teutonic Cross III
aka Cross Potent, Marian Cross

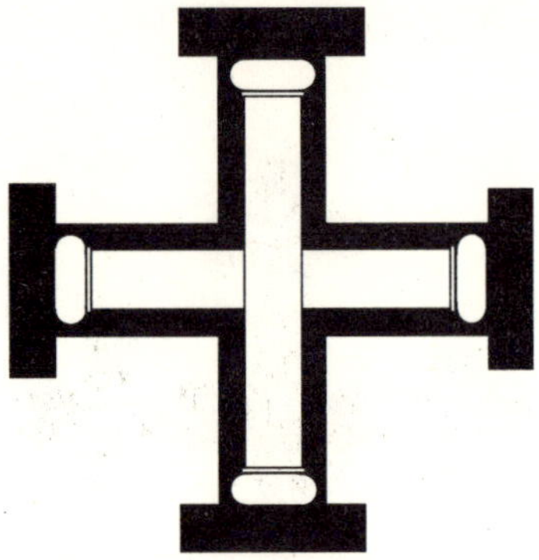

Masonic Teutonic Cross

The Masonic Teutonic Cross is a combination of crosses — i.e. a Teutonic Cross and a Capiteau Cross. It is one of the numerous variations of the Greek Cross and a cross that is employed in the heraldry of Masonic Order. It possesses no ecclesiastical association.

St. Chad's Cross I

The St. Chad's Cross I is related, *en forme,* to the Teutonic Cross and Potent Cross. The symbolism regards the central square which represents the world and the arms refer to the teachings that spread to the four corners of the world. The four potent quarters or arms are also seen as the four nails of the crucifixion. The St. Chad's Cross I is a variation of the Greek Cross and a cross that is almost exclusively found in heraldry.

Snowflake Cross II
aka Ukranian Kyiv (Kiev) Cross

The Snowflake Cross II is a variation of Snowflake Cross I (*see* Latin Crosses: Variations, Snowflake Cross I). It is a cross that is almost exclusively found in Ukraine and Armenia. The Snowflake Cross II is a variation of the Greek Cross and a cross form that is employed in heraldry as well as in ecclesiastical situations, particularly engraved in stone. It is also referred to as the Ukrainian Kyiv (Kiev) Cross.

The Cross Crosslet Crossed II is related to the Cross Crosslet Crossed I (*see* Latin Crosses: Triple Crosspiece Variation, Cross Crosslet Crossed I). It is a cross that is found in ecclesiastical situations — i.e. engraved in stone or in two-dimensional manifestations. The inner portion of the four crosslets may be seen to form a fifth crosslet, while the whole comprises a sixth form. The Cross Crosslet Crossed II is a variation of the Greek Cross and is not to be confused with Jerusalem Cross. It is also referred to as Cross Crosslet Double Crossed, Cross Crosslet Crossly, Cross Double Crossed, Cross Crosslet Crossed and Rune Cross.

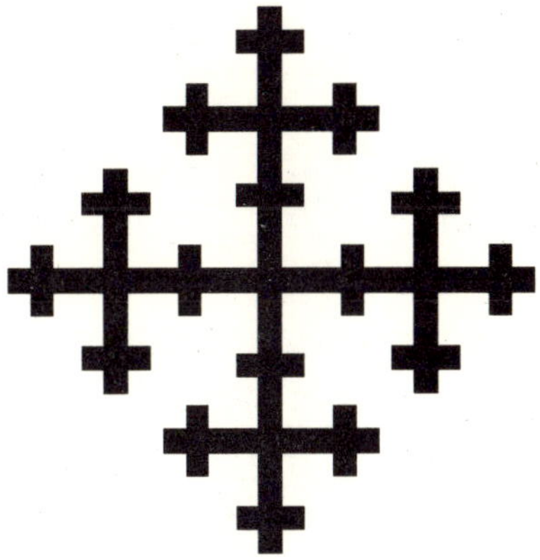

Cross Crosslet Crossed II
aka Cross Crosslet Double Crossed, Cross Crosslet Crossly, Cross Double Crossed, Rune Cross

Greek Crosses: Coptic Variation

The Coptic Church is considered as to be one of the earliest sustained churches in Christendom being established by St. Mark. They are doctrinally different from both the Orthodox and Roman churches. The Coptic Patriarch of Alexandria was the first to be called pope. Tradition states that the Arc of the Covenant was secreted out of Israel and brought to Egypt and later placed into the care of the Coptic Church. The iconography of the Coptic Church is borrowed and transmuted from both Orthodox and Roman traditions. In essence, their symbolic heritage is rich and highly varied, elaborate, often with filigree (see p. 220). Generally, one finds numerous Coptic crosses that are derived from the Greek Cross.

Coptic Cross V

The Coptic Cross V is one of a number of crosses derived from the Coptic faith (*see* Coptic Cross I in Latin Crosses section). This cross is based upon a simple Greek Cross and possesses elements of the Sun Cross. The additions of nails refer to those employed in the crucifixion of Christ — i.e. piercing his hands and feet. It is a Greek Cross variation related to the Solar Cross, but with four Tau crosses, and is a cross that is frequently employed in heraldry.

Coptic Cross VI
aka Ethiopian Cross

The Coptic Cross VI is one of a number of crosses derived from the Coptic faith, and consists of a Bouttonnée II Cross placed over a solar disc. It is believed that the solar disc was an adaptation from the ring or disc atop Ansata Cross I and II. However, it appears to be a variation of the Greek Cross that found favour in north-eastern Africa in the early centuries of the Common Era (*see* Coptic Cross I in Latin Crosses section). It is also referred to as the Ethiopian Cross.

The Coptic Cross VII is one of a number of crosses derived from the Coptic faith as well as one of the simplest. It is one of the oldest variations of the Greek Cross as a Christian symbol (*see* Coptic Cross I in Latin Crosses section). The Coptic Cross VII is a variation of the Greek Cross and is related to the Byzantine Cross. It is a cross that is employed in heraldry as well as in ecclesiastical situations.

Coptic Cross VII
aka Ethiopian Cross

The Coptic Cross VIII is a Greek Cross equivalent of Coptic Cross I variation. It appears to be a variation of the Greek Cross that found favour in north-eastern Africa in the early centuries of the Common Era. The Coptic Cross V is a symbol that is frequently employed in heraldry as well as in ecclesiastical situations. It is also referred to as the Ethiopian Cross.

Coptic Cross VIII
aka Ethiopian Cross

The Coptic Cross IX is one of a number of crosses derived from the Coptic faith. The terminations resemble *fleur-de-lys* in form only. They are made up of two triangles and may also be referred as triple fitchy. The Coptic Cross VI is a variation of the Greek Cross and a cross that is employed in heraldry as well as in ecclesiastical situations. It is also referred to as the Ethipoian Cross and Triple Fitch Cross.

Coptic Cross IX
aka Ethiopian Cross, Triple Fitch Cross

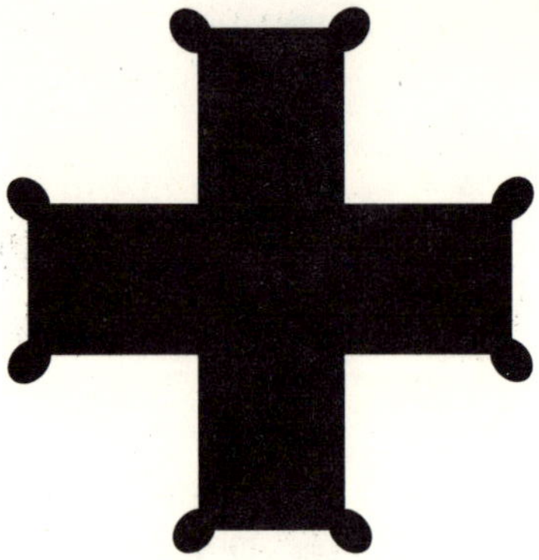

Coptic Cross X

The Coptic Cross X is one of a number of crosses derived from the Coptic faith and one of the simpler examples, *en forme*. The Coptic Cross VII is a variation of the Greek Cross and is employed in heraldry as well as in ecclesiastical situations.

Coptic Cross XI

The Coptic Cross XI is a variation of Coptic Cross IV and the Greeck Cross. It is one of a number of crosses derived from the Coptic faith. The Coptic Cross VIII is employed in heraldry as well as in ecclesiastical situations.

Greek Crosses: Interlaced Variation

There are a number of crosses that are variations of the Greek Cross that may be characterized as appearing to be interlocked or interlaced. All of these crosses are heraldic in nature. The partée and cottised crosses may be seen to be allied to and / or with militaristic implications.

The Solomon's Knot I is a cruciform that denotes peace. It refers to the Old Testament King who, through his wisdom, was able to maintain a peaceful balance in difficult situations. The Solomon's Knot I is a variation of the Greek Cross and a form that is employed in heraldry almost exclusively.

Solomon's Knot I

The Knotted Cross is an example of a cross that is constructed from a simple material. It refers to the four mysteries of the cross. The Knotted Cross is a variation of the Greek Cross and is a cross that is employed in heraldry.

Knotted Cross

The St. Brighid's Cross is a cross that is also constructed of a common material — in this case, straw. The St. Brighid's or St. Bridgit or St. Brighid was an Irish Druid priestess who converted and became a prioress of an abbey. The St. Brighid's Cross is a variation of the Greek Cross and a symbol that is found in heraldry and may, at times, be found as simple straw crosses used to decorate a home. It is also referred to as St. Bridgit's Cross and St. Bride's Cross.

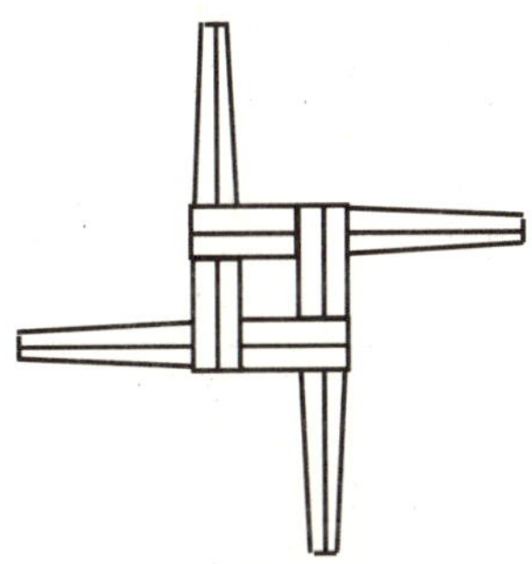

St. Brighid's Cross
aka St. Bridgit's Cross, St. Bride's Cross

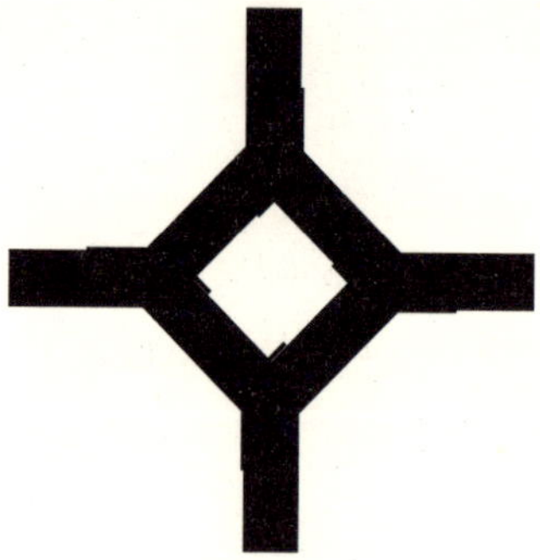

Nowy Masculy Cross

The Nowy Masculy Cross is a cross consisting of a central portion or lozenge (nowy) which is hollowed out or voided (masculy). It symbolizes persuasiveness. Also, a cross in which the centre lozenge is open (voided) refers to a divorced woman. The Nowy Masculy Cross is a variation of the Greek Cross and is employed in heraldry.

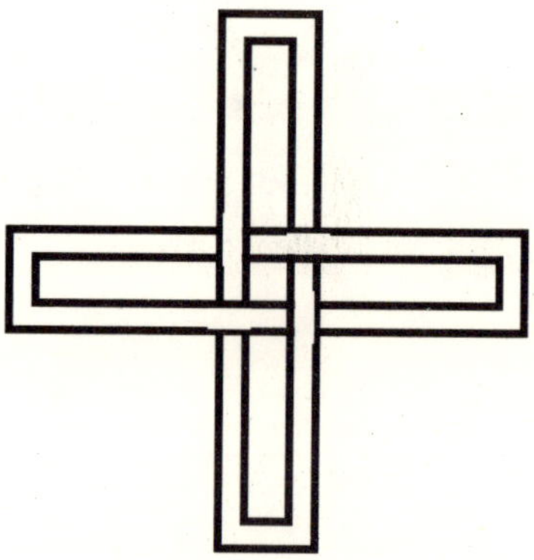

Interlaced Cross

The Interlaced Cross refers to the intertwining of faith and glory. The Interlaced Cross is a variation of the Greek Cross and a symbol that is employed in heraldry.

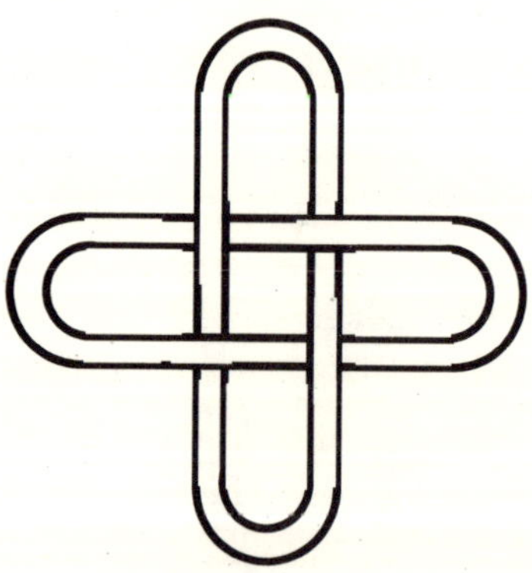

Looped Cross

The Looped Cross is related to the Interlaced Cross. It is a variation of the Greek Cross and a symbol that is frequently employed in heraldry.

Greek Crosses: Interlaced Variation (Continued)

The Partée Double Cross is the simplest form of a number partée and fretted crosses with their variations. It is similar to the employment of a cottise (the shield suspender) and is a referent to defence, protection and support. The Partée Double Cross is a variation of the Greek Cross and a symbol that is employed in heraldry. It is also referred to as Biparted Cross.

Partée Double Cross
aka Biparted Cross

The Partée Double and Fretted Cross is a variation of the Partée Double Cross. It is similar to the employment of a cottise and is a referent not only to defence, protection and support, but also strength through co-operation. The Partée Double and Fretted Cross is a variation of the Greek Cross and a cross that is employed in heraldry.

Partée Double and Fretted Cross

The Triple Parted Cross is an extension of the Partée Double Cross. It is similar to the employment of a cottise and is a referent to defence, protection and support. The Triple Parted Cross is a variation of the Greek Cross and a symbol that is employed in heraldry.

Triple Parted Cross

Triple Parted and Fretted Cross

The Triple Parted and Fretted Cross is the embodiment of the interwoven Triple Parted Cross that is interwoven. Like the former, it is a referent to defence, protection and support. The Triple Parted and Fretted Cross is a variation of the Greek Cross and a symbol that is employed in heraldry.

Roman Sacred Cross

The Triple Parted and Fretted Cross is the basis for the Roman Sacred Cross. The design of this cross reveals a Sunwise Fylfot Cross in the centre and as such is a referent to the male and dominance. The Roman Sacred Cross is a variation of the Greek Cross and a symbol that is employed in heraldry.

Masculy Cross I
aka Masclée Cross, Masculy Interlaced Cross, Bowen Cross

The Masculy Cross I is an interlaced cruciform that recalls the interlaced Saxon and Celtic crosses. It is a variation of the Greek Cross and a symbol that is only employed in heraldry. It is also referred to as Masclée Cross, Masculy Interlaced Cross and Bowen Cross.

Greek Crosses: Gammadia Variation

The Greek letter gamma (γ) when employed in mathematics has a rather precise meaning. However, in Christian symbolism, its meaning varies somewhat, but generally is associated with the crucifixion. It is of further interest to note that the Greek letter gamma resembles a gibbet (see Introduction, p. 16). However, as the third letter in the Greek alphabet, it also refers to the Trinity.

The spelling of the term "sarcelly" as in Sarcelly Disjointed Cross is a variation on *recercelée*. The Sarcelly Disjointed Cross is further a variation of the Gammadia Cross II (following) as well as a Moline Cross. It is a cross that is exclusively employed in heraldry. It is also referred to as the Fimbriated Cross, Gammadia Cross and Fylfot Cross.

Sarcelly Disjointed Cross
aka Fimbriated Cross, Gammadia Cross, Fylfot Cross

The Gammadia Cross I receives its name from the simplified use of the Greek letter *gamma* (*see* Gamma Cross, following). *Gamma* is shown here in the lower right hand quadrant and then repeated and rotated to form the cross. The Gammadia Cross is also seen to be related to the Fylfot Cross. It is a variation of the Greek Cross, and is a form that is solely employed in heraldry. It is also referred to as Fimbriated Cross, Voided Cross and Fylfot Cross.

Gammadia Cross I
aka Fimbriated Cross, Voided Cross, Fylfot Cross

Gammadia Cross II
aka Fimbriated Cross, Sarcelly Disjointed Cross, Fylfot Cross

The Gammadia Cross II is a variation of the Gammadia Cross I, Moline Voided Cross and closely related to Gamma Cross, following. The Gammadia Cross II is also seen to be related to the Fylfot Cross. It is a variation of the Greek Cross and is exclusively employed in heraldry. It is also referred to as the Fimbriated Cross, Sarcelly Disjointed Cross and Fylfot Cross.

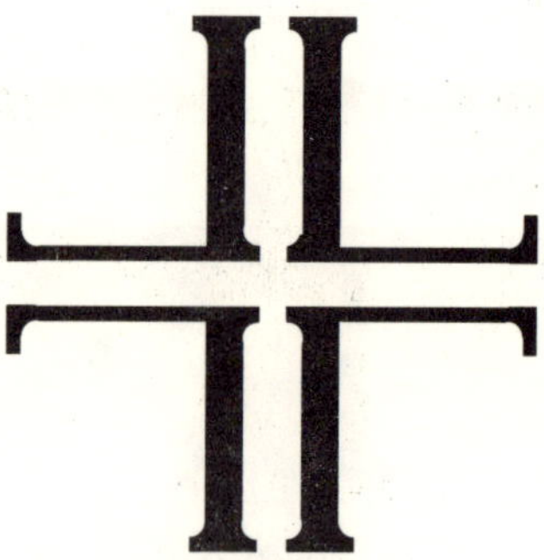

Gamma Cross
aka Gammadia Cross

The Gamma Cross is closely related to the Gammadia Cross I and II. It consists of four Greek gammas arranged to form a cross. It is a symbol that is generally employed only in heraldry. It is also referred to as the Gammadia Cross.

Cottised Cross
aka Croix Coticée

The Cottised Cross is derived from Sarcelly Disjointed Cross and was utilized as the battle cross for the Germans during the Second World War. The Cottised Cross is a variation of the Greek Cross and a form that is exclusively employed in heraldry as in well as military situations. It is also referred to as the Croix Coticée.

Greek Crosses: Boton/Pommé Variation

One of the many terminations that are employed with the basic Greek cross as a starting point is the addition of a solid circular form referred to as a "boton" or "pommé". The "pommé" is often erroneously associated with an apple (pomme). However, it refers to a pommel or a rounded termination on the hilt of a sword or found on a saddle. When doubled it is often called "sarcelée", but unlike the normal form of the sarcelé (recercellée) the terminations are not open (*see* Latin Crosses: Moline, Recercelée, Fleurée Variations; Recercellée Cross I and II) but turn in completely upon themselves forming a distinct double bud which may be seen to resemble cross bones, but not saltire. When tripled the cross is named "tréfflée", trefoil, boton or bouttonnée. The "boton" or "pommé" termination is frequently encountered.

The Bouttonnée Cross II is related to the Gothic Cross, and like the Gothic Cross, it refers to the trinity; in addition, it is a Greek Cross variation of Bouttonnée Cross I. It is a Celtic–Druid symbol of earth, sky and sea. It also possesses references to the twelve months of the year. The Bouttonnée Cross II is a symbol that is frequently employed in heraldry and occasionally encountered in ecclesiastical situations. It is also referred to as the Botonny Cross, Budded Cross, Croix Tréfflée and Trefoil Cross.

Bouttonnée Cross II
aka Botonny Cross, Budded Cross, Croix Tréfflée, Trefoil Cross

The Pomy Cross III is the Greek Cross version of Pomy Cross I. It possesses four pomels at the four terminations. The term "pomel" refers to the knobs or pomels that are found on the hilt of a sword and its guard piece. Since the pomel is also found at the foot of this cross, the militaristic application is not entirely applicable. The Pomy Cross II is a symbol that is frequently employed in heraldry. It is also referred to as the Croix Pommée, Pommelly Cross, Croix Bourdonnée, and Bishop's Cross.

Pomy Cross III
aka Croix Pommée, Pommelly Cross, Croix Bourdonnée, Bishop's Cross

Serbian Cross

The Serbian Cross is a version of the Pomy Cross III. It possesses four pomels at the four terminations and the Cyrilic letter "C" in each of the quadrants. The Cyrilic letter "C" refers to Serbia. The Serbian Cross is a variation of the Greek Cross and a symbol that is only employed in heraldry.

Pommée Cross IV
aka Bezant Cross

The Pommée Cross IV is a version of Pomy Cross III. It possesses four large circular terminations or pommels. The Pommée Cross IV is a variation of the Greek Cross and a symbol that is employed in heraldry. It is also referred to as the Bezant Cross.

Sarcelée Cross III
aka Cercely Cross, Croix Cercelée, Croix Recercellé, Croix Rocercellé, Croix Recercelée, Croix Recercelée, Recersile Cross, Resarcellée Cross, Resarcelled Cross, Sarcelly Cross

The Sarcelée Cross III possesses a glut of spelling variants. It is a Greek Cross variation. Sarcelée Cross III is related to the Moline Cross but displays an unusual configuration in that the "moline"-like terminations curve into themselves and create a double bud-like form reminiscent of crossed bones. The Sarcelée Cross III is frequently encountered in heraldry but rarely in ecclesiastical situations. It is also referred to as the Cercely Cross, Croix Cercelée, Croix Recercellé, Croix Rocercellé, Croix Recercelée, Croix Recercelée, Recersile Cross, Resarcellée Cross, Resarcelled Cross and Sarcelly Cross.

The Lazarus Cross I is a variation of the Greek Cross and a cross that is employed in heraldry. Essentially it is composed of four Pomy Cross I joined at their base. The twelve pomels may refer to the twelve daylight hours, the twelve months of the year or the twelve disciples. Or, four groups of three pomels each, the three pomels referring to the Trinity and the four groups referring to the four days that Lazarus lay in the tomb. The Lazarus Cross I is rarely found in ecclesiastical situations and it is a variation similar to a Maltese Cross, but green in colour.

Lazarus Cross I

The Lazarus Cross II is a variation of the Lazarus Cross I, except the circles are touching, bouttonné-like. The iconography remains as seen in the Lazarus Cross I. It is exclusively a heraldic cruciform.

Lazarus Cross II

Greek Crosses: Annuleted Variation

The Annuleted Cross specifically has rings or annulets at the angle of the termination of the crosspieces. There are a number of other crosses that possess similar forms, although not noted a "rings". Annuleted variations, in this consideration, may display the annulet as a ring — e.g. Anulety Cross I-III — or as a loop — e.g. Occitan Cross I-IV. The annulet is not to be confused with the Pommée or Sarcellée or Boutonnée crosses as the annulets tend to be smaller, ring-like and distinctly separated.

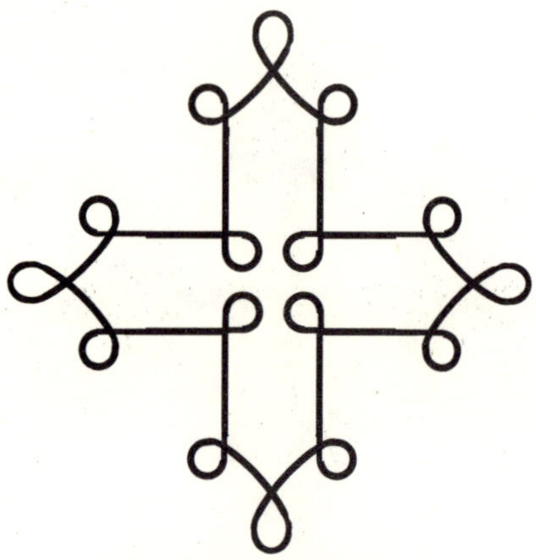

Entrailed Cross

The Entrailed Cross may be seen as a variation of the Occitan crosses. Essentially its never-ending line is a referent to eternity and is related to the Buddhist "never ending knot". In addition there are three loops or annulets at each termination referring to the Holy Trinity. The Entrailed Cross is a variation of the Greek Cross and a cross that essentially found in heraldry.

Annulety Cross I
aka Annuleted Cross, Humetty Cross Ringed

The Annulety Cross I is a cross that is Byzantine in origin and may refer to the suspended crosses in the Greek Orthodox tradition. The rings are symbols of nobility and jurisdiction. The Annulety Cross is a variation of Greek Cross and a form that is frequently employed in heraldry. It is also referred to as the Annuleted Cross and Humetty Cross Ringed.

The Annulety Cross II is a variation of Annulety Cross I. It is a further variation of the Greek Cross and a form that is frequently employed in heraldry. It is also referred to as the Annuleted Cross and Humetty Cross Ringed.

Annulety Cross II
aka Annuletted Cross, Humetty Cross Ringed

The Annulety Cross III is a variation of the Annulety Cross II. It is a further variation of Greek Cross and a form that is frequently employed in heraldry. It is also referred to as the Annuleted Cross, Annuleted Rebated Cross and Humetty Cross Ringed.

Annulety Cross III
aka Annuletted Rebated Cross, Annuletted Cross, Humetty Cross Ringed

The Annulety Fretted Cross is a cross that is Byzantine in origin and may refer to the suspended crosses in the Greek Orthodox tradition. The Annulety Fretted Cross is a variation of the Greek Cross as well as Annulety Cross. It is frequently employed in heraldry.

Annulety Fretted Cross

Occitan Cross I
aka Toulouse Cross I, Languedoc Cross I

The Occitan Cross I was first employed prior to the First Crusade. It was later carried by the Count of Toulouse into the First Crusade. It is often referred to as Cathar Cross, but since the Cathars detested the representation of the cross, this is an erroneous attachment. This cross is associated with the Languedoc region of France and the cross appears on the flag of Toulouse. Occitan was the language spoken in the Languedoc region. It is a variation of the Greek Cross, and is frequently employed in heraldry. It is also referred to as the Toulouse I and Languedoc Cross I

Occitan Cross II
aka Toulouse Cross II, Languedoc Cross II

The Occitan Cross II is a variation of the Occitan Cross I and a symbol that is exclusively employed in heraldry. It is also referred to as the Toulouse Cross II and Languedoc Cross II.

Occitan Cross III
aka Toulouse Cross I, Languedoc Cross III

The Occitan Cross III is a variation of the Occitan Cross I and a symbol that is always employed in heraldry. It is also referred to as the Toulouse Cross III and Languedoc Cross III.

The Occitan Cross IV is a variation of the Occitan Cross I and III, and a symbol that is always employed in heraldry. It is also referred to as the Toulouse Cross and Languedoc Cross.

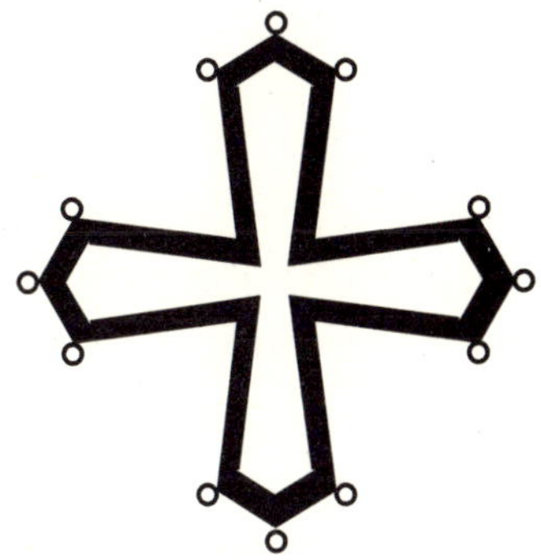

Occitan Cross IV
aka Toulouse Cross, Languedoc Cross

Greek Crosses: Pattée and Patonce Variation

Variously spelled — paty, pate, patee, pattee, paté, patée, pattée — this cross variation is characterized by the flaring or splaying of the crosspieces towards their end. The patonce style cross is closely related to the pattée style crosses in that the flaring at the ends of the crosspieces is separated into three points. This termination has been referred to as being "paw-like". They are separate and not to be confused. The term pattee is described as a paw or foot that may be applied to a bird or animal. It also is applied to a crossroad. In heraldry it symbolizes the younger branch of a family.

Pattée Cross I
aka Paty Cross, Pate Cross,
Patee Cross, Pattee Cross, Paté Cross,
Patée Cross, Cossack Cross, Formée Cross

The Pattée Cross I is a variation of the Greek Cross and is frequently employed in heraldry as well as in ecclesiastical situations, particularly it is that cross forms that is often seen affixed to the top of a crown. Unlike other forms of patte crosses, its crosspieces do not flare as much as others and appear to the Greek Cross equivalent of the Latin Cross variation, known as Byzantine Cross II. It is also referred to as the Paty Cross, Pate Cross, Patee Cross, Pattee Cross, Paté Cross, Patée Cross and Formée Cross.

Pattée Cross II
aka Iron Cross, Maltese Cross,
Regeneration Cross, St. John's Cross,
Paty Cross, Pate Cross, Patee Cross,
Pattee Cross, Paté Cross, Patée Cross,
Formée Cross

A variation of the Pattée Cross I, the shape of which was used by the Germans as a military decoration since the nineteenth century. It is essentially a cross found in heraldry. Pattée Cross II is also referred to as the Iron Cross, Maltese Cross, Regeneration Cross, St. John's Cross, Paty Cross, Pate Cross, Patee Cross, Pattee Cross, Paté Cross, Patée Cross and the Formée Cross.

A variation of the Pattée Cross I and II, and the Greek Cross, Pattée Cross III is frequently employed in heraldry. It is also referred to as the Paty Cross, Pate Cross, Patee Cross, Pattee Cross, Paté Cross, Patée Cross and Formée Cross.

Pattée Cross III
aka Iron Cross, Paty Cross, Pate Cross, Patee Cross, Pattee Cross, Paté Cross, Patée Cross, Formée Cross

A variation of Pattée Cross I and II, Pattée Cross IV is derived from the Greek Cross. It is frequently employed in heraldry and seldom, if ever, in ecclesiastical situations. It is also referred to as Paty Cross, Pate Cross, Patee Cross, Pattee Cross, Paté Cross, Patée Cross and Formée Cross.

Pattée Cross IV
aka Iron Cross, Paty Cross, Pate Cross, Patee Cross, Pattee Cross, Paté Cross, Patée Cross, Formée Cross

The Knights Templar Cross is of a particular form that is related to the Crux Pattée and/or the Cross Formée. It is a variation of the Greek Cross and is a symbol that is frequently employed in heraldry. It is also referred to as Alisée Cross or Alaisé Cross.

Knights Templar Cross
aka Alisée Cross, Alaisé Cross

Patonce Pattée Cross I
aka Cross Patonce, Cross Enhendee,
Cross Pattee Fleuron

The Patonce Pattée Cross I is a cross that is related to the Crux Patté and Gothic Cross. *Patonce* refers to the "paw-shaped" terminations which may be seen to be related to the *fleur-de-lys*. The triple terminations are seen to be symbolic of the Trinity. The Patonce Pattée Cross I is a variation of the Greek Cross and is a form that is exclusively employed in heraldry. It is also referred to as the Cross Patonce, Cross Enhendee and Cross Pattee Fleuron.

Patonce Pattée Cross II
aka Cross Patonce, Cross Enhendee,
Cross Pattee Fleuron

The Patonce Pattée Cross II is a variation of the Patonce Pattée Cross I and as such it is a variation of the Greek Cross and a cross form that is frequently employed in heraldry. It is also referred to as the Cross Patonce, Cross Enhendee and Cross Pattee Fleuron.

Patonce Pattée Cross III

The Patonce Pattée Cross III is a variation of Patonce Pattée Cross I and as such it is a variation of the Greek Cross. It is a cruciform form that is exclusively employed in heraldry.

The Pattée Quadrate Cross is essentially composed of both a Patté Cross II and a St. Chad Cross. The symbolism regarding the central square which represents the world and the arms refers to the teachings that spread to the four quarters of the world. The Pattée Quadrate Cross is a variation of the Greek Cross and a form that is only employed in heraldry.

Pattée Quadrate Cross

Greek Crosses: Star/Flame Variation

A number of crosses, based upon the Greek Cross, are called Star crosses. This would seem to be a logical variation of the Greek Cross. The star is a referent to the Star of Bethlehem and to glory. The star is also a symbol of a guiding light and in the case of heraldic crosses, it is a referent to Christian teachings as a guide to the hereafter. The Flaming crosses refer to the burning truth as espoused by Christianity. It may also refer to martyrdom, but, never to the burning cross of certain right-wing political groups.

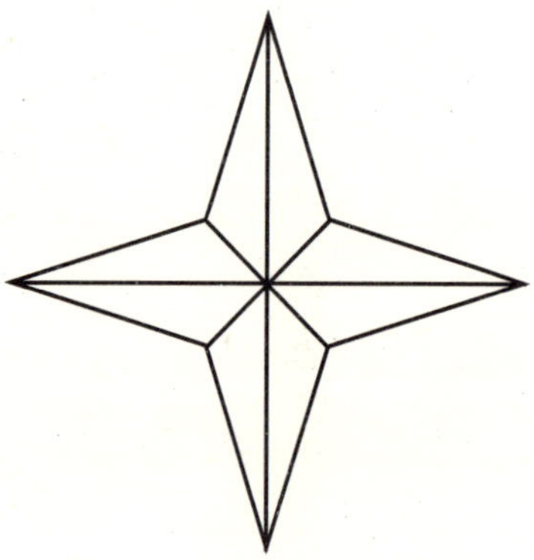

Star Cross I
aka Croix Estoilée

The Star Cross I is seen to represent the light of the true faith as well as a referent to the Star of Bethlehem. It may be seen to be composed of four overlapping lozenges. It may also be seen as being made up of four fitché elements. The Star Cross I is a variation of the Greek Cross and a form that is frequently employed in heraldry. It is also referred to as Croix Estoilée.

Star Cross II
aka Croix Estoilée, Fitchy at All Points Cross

The Star Cross II is a variation of the Star Cross I and mirrors similar iconography. It is a symbol that is employed in heraldry. Star Cross II is also referred to as the Croix Estoilée and Fitchy at All Points Cross.

The Star Cross III consists of wavy elements proceeding from a quadrate form. The symbolism, obviously, refers to the Christian teaching expanding to the four corners of the world and may also refer to the Star of Bethlehem. It is a variation of the Greek Cross and a symbol that is employed in heraldry. It is also referred to as the Croix Estoilée.

Star Cross III
aka Croix Estoilée

The Star Cross IV is a variation of the Greek Cross. In this case, four, six-pointed stars are found at the terminations which is a referent to celestial goodness. The Star Cross IV is a variation of the Greek Cross and a symbol that is employed in heraldry. It is also referred to as the Croix Estoilée and Crux Stellata.

Star Cross IV
aka Croix Estoilée, Crux Stellata

The Flaming Cross I possesses two possible meanings. First, it is seen to refer to the Holy Spirit which is frequently shown in the visual arts as a flame. Second, it also is seen to refer to those martyrs who were burned at the stake and, therefore, to zealousness. The Flaming Cross I is a variation of the Greek Cross, and is a cross that is exclusively employed in heraldry. It is also referred to as the Crux Flamant.

Flaming Cross I
aka Crux Flamant

Flaming Cross II
aka Crux Flamant

The Flaming Cross II is a variation of the Flaming Cross I. Its iconography is associated with the brilliant flame of truth that is directed to the four points of the world. The Flaming Cross II is also a variation of the Greek Cross, and is a symbol that is employed exclusively in heraldry. It is also referred to as the Crux Flamant.

Greek Crosses: Jerusalem Variation

The Jerusalem Cross is a form that grew out of the crusades and the banner given to the crusaders by Pope Urban II. Therefore, it may be considered as a cross form with military implications. However, nowadays it has assumed, predominantly, an ecclesiastical character and use. Fundamentally it is a Greek Cross in which smaller Greek crosses appear in each quadrant. It was a cross that appeared subsequently to the First Crusade. The four small crosses are said to represent the Four Gospels and/or the four corners of the world. Together, the five crosses are seen to represent the five wounds suffered by the Christ at his crucifixion.

The Jerusalem Cross I is a Greek Cross variation. This is the simplest of Jerusalem crosses being made of five Greek crosses. The Jerusalem Cross I is a cross that is often employed in heraldry as well as in certain ecclesiastical situations. It is also referred to as Crusader's Cross, Knights of Jerusalem Cross, Franciscan Custody of the Holy Land Cross, Fivefold Cross and Crusader Kingdom of Jerusalem Cross.

Jerusalem Cross I
aka Crusader's Cross, Knights of Jerusalem Cross, Franciscan Custody of the Holy Land Cross, Fivefold Cross, Crusader Kingdom of Jerusalem Cross

The Jerusalem Cross II is a variation of the Jerusalem Cross I. It is based upon the Teutonic Cross. It is also known as a Fivefold Cross made up of four Tau crosses or Potent crosses forming the major cross and four Greek crosses in the quadrants. It is derived from the Greek Cross, and is frequently employed in heraldry. It is also referred to as the Crusader's Cross, Knights of Jerusalem Cross, Franciscan Custody of the Holy Land Cross, Fivefold Cross, Crusader Kingdom of Jerusalem Cross.

Jerusalem Cross II
aka Crusader's Cross, Knights of Jerusalem Cross, Franciscan Custody of the Holy Land Cross, Fivefold Cross, Crusader Kingdom of Jerusalem Cross

Greek Crosses: Jerusalem Variation (Continued)

Jerusalem Cross III
aka Crusader's Cross, Knights of Jerusalem Cross, Franciscan Custody of the Holy Land Cross, Fivefold Cross, Crusader Kingdom of Jerusalem Cross

The Jerusalem Cross III is a variation of the Jerusalem Cross I. It is the most elaborate of the Jerusalem crosses as each cross consists of a Cross Potent. This form is not as popular as the Jerusalem Cross I and II. It is derived from the Greek Cross, and is frequently encountered in heraldry but rarely in ecclesiastical situations. It is also referred to as the Crusader's Cross, Knights of Jerusalem Cross, Franciscan Custody of the Holy Land Cross, Fivefold Cross and Crusader Kingdom of Jerusalem Cross.

St. Chad's Cross II

The St. Chad's Cross II is a variation of the Jerusalem Cross II. It is made of a Teutonic Cross or four Potent crosses with four small Greek crosses in the quarters. A quadrate form occupies the centre. The St. Chad's Cross II is a variation of the Greek Cross and is often employed in heraldry as well as in ecclesiastical situations.

St. Chad's Cross III

The St. Chad's Cross III is a variation of the St. Chad's Cross II. It is made of a Teutonic Cross or four Potent crosses with four small Pattée crosses in the quadrants. A quadrate form occupies the centre. The St. Chad's Cross II is a variation of the Greek Cross and is often employed in heraldry as well as in ecclesiastical situations.

The Georgia's Cross is a variation of the Jerusalem Cross I. The main form is made of a Greek Cross with four Cross crosslets in the quadrants. This particular cross is part of the insignia of Georgia, formerly of the USSR and is exclusively found in heraldry. It is also referred to as the Crusader's Cross.

Georgia's Cross
aka Crusader's Cross

Greek Crosses: Plant/Animal Variation

A number of the Greek style crosses employ plant or animal components in their make-up. These crossess are exclusively found in heraldry and only in the most remote cases are associated with ecclesiastical use. The plant or animal components exemplify the vast variety of forms that heraldic crosses utilize.

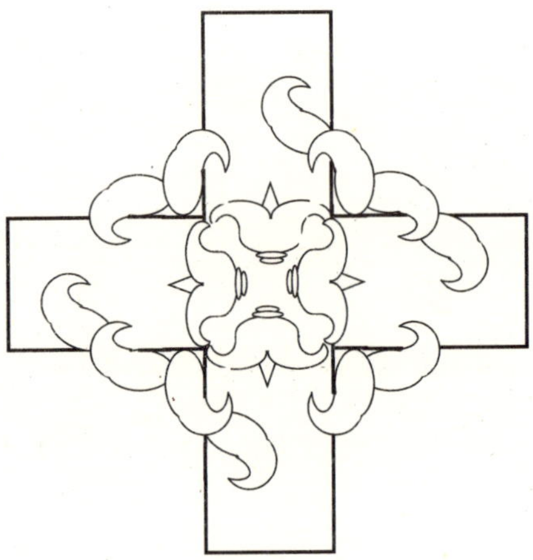

Slipped Cross

The Slipped Cross refers to flowers or buds that are on their stems and often is exhibited by a number of flowers on the cross. It is a variation of the Greek Cross, and is a cross that is only employed in heraldry.

Gringolee Cross
aka Croix Gringolée, Croix Guivrée

The Gringolee Cross is composed of a simple Greek Cross from which snake-like forms issue from the terminations. It is a variation of the Greek Cross and a symbol that is exclusively employed in heraldry. It is also referred to as the Croix Gringolée, and/or Croix Guivrée.

The Avellane Cross I is composed of four filberts (Fr.: *nuces avellance*) or hazel nuts. Its iconography is unknown, but it may have been employed for its purely decorative nature. It is a variation of the Greek Cross, and is frequently employed in heraldry. It is also referred to as the Avellan Cross.

Avellane Cross I
aka Avellan Cross

The Avellane Cross II is a variant of the Avellane Cross I. The terminations of this particular variation resembles a *fleur-de-lys*. It is also a variation of the Greek Cross, and is a cross that is exclusively employed in heraldry. It is also referred to as the Avellan Cross.

Avellane Cross II
aka Avellan Cross

The Avellane Pommelled Cross is a variation of the Avellane Cross I. The terminations of this particular variation are pomels. It is also a variation of the Greek Cross. The Avellane Pommelled Cross is a cross that is exclusively employed in heraldry. It is also known as the Avellan Pommelled Cross.

Avellane Pommelled Cross
aka Avellan Pommelled Cross

Avellane Invected Cross
aka Avellan Invected Cross

The Avellane Invected Cross is a variation of the Avellane Cross I. It is composed of four filberts (Fr.: *nuces avellance*) or hazel nuts facing inward — i.e. towards the crossing. Its iconography is unknown. The Avellane Invected Cross is a variation of the Greek Cross, and is frequently employed in heraldry. It is also referred to as the Avellan Invected Cross.

Avellane Doubled Cross
aka Avellan Doubled Cross, Double Fruitage Cross, Double Avellaney Cross

The Avellane Doubled Cross is a variation of the Avellane Cross I, but the buds are doubled. Its iconography is unknown. It is a variation of the Greek Cross. The Avellane Doubled Cross is exclusively employed in heraldry. It is also called as the Avellan Doubled Cross, Double Fruitage Cross and Double Avellaney Cross.

Fruitagee Cross
aka Croix Fruitagée

The Fruitagee Cross is one of a number of cross forms that employ natural forms. It implies the fruitfulness of the faith, and as it seems to represent pomegranets, it would imply resurrection. The Fruitagee Cross is a variation of the Greek Cross and is a symbol that is only employed in heraldry. It is also referred to as the Croix Fruitagée.

Greek Crosses: Plant/Animal Variation (Continued)

The Batonée Cross is composed of a cluster of three leaf forms at the four terminations. It is a device that refers to perpetuity as well as the months of the year, the Apostles, the Trinity and the spreading of the word to the four quarters of the world. The Batonée Cross is a variation of the Greek Cross, related to the Trefly Cross, and is only employed in heraldry.

Batonée Cross

The Trefly Cross is a cross that employs a vine-like component. It is a variation of the Greek Cross and is a symbol that is only employed in heraldry. It is also referred to as the Croix Trèfle.

Trefly Cross
aka Croix Trèfle

Nestorius was the Eastern Orthodox Metropolitan and Patriarch of Constantinople who was branded a heretic by Rome. He felt that the divine and human natures were not merged in the Christ. Nestorianism became popular in Asia as far as China. This Nestorian Cross is related to the Armenian Cross and the appearance of the elephant's heads may connect this form with India. It is a variation of the Greek Cross and a symbol that is only employed in heraldry.

Nestorian Cross

Quatrefoil Cross

The Quatrefoil Cross is composed of four leaf forms. It is a variation of the Greek Cross and a form that is only employed in heraldry.

Ermine Cross
aka Croix Erminée

The Ermine Cross is a cross form that is composed of the representation of four tails of ermine. It is a cross that implies nobility and status. The Ermine Cross is a variation of the Greek Cross and a symbol that is only employed in heraldry. It is also referred to as the Croix Erminée.

Swallow Tail Cross

The Swallow Tail Cross is so named because of the bifurcation of the foot of the cross resembling the tail of a swallow. It is a variation of the Greek Cross and is a cross form that is only employed in heraldry.

Greek Crosses: Anchry, Milrine, Moline, Recercelée Variation

Probably no cross variation is more confusing than those crosses which have bifurcated terminations and are related to pre-existent forms or means of support — e.g. the metal braces on a millstone. These bifurcations may be blunted or end in pointed terminations. None the less, they are variously called: Anchry Cross, Milrine Cross, Moline Cross and Recercelée Cross. The latter — i.e. Recercelée Cross — is even more confusing and identical, or virtually identical cross form that is variously entitled: Croix Recercellée, Croix Recercellé, Recercele Cross, Recercely Cross, Croix Rocercellé, Sarcelly Cross, Cercelée Cross, Croix Fourché, Forked Cross, Fourchy Cross, Miller's Cross and Miller Rebated Cross.

The Anchor Cross II is related to the Moline Cross and symbolizes hope. It is composed of four anchor-like forms without the crosspiece and loop seen in Anchor Cross I. The Anchor Cross II is a variation of the Greek Cross and a form that is only employed in heraldry. It is also referred to as the Anchry Cross and Croix Ancre.

Anchor Cross II
aka Anchry Cross, Croix Ancre

The Anchor Cross III is a variation of the Anchor Cross II and is only employed in heraldry. It is also referred to as the Anchry Cross and Croix Ancre.

Anchor Cross III
aka Anchry Cross, Croix Ancre

Anchor Cross IV
aka Anchry Cross, Croix Ancre

The Anchor Cross IV is a variation of the Anchor Cross II and a cross form that is only employed in heraldry. It is also referred to as the Anchry Cross and Croix Ancre.

Cercelée Cross
aka Anchory Cross, Cross Ancrée, Croix Recercellée, Croix Recercellé, Recercele Cross, Croix Rocercellé, Sarcelly Cross, Recercely Cross

The Cercelée Cross is a variation of the Anchor Cross IV and is a cross that is only employed in heraldry. It is also referred to as the Anchory Cross, Cross Ancrée, Croix Recercellée, Croix Recercellé, Recercele Cross, Croix Rocercellé, Sarcelly Cross and Recercely Cross.

Recercely Cross
aka Anchory Cross, Cross Ancrée, Croix Recercellée, Croix Recercellé, Recercele Cross, Croix Rocercellé, Sarcelly Cross, Cercelée Cross

The Recercely Cross is a variation of the Anchor Cross IV and a cross that is only employed in heraldry. It is also referred to as the Anchory Cross, Cross Ancrée, Croix Recercellée, Croix Recercellé, Recercele Cross, Croix Rocercellé, Sarcelly Cross and Cercelée Cross.

Although its form suggests that it is closely related to the Recercely Cross or Anchor Cross IV, the Milrine Cross III is, by name, associated with Milrine Cross I and II, following. The Milrine Cross I is a variation of the Greek Cross and a symbol that is frequently employed in heraldry. It is also referred to as the Miller Cross, Mill-iron Cross, Millrind Cross and Moline Cross.

Milrine Cross I
aka Miller Cross, Mill-iron Cross, Millrind Cross, Moline Cross

The Milrine Cross II is related to the Moline Cross, and refers to bracing or reinforcing irons on a millstone. It is a variation of the Greek Cross and a cross that is only employed in heraldry. It is also referred to as the Miller Cross, Mill-iron Cross, Millrind Cross and Moline Cross.

Milrine Cross II
aka Miller Cross, Mill-iron Cross, Millrind Cross, Moline Cross

The Milrine Cross III is a modification of the Milrine Cross II and indicates the innovations this form may have. It is a variation of the Greek Cross and a cross that is only employed in heraldry. It is also referred to as the Miller Cross, Mill-iron Cross, Millrind Cross and Moline Cross.

Milrine Cross III
aka Miller Cross, Mill-iron Cross, Millrind Cross, Moline Cross

Greek Crosses: Anchry, Milrine, Moline, Recercelée Variation (Continued)

Hameḍon Cross
aka Hamecon Cross

The Hameḍon Cross is seen to be related to the Anchor Cross IV, *en forme*. In this cross the final terminations resemble fish-hooks. The Hameḍon Cross is a variation of the Greek Cross and a symbol that is employed in heraldry. It is also referred to as the Hamecon Cross.

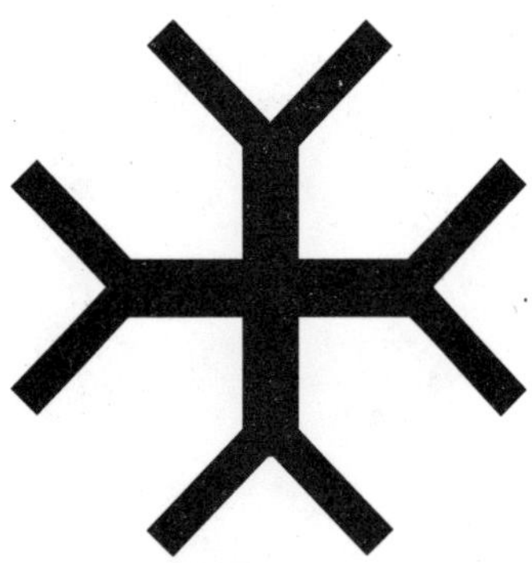

Fourché Cross I
aka Forked Cross, Miller Rebated Cross, Pall Cross

The Fourché Cross is related to the Milrine Cross in that its shape recalls the form used on a millstone. Its forked terminations also recall the admonition to take Christianity to all corners of the world. The Fourché Cross is a variation of the Greek Cross and a form that is only employed in heraldry. It is related to the Thieves' and Pall Crosses. It is also referred to as the Forked Cross, Miller Rebated Cross and Pall Cross.

Fourché Cross II
aka Forked Cross, Miller Rebated Cross, Pall Cross

The Fourché Cross II is a variation of the Fourché Cross I. Its forked terminations are not as angular as the former. The Fourché Cross II is a variation of the Greek Cross. It is only employed in heraldry. It is also referred to as the Forked Cross, Miller Rebated Cross, and Pall Cross.

The Anchor Double Parted Cross is a variation of the Anchor Cross II. Although the form of the terminations is less "ancry" than *fleur-de-lys*. It is a variation of the Greek Cross and exclusively found in heraldry.

Anchor Double Parted Cross

The Lithuanian Cross is related to the Fourché Cross, *en forme*. The central diamond form holds a simple Greek Cross. The Lithuanian Cross is a variation of the Greek Cross and a symbol that is only employed in heraldry.

Lithuanian Cross

The Voided Milrine Cross is related to the Milrine Cross II, and refers to bracing or reinforcing irons on a millstone. It is a variation of the Greek Cross and a cross that is exclusively employed in heraldry. It is also referred to as the Voided and Disjointed Milrine Cross.

Voided Milrine Cross
aka Voided and Disjointed Milrine Cross

Moline Nowy Masculy Cross

The Moline Nowy Masculy Cross is related to the Milrine Cross I. It is a variation of the Greek Cross and a cross that is only employed in heraldry.

Moline Pierced Lozengy Cross

The Moline Pierced Lozengy Cross is nearly identical to the Moline Nowy Masculy Cross. It is a variation of the Greek Cross and a cross that is solely employed in heraldry.

Greek Crosses: Militaristic Variation

Prior to the crusades the various types of crosses — i.e. Tau, Latin, Greek, Solar and Saltire — were represented in finite variations and were seen in common use. Only the cruciforms of the Coptics exhibited numerous, rich, varied and distinctive forms. However, from the eleventh century, the variations of the cruciform became infinite in form, myriad in variations and nearly limitless in number.

The crusades seem to have spawned the numerous militaristic cruciform variations. The teachings of brotherhood, "love thy neighbour, and a pacific approach to ones" fellowmen were thrown aside in the pseudo-religious frenzy engendered by the crusades. The crosses reflected this bloody intent. Many of these cross variations were connected with military orders that were associated with the crusades. In addition, numerous personal coats of arms held crosses that were derived from implements of war — e.g. swords, arrow heads, lance tips, daggers, etc. The vast majority of these militaristic crosses were variations of the Greek Cross and could and were easily employed in coats of arms.

The Pheon Cross is made up of four pheons or broad-arrowheads. This form, this arrowhead, is one of the most obviously deadly of the symbols applied to the cross. It is one of the numerous variations of the Greek Cross which has obvious militaristic implications. The Pheon Cross is a symbol that is only employed in heraldry. It is also referred to as the Cross of Pheons, and Croix Pheonée.

Pheon Cross
aka Cross of Pheons, Croix Pheonée

The Bretesse Cross I is a cross in which there appears crenellations as found in a castle. It is one of the numerous variations of the Greek Cross which has militaristic implications and related to Double Potent Cross. The Bretesse Cross I is a symbol that is generally only employed in heraldry. It is also referred to as the Crenel Cross, Embattled Cross, Cross Potent Cross and Double Potent Cross.

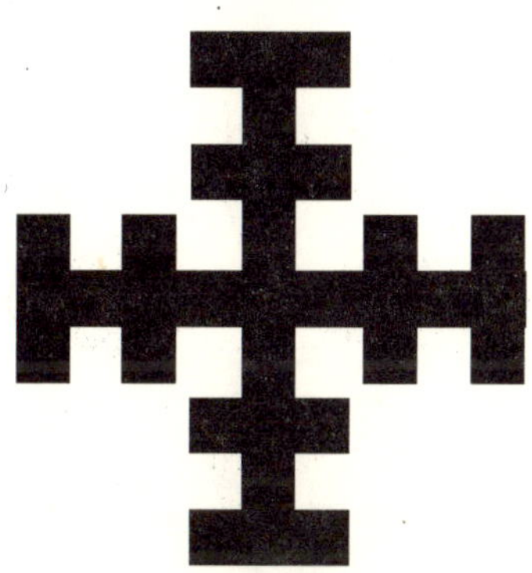

Bretesse Cross I
aka Crenel Cross, Embattled Cross,
Cross Potent Cross, Double Potent Cross

Bretesse Cross II
aka Crenel Cross, Embattled Cross, Cross Potent Cross

The Bretesse Cross II is a variation of the Bretesse Cross I. It is a cross in which there appears crenellations as found in a castle. It is one of the numerous variations of the Greek Cross which has militaristic implications. The Bretesse Cross II is a form that is generally only employed in heraldry. It is also referred to as the Crenel Cross, Embattled Cross and Cross Potent Cross.

Cross Crosslet Double Fitched of all Four Rebated

The Cross Crosslet Double Fitched of all Four Rebated is one of the numerous variations of the Greek Cross which has militaristic implications. Its connection with the fitchy — i.e. dagger form — establishes this affiliation. Its terminations also resemble crenellations. It is a form that is only employed in heraldry.

Fusil Cross I
aka Lozengy Cross

The Fusil Cross I is a cross which is based upon a spindle (*fuscan*) or a fuse (*fuisil*) or a diamond shape (lozenge). It also may be a referent to a spearhead. The Fusil Cross I is one of the numerous variations of the Greek Cross which has militaristic implications. It is a symbol that is only employed in heraldry. It is also referred to as the Lozengy Cross and is related to the Clechée Cross.

The Fusil Cross II is a variation of the Fusil Cross I. It is a cross which is based upon a spindle (*fuscan*) or a fuse (*fuisil*) or a diamond shape (lozenge). It also may be a referent to a spearhead. The Fusil Cross II is one of the numerous variations of the Greek Cross which has militaristic implications. It is a symbol that is exclusively employed in heraldry. It is also referred to as the Lozengy Cross and is related to the Clechée Cross.

Fusil Cross II
aka Lozengy Cross

The Urdée Cross is composed of lozenges at the terminations. This term *urdé* refers to a sharpened projection. The Urdée Cross is one of the numerous variations of the Greek Cross which has militaristic implications. It is a cross form that is solely employed in heraldry. It is also referred to as the Urdy Cross, Champaine Cross, Croix Aiguisée and Verdy Cross.

Urdée Cross I
aka Urdy Cross, Champaine Cross, Croix Aiguisée, Verdy Cross

The Knights of Christ's Cross I belongs to an ancient Portuguese order related to the Templars (Order of the Temple). It is one of the numerous variations of the Greek Cross which has militaristic implications. Essentially, it consists of a Teutonic or Templar's Cross with a simple voided Greek Cross. The Knights of Christ's Cross I is a cross form that is generally only employed in heraldry. It is also referred to as the Order of Christ Cross.

Knights of Christ's Cross I
aka Order of Christ Cross

Knights of Christ's Cross II
aka Order of Christ Cross, Templars' Cross

The Knights of Christ's Cross II is a variation of the Knights of Christ's Cross I and belongs to a Portuguese order and was found on the sails of ships. It is one of the numerous variations of the Greek Cross which has militaristic implications — i.e. associated with a militaristic order. The Knights of Christ's Cross II is a symbol found in heraldry, and occasionally appears in ecclesiastical situations and environs. It is also referred to as the Order of Christ Cross and Templars' Cross.

Barbée Cross I
aka Croix Tournée, Croix Cromponnée, Arrow Cross

The Barbée Cross I symbolizes expansion and Christian evangelism. It was adopted by the Hungarian Fascist in the twentieth century. It is also described as a cross with four fish hooks or arrows. It is also known as a fascist's Arrow Cross. The Barbée Cross I is a variation of the Greek Cross with militaristic implications, and is a cross that is only employed in heraldry. It is also referred to as Croix Tournée, Croix Cromponnée and Arrow Cross.

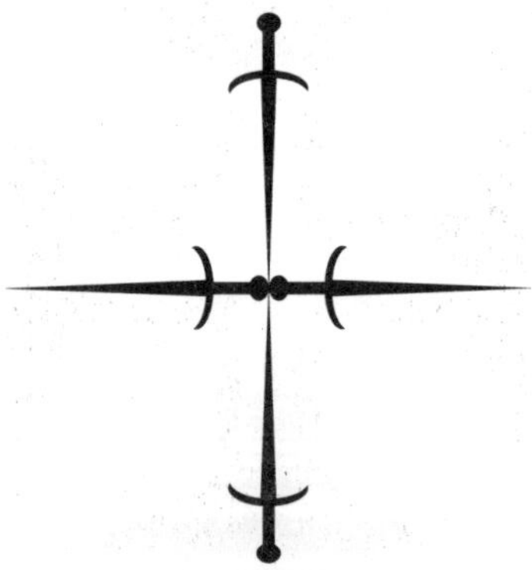

Damascus Cross
aka Cross Damaḍon

The Damascus Cross is composed of four swords making it one of the most obvious militaristic of the crosses. Damascus was known to produce very fine swords, knives and daggers. The Damascus Cross is one of the numerous variations of the Greek Cross. It is a symbol that is generally only employed in heraldry. It is also known as the Cross Damaḍon.

Greek Crosses: Militaristic Variation (Continued)

The Demisarcel Cross is related to the Dymock Cross. *Sarcel* means "cut through the middle". It is seen by some to represent a crenulation. It is one of the numerous variations of the Greek Cross which has militaristic implications. The Demisarcel Cross is a cross form that is generally only employed in heraldry.

Demisarcel Cross

The Dymock Cross is related to the Cross Pattée as well as the Demisarcel Cross. It is one of the numerous variations of the Greek Cross which has militaristic implications. The Dymock Cross is a cross form that is generally only employed in heraldry. It is also referred to as the Pattée Notched Cross.

Dymock Cross
aka Pattée Notched Cross

The Double Fitched and Rebated Cross is related to the Cross Crosslet Double Fitched of all Four Rebated and Bretesse Cross in which there appears crenellations as found in a castle. It is one of the numerous variations of the Greek Cross which has militaristic implications. The Double Fitched and Rebated Cross is a cross form that is only employed in heraldry.

Double Fitched and Rebated Cross

Pommée Cross
aka Pommelly Cross, Croix Bourdonnée, Bishop's Cross

The Pommée Cross is related to the Boutonée Cross, Pommée refers to pomels, apples or head, either of which may apply to this cross. Apples are the reward of a good life. The ends also resemble the pomel of a sword hilt and are symbols of authority. It is a variation of the Greek Cross and a cross that is frequently employed in heraldry. It is also referred to as the Pommelly Cross, Croix Bourdonnée and Bishop's Cross.

Fouchy Cross
aka Croix Fouché, Croix de Fourchette

The Fouchy Cross is a heraldic device that is found exclusively in France. Its form is unique and is stated that it represents the forked iron stand upon which soldiers rest their muskets. The Fouchy Cross is a variation of the Greek Cross and a form that is only employed in heraldry. It is also referred to as the Croix Fouché and Croix de Fourchette.

Greek Crosses: Militaristic, Fleur-de-lys Variation

A number of Greek crosses which have militaristic implications were derived from the *fleur-de-lys*. In these instances, the flower, the *fleur-de-lys*, are seen to represent an elaborate and fearful lance or spear tip. They, generally, are not necessarily associated with France. As a matter of fact, many are Spanish in origin and were adopted by the four main Iberian orders — i.e. the Order of Alcantara, Calatrava, Montesa and Santiago (*see* Latin Crosses Fitchy Militaristic Variations). These orders were established, in part, to rid the peninsula of the Moors and were then involved in the crusades.

The Order of Alcantara Cross I is associated with the city of Alcantara in Leon, near the Portuguese border. It was established in defence against the Moors. The Order of Alcantara was one of the four major religio-military orders established in Spain. The Order of Alcantara Cross is one of the numerous variations of the Greek Cross which has militaristic implications — i.e. associated with a militaristic order. It is a cross form that is generally only employed in heraldry.

Order of Alcantara Cross I

The Order of Alcantara Cross II is a florid variation of the Order of Alcantara Cross I. It is one of the numerous variations of the Greek Cross which has militaristic implications. It is a cross form that is generally only employed in heraldry.

Order of Alcantara Cross II

Order of Avis's Cross
aka Croix Fleur-de-lys, Orden Nova Cross, Orden de Milica Cross

The Order of Avis's Cross is the cross of a warrior–monastic order. Created as a defence of the city Mvora against the Moors. It is one of the numerous variations of the Greek Cross which has militaristic implications — i.e. associated with a militaristic order. The Order of Avis's Cross is a symbol that is generally only employed in heraldry. It is also referred to as the Croix Fleur-de-lys, Orden Nova Cross and Orden de Milica Cross.

Order of Santo Domingo's Cross
aka Crux Militia Jesus Christi, Iberian Cross

The Order of Santo Domingo's Cross is associated with a Spanish warrior–monastic order. It is one of the numerous variations of the Greek Cross which has militaristic implications — i.e. associated with a militaristic order. The Order of Santo Domingo's Cross is a cross form that is generally only employed in heraldry. It is also referred to as the Crux Militia Jesus Christi and Iberian Cross.

Order of Calatrava's Cross I
aka Valencia Cross

The Order of Calatrava's Cross I is derived from Order of Avis's Cross and voided by a Greek Cross. It is a Castillian order of reconquest by the Knights of Calatrava. The Order of Calatrava was one of the four major Spanish religio-militaristic orders. It is one of the numerous variations of the Greek Cross which has militaristic implications. The Order of Calatrava's Cross I is a cross form that is generally only employed in heraldry. It is also referred to as the Valencia Cross.

The Order of Calatrava's Cross II is a florid variation of the Order of Calatrava's Cross I. It is one of the numerous variations of the Greek Cross which has militaristic implications — i.e. associated with a militaristic order. The Order of Calatrava's Cross II is a cross form that is generally only employed in heraldry. It is also referred to as the Valencia Cross.

Order of Calatrava's Cross II
aka Valencia Cross

The Order of Montessa Cross is a variation of the Order of Calatrava's Cross II . The Order of Montessa was one of the four major Iberian religio-militaristic orders. It is isolated to the Kingdom of Aragon, Spain. It is one of the numerous variations of the Greek Cross which has militaristic implications and is only employed in heraldry.

Order of Montessa Cross

Greek Crosses: Militaristic, Fitchy Variation

As with the Latin Cross, a good number of Greek crosses sport the fitchy (fiché) foot. This addition is seen by some as a simple device by which a cross may be driven into the earth by those who wished to pray and there was no church or chapel nearby — i.e. a cross that may be employed by pilgrims. Others see the fitchy foot as an offensive/defensive extension — i.e. a dagger or knife blade — and the weapon of a warrior. Generally, fitchy applies to those crosses that taper from the crosspiece, while fitchy footed apply to those which are pointed at the bottom section. This definition does not always apply.

Quad Fitchy Cross
aka Fitchy of Four Cross, Sixteen-point Cross

The Quad Fitchy Cross is one of a number of fitchy variations. Fitchy footed does not apply as all four terminations are identical. It is one of the numerous variations of the Greek Cross which has militaristic implications and is only employed in heraldry. It is also known as the Fitchy of Four Cross and Sixteen-point Cross.

Cronel Cross
aka Burre Cross, Coronel Cross,
Triple Fichée Cross

The Cronel Cross is derived from the cronel or the lance point with three sharpened elements. It is related to the Double Fitch crosses. The Cronel Cross is one of the numerous variations of the Greek Cross which has militaristic implications. It is a cross form that is only employed in heraldry. The Cronel Cross is also known as the Burre Cross, Coronel Cross and Triple Fichée Cross.

Greek Crosses: Militaristic, Fitchy Variation (Continued)

The Double Fitch Cross I is so designed to form two points on each termination, similar to the points on a lance. It is one of the numerous variations of the Greek Cross which has militaristic implications. The Double Fitch Cross I is a cross form that is exclusively employed in heraldry. It is also referred to as the Double Fiché Cross.

Double Fitch Cross I
aka Double Fiché Cross

The Double Fitch Cross II is a variation of the Double Fitch Cross I. It is one of the numerous variations of the Greek Cross which has militaristic implications. the Double Fitch Cross II is a cross form that is only employed in heraldry. It is also referred to as the Double Fiché Cross.

Double Fitch Cross II
aka Double Fiché Cross

The Double Fitch Cross III is a variation of the Double Fitch Cross I. It is one of the numerous variations of the Greek Cross which has militaristic implications. The Double Fitch Cross III is a cross form that is solely employed in heraldry. It is also referred to as the Double Fiché Cross.

Double Fitch Cross III
aka Double Fiché Cross

Double Fitchy Quartered Cross

The Double Fitchy Quartered Cross is a variation of the Double Fitch Cross II. It is one of the numerous variations of the Greek Cross which has militaristic implications. It is a cross form that is unique to heraldry.

Rousset Cross
aka Greek Cross Fichy

The Rousset Cross is composed of a simple Greek Cross in which the foot is fitched. It is one of the numerous variations of the Greek Cross which has militaristic implications. The Rousset Cross is a cross form that is only employed in heraldry. It is also referred to as the Greek Cross Fichy.

Urdée Cross II
aka Urdy Cross, Champaine Cross,
Croix Aiguisée, Verdy Cross

The Urdée Cross II is a variation of the Urdée Cross I and the Aiguisée Cross I. It is based on the Greek Cross in which the ends of the terminations are pointed. It is one of the numerous variations of the Greek Cross which has militaristic implications. It is a cross form that is unique to heraldry and is also known as the Urdy Cross, Champaine Cross, Croix Aiguisée and Verdy Cross.

The Voided Urdée Cross is a variation of the Urdée Cross II. It is a cross form that is found only in heraldry and is also known as the Voided Urdy Cross and Voided Champaine Cross and Voided Verdy Cross.

Voided Urdé Cross
aka Voided Urdy Cross, Voided Champaine Cross, Voided Verdy Cross

The Bordered Urdée Cross is a variation of the Urdée Cross II. It is a cross form that is found exclusively in heraldry.

Bordered Urdée Cross

The Fitchy at All Points Cross is similar to the Star Cross I and mirrors similar iconography. It is a symbol that is employed in heraldry. Star Cross II is also referred to as the Croix Estoilée and Star Cross II.

Fitchy at All Points Cross
aka Croix Estoilée, Star Cross II

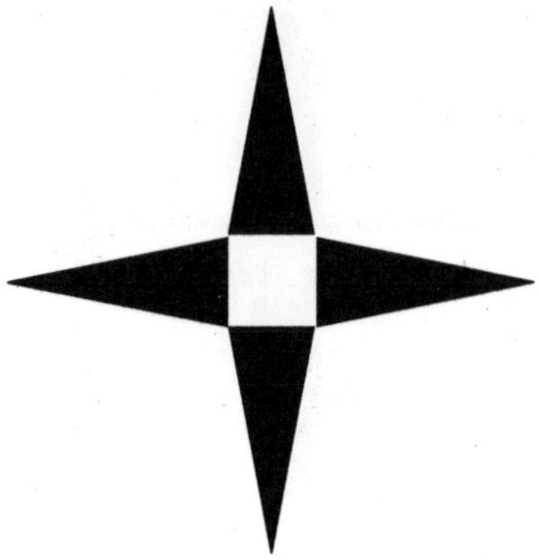

Fitchy at All Points and Quarter Pierced Cross

The Fitchy at All Points and Quarter Pierced Cross is a variation of the Fitchy at All Points Cross. It is a symbol that only appears in heraldry.

Fitchy Foot at All Points Cross

The Fitchy Foot at All Points Cross is a variation of the Urdée Cross II. It is based on the Greek Cross in which the ends of the terminations exhibit a pointed element. It is one of the numerous variations of the Greek Cross which has militaristic implications. The Fitchy Foot at All Points Cross is a cross form that is unique to heraldry.

Fitchy at All Points and Quartered Cross

The Fitchy at All Points and Quartered Cross is a variation of the Fitchy Foot at All Points Cross. It is one of the numerous variations of the Greek Cross which exhibits militaristic implications. The Fitchy at All Points and Quartered Cross is a cross form that is exclusively seen in heraldry.

A variation of the Pattée Cross II, the Patée Fitchy Disjointed Cross is essentially a cross found only in heraldry. It is a cruciform which has militaristic implications.

Patée Fitchy Disjointed Cross

A variation of the Pattée Cross II, the Patée Fitchy Cross is exclusively found only in heraldry. It is a cruciform which has obvious militaristic implications.

Patée Fitchy Cross

The Endented Cross is one of the numerous variations of the Greek Cross which has militaristic implications. It is a cross form that is generally only employed in heraldry.

Endented Cross

Fleury Fitchée
aka St. Jame's Cross

A variation of the Greek Cross as well as the Order of Avis Cross, the Fleury Fitchée Cross is essentially a cross found only in heraldry. It is a cross form which has militaristic implications. It is also referred to as the St. Jame's Cross.

Greek Crosses: Militaristic, Maltese Variation

The Maltese Cross variation is derived from the cross that was associated with the Knights of St. John of Jerusalem of Rhodes and of Malta. It is fundamentally a cross that is associated with a military order and awards — e.g. Polish Military Cross, Knight's Cross (Germany) and Military Cross (King's Royal Rifle Corps). The Maltese Cross with its eight prominent points are created from a Patté Cross in which the terminations have been deeply indented. Eight is a holy number that is seen by some to refer to the beatitudes is also a number that symbolizes regeneration.

The Maltese Cross I is a cross that found its genesis in militaristic orders. It is associated with the Knights of St. John who were driven from Rhodes where the fled after the fall of Jerusalem. They were further driven to the Island of Malta by the Turks. Some see that the elements of the cross are composed of arrowheads. It is a variation of the Greek Cross, and is a cross that is essentially employed in heraldry. It is also known as the Eight-point Cross, Regeneration Cross, St. John's Cross, St. John of Jerusalem's Cross, Order of St. John of Jerusalem of Rhodes and of Malta Cross, Fishtail Cross and Knights Hospitalier Cross.

Maltese Cross I
aka Eight-point Cross, Regeneration Cross, St. John's Cross, St. John of Jerusalem's Cross, Order of St. John of Jerusalem of Rhodes and of Malta Cross, Fishtail Cross, Knights Hospitalier Cross

The Maltese Cross II is a variation of the Maltese Cross I. In this variation, the pointed forms are more prominent, and may be seen as four arrowheads joined at their points. The Maltese Cross II is a variation of the Greek Cross, and is a cross that is employed only in heraldry. It is also referred to as the Eight-point Cross, Regeneration Cross, St. John's Cross, St. John of Jerusalem's Cross, Order of St. John of Jerusalem of Rhodes and of Malta Cross, Fishtail Cross and Knights Hospitalier Cross.

Maltese Cross II
aka Eight-point Cross, Regeneration Cross, St. John's Cross, St. John of Jerusalem's Cross, Order of St. John of Jerusalem of Rhodes and of Malta Cross, Fishtail Cross, Knights Hospitalier Cross

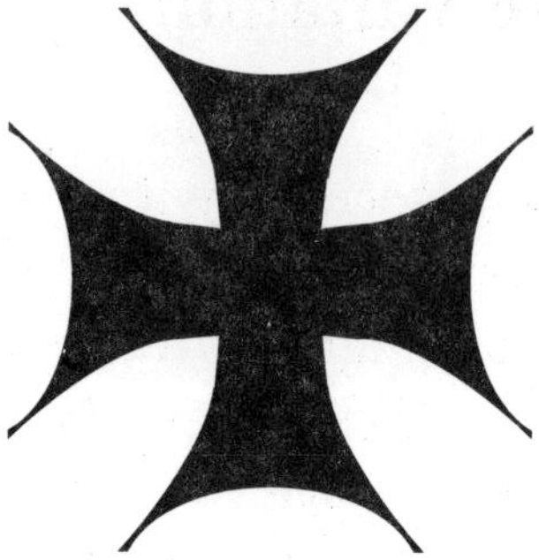

Maltese Cross III
aka Eight-point Cross, Regeneration Cross, St. John's Cross St. John of Jerusalem's Cross, Order of St. John of Jerusalem of Rhodes and of Malta Cross, Fishtail Cross, Knights Hospitalier Cross

The Maltese Cross III is a variation of the Maltese Cross I and one that is not seen as often as the other varieties noted above. It is a variation of the Greek Cross, and is a cross that is frequently employed in heraldry. It is also known as the Eight-point Cross, Regeneration Cross, St. John's Cross St. John of Jerusalem's Cross, Order of St. John of Jerusalem of Rhodes and of Malta Cross, Fishtail Cross and Knights Hospitalier Cross.

Maltese Cross IV
aka Eight-point Cross, Fishtail Cross

The Maltese Cross IV is associated with the "Sovereign Military Order of Malta". This cross consists of four spear points in which the points turn inwards and are, thereby, neutralized as a weapon of war. The Maltese Cross IV is one of the numerous variations of the Greek Cross which has militaristic implications — i.e. associated with a militaristic order. It is a cross that is generally only employed in heraldry. It is also referred to as the Eight-point Cross and Fishtail Cross.

Huguenot Cross

The Huguenot Cross is similar to the Russian Knights of St. John of Jerusalem Cross and a dove was added. It was the cross associated with the French Protestants of the sixteenth century, hence the *fleur-de-lys*. The dove refers to the Holy Spirit and the message that the Huguenots they carried. The Huguenot Cross is a variation of the Greek Cross and a symbol that was employed in heraldry.

The Order of Holy Spirit Cross is derived from the Huguenot Cross. The Order was established by the last Valois king, Henri III. The appearance of the voided dove in the centre relates this cross to the Huguenot Cross. It was during the reign of the Valois that the Huguenots were persecuted, particularly during the St. Bartholomew's Eve Massacre. The Order of Holy Spirit Cross is a variation of the Greek Cross and a symbol that is employed in heraldry. It is also referred to as the Croix du Chevaliers du Saint-Esprit.

Order of the Holy Spirit Cross
aka Croix du Chevaliers du Saint-Esprit

The Russian Knights of St. John of Jerusalem Cross is derived from the Maltese Cross with an addition of *fleur-de-lys* (normally considered as a French device). The use of Maltese Cross here indicates the popularity that the cross possessed in militaristic orders. The Russian Knights of St. John of Jerusalem Cross is a variation of the Greek Cross and a symbol that is solely employed in heraldry.

Russian Knights of St. John of Jerusalem Cross

The Maltese Knights of Bath Cross is one of the numerous variations of Greek Cross which has militaristic implications — i.e. associated with a militaristic order. It is a combination of a Maltese Cross and four *fleur-de-lys*. It is a cross form that is generally only employed in heraldry.

Maltese Knight's of Bath Cross

Order of St. Lazarus of Jerusalem Cross I

The Order of St. Lazarus of Jerusalem Cross I is green in colour. It is one of the numerous variations of the Greek Cross which has militaristic implications — i.e. associated with a militaristic order — and related to the Maltese Cross. It is a cross form that is generally employed only in heraldry.

Order of St. Lazarus of Jerusalem Cross II

The Order of St. Lazarus of Jerusalem Cross II is green in colour and a variation of the Order of St. Lazarus of Jerusalem Cross I. It is one of the numerous variations of the Greek Cross which has militaristic implications — i.e. associated with a militaristic order. It is a cross form that is generally employed only in heraldry.

Voided or Bordered Maltese Cross

The Voided or Bordered Maltese Cross is a variation of Maltese Cross II. It is a variation of the Greek Cross and is a cross that is only employed in heraldry.

The Venerable Order of St. John Cross is derived from the Maltese Cross with an the addition of *fleur-de-lys*. The use of Maltese Cross here indicates the popularity that the cross possessed in militaristic orders. The Venerable Order of St. John Cross is a variation of the Greek Cross and a symbol that is solely employed in heraldry.

Venerable Order of St. John Cross

The Russian Grand Priory of the Knights of St. John of Jerusalem Cross is derived from the Maltese Cross with an the addition of *fleur-de-lys*, not a Russian device. It is a variant of the Russian Knights of St. John of Jerusalem Cross. The Russian Grand Priory of the Knights of St. John of Jerusalem Cross is a variation of the Greek Cross and a symbol that is solely employed in heraldry.

Russian Grand Priory of the Knights of St. John of Jerusalem Cross

The Maltese Cross V is a rare variation of the Maltese Cross I. It is found associated with Priory of Manosque, France. It is a variation of the Greek Cross, and is a cross that is essentially employed in heraldry.

Maltese Cross V

Greek Crosses: Fylfot/Svastika Variation

An Apologia

I find *svastika* the most repugnant of all symbols! Yet, here it is, occupying a sizeable section in this consideration.

I can clearly remember the day when I visited an old, wooden temple in Kuala Lumpur. This simple temple sat on a little knoll across Jalan Stadium from the highly elaborate Chan See Shu Yuen Temple. Locally, this temple was important for its production of joss sticks of varying sizes. Its architecture was of middling interest. Alas, it has since burned to the ground. As I climbed the stairs, I found tucked away at the rear of the temple. On the second floor, in a small sanctuary, I first beheld a large Buddha image sitting peacefully in the *mudrā* of contemplation.

I was emotionally, psychologically and physically repelled. On the image's chest was a *svastika* — more precisely, a *sauvastika*. I had lived through the Second World War and witnessed, second hand, the untold horrors of the psychologically depraved Nazi regime of Germany, particularly the death camps with bodies stacked like cord-wood. The image of the Nazi flag — i.e. a black *svastika* turned 45°, within a white circle upon a red field — was an image that is utterly contemptible in my eyes. *Svastika* was anathema to me, I hated it because of what it implied! Yet here in this sacred, peaceful locale was an image of the pacific Prince Siddhārtha Gautama with that most hated icon emblazoned upon his chest — a *sauvastika*. Still to this day, some twenty-five years later the memory of seeing that sign creates a relict so strong that I still cringe.

Yet, it is a sign, a symbol that is thousands of years old. Numerous scholars declare it the arch-symbol. It is found in the remote areas of prehistory. The Buddhists, Hindus and Jainas view the *sauvastika/svastika* as an auspicious symbol of good luck. It has appeared in the early Abrahamic religion. It is found represented by the ancient peoples of Egypt, Tibet, Turkey, Bali and Burma; the Aztecs, Maya and Incas and native North Americans; the Romans, Greeks, Chinese, Koreans and Japanese; Christians before the fourth century. Virtually every civilization in the world has employed *sauvastika/svastika* at one time or another. For these far-flung peoples, *sauvastika/svastika* is an icon parallel in use and importance to that of the Christian cross.

By many, *sauvastika/svastika* is seen as a sun symbol. By others is a representation of heavenly lightening. In Buddhism it is an auspicious sign of luck and often associated with the Buddha, while in Hinduism, it represents well being. In the West, until the second third of the twentieth century, it was considered to be a good luck charm.

Although a number of forms do not fall within the parameters of Solar Cross — i.e.

employing a circular element — none the less, its importance is such that all are considered here within this section of the Greek crosses.

The names vary: fylfot cross, hooked cross, cramponed cross, ugunskrust (fire cross), perkonkrust (thunder cross), kaskrust (hooked cross), Laima's cross, double cross, gammadion cross, tetragammadion cross, hakenkreuz (hook cross), Sun wheel, tetraskelion, wan, mundilfari and *svastika*.

The Widdershins Fylfot Cross is the most ancient symbol. Found in Neolithic Eurasia, the Crux Gamata is sacred to Buddhism, Hinduism, Jainism, Zoroastrianism and Pre-Colombian Americas. The term "fylfot" may come from the Anglo Saxon *fíer fóte*, meaning four feet. The arms face to the left, therefore, by the ancient tradition, it is the female symbol and associated with the moon. The Widdershins Fylfot Cross is one of the numerous variations of the Greek Cross and a cross that is frequently employed in heraldry, rarely in ecclesiastical situations and is a symbol of Kālī. It is also referred to as the Crux Gammata, Crux Dissimulata, Crux Gammadion, Hooked Cross, Rebated Cross Potent, Bent Cross, Indian Cross and Cross Cramponned.

Widdershins Fylfot Cross
aka Crux Gammata, Crux Dissimulata, Crux Gammadion, Hooked Cross, Rebated Cross Potent, Bent Cross, Indian Cross, Cross Cramponned

The Sunwise Fylfot Cross is also the most ancient symbol. Found in Neolithic Eurasia, the Crux Gamata is sacred to Buddhism, Hinduism, Jainism, Zoroastrianism and Pre-Colombian Americas. The arms face to the right, therefore, by the ancient tradition, it is the male form — i.e. the sun being the male component. This particular form was incorporated into Nazi symbolism. The Sunwise Fylfot Cross is one of the numerous variations of the Greek Cross and a cross that is frequently employed in heraldry, rarely in Christian ecclesiastical situations and a symbol of Lord Viṣṇu and of Sūrya. It is also referred to as the Crux Gammata, Crux Dissimulata, Crux Gammadion, Hooked Cross, Rebated Cross Potent, Bent Cross, Indian Cross and Cross Cramponned.

Sunwise Fylfot Cross
aka Crux Gammata, Crux Dissimulata, Crux Gammadion, Hooked Cross, Rebated Cross Potent, Bent Cross, Indian Cross, Cross Cramponned

Potent Sunwise Fylfot
aka Potent Rebated Cross

The Potent Sunwise Cross is made up of eight potents. It is related to the Fylfot crosses. The Potent Sunwise Cross is one of the numerous variations of the Greek Cross and a symbol that is frequently employed in heraldry. It is also known as the Potent Rebated Cross.

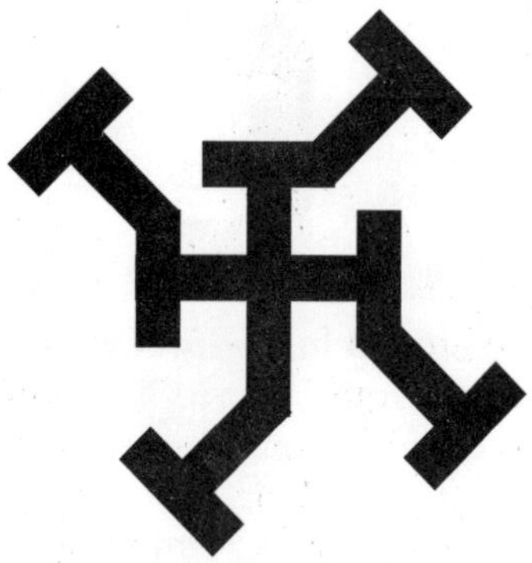

Potent–Repotent Cross
aka Potent-repotent in Four Points Cross

The Potent–Repotent Cross is made up of eight potents attached at a 45° angle to a Potent Cross. It is related to the Fylfot crosses. The Potent–Repotent Cross is one of the numerous variations of the Greek Cross and a symbol that is exclusively employed in heraldry. It is also known as the Potent–Repotent in Four Points Cross.

Gurgity Cross
aka Anserated Cross

The Gurgity Cross appears to be related to the Sunwise Fylfot Cross. It is a cross form that seldom appears in heraldry. The Gurgity Cross is one of the numerous variations of the Greek Cross and a symbol that is only employed in heraldry. It is also referred to as the Anserated Cross.

The Rhodes Fylfot Cross is related to the Widdershins Fylfot Cross. It is a cross form that is found upon a tray from Rhodes (*c.* 585 BCE) and is similar to one found in a Greek bowl (*c.* 165 BCE). The Rhodes Fylfot Cross is a cross that appears to be essentially decorative and is found neither in ecclesiastical situations nor does it appear in heraldry.

Rhodes Fylfot Cross

The Kuna (aka: Cuna) Fylfot Cross is related to the Sunwise Fylfot Cross. It is a cross form that is found in the mola — i.e. reversed and multi-level applique — of the Cuna tribe in Central America. It is a form that is exclusively decorative in application and is neither ecclesiastical nor heraldic.

Kuna Fylfot Cross

The Boreyko Fylfot Cross is related to the Widdershins Fylfot Cross and is utilized by the Polish family of the same name. It is a fylfot cross form that is somewhat unique inasmuch as it is not symmetrical. The Boreyko Fylfot Cross is exclusively found in Polish heraldry.

Boreyko Fylfot Cross

Bosnia Fylfot Cross

The Bosnia Fylfot Cross is related to the Sunwise Fylfot Cross and is found engraved upon Bosnian grave markers. It is a fylfot cross form that is somewhat unique. The Bosnia Fylfot Cross is nearly always found adorning a church or other related accoutrements.

Greek Fylfot Cross

The Greek Fylfot Cross is related to the Sunwise Fylfot Cross, Rhodes Fylfot Cross as well as the Kuna Fylfot Cross and it appears before the Common Era (BCE). It is a fylfot cross form that is somewhat unique. The Greek Fylfot Cross is a cross that appears to be essentially decorative and is found neither in ecclesiastical situations nor does it appear in heraldry.

Thunder Cross
aka Perkons Cross

The Thunder Cross predates Christianity or Christian influence in the Baltic region. It is a fylfot cross form that is somewhat unique and is seen as either a solar symbol or associated with Perkons (Perkunis), the Baltic (Lithuania) god of thunder and fertility who is related to Thor. The Thunder Cross is also known as the Perkons Cross.

The Hirosaki Fylfot Cross is related to the Widdershin Fylfot Cross and is found as the symbol on the flag of Hirosaki, Aomori, Japan. It is a fylfot cross form that is somewhat unique as it is based upon a nine element square. The Hirosaki Fylfot Cross is only encountered in heraldry.

Hirosaki Fylfot Cross

The Book of Silk Fylfot Cross is related to the Sunwise Fylfot Cross and is found in the *Book of Silk* (*c.* 400 BCE) an ancient Chinese astronomy manuscript. It is a fylfot cross form that is somewhat unique. The Book of Silk Fylfot Cross may represent a comet. It is a cross that appears to be essentially astronomical and is found neither in ecclesiastical situations nor does it appear in heraldry.

Book of Silk Fylfot Cross

The Tursaansydan Cross I is related to the Sunwise Fylfot Cross and is an ancient Finnish symbol. It refers to the "heart of Tursas" — i.e. the deity of war — and/or the "heart of the walrus" (mursunsydamet). The Tursaansydan Cross I is a cross that appears to be associated with the ancient Finnish magic/religious practices unrelated to Christianity. It does not appear in heraldry.

Tursaansydan Cross I

Tursaansydan Cross II

The Tursaansydan Cross II is related to the Sunwise Fylfot Cross and is an ancient Finnish symbol related to Norse deities as well as a variation of the Tursaansydan Cross I. It is a fylfot cross form that is somewhat unique. The Tursaansydan Cross II is a cross that appears to be associated with the ancient Finnish magic/religious practices unrelated to Christianity. It does not appear in heraldry.

Finnish Liberty Cross
aka Order of the Cross of Liberty

The Finnish Liberty Cross is related to the Sunwise Fylfot Cross and is derived from an ancient Finnish symbol (see Tursaansydan Cross I and II). It is exclusively encountered in heraldry. It is also known as the Order of the Cross of Liberty.

Widdershins Fylfot Solar Cross

The Widdershins Fylfot Solar Cross is the Solar Cross adaptation of the Widdershins Fylfot Cross. It is one of the numerous variations of the Solar Cross and a symbol that is frequently employed in heraldry.

The Sunwise Fylfot Solar Cross is an adaption of the Widdershin Fylfot Cross. It is one of the numerous variations of the Solar Cross and a symbol that is frequently employed in heraldry.

Sunwise Fylfot Solar Cross

The Viking Sunwise Fylfot Cross is an ancient Norse adoption of the Sunwise Fylfot Cross. It is one of the numerous variations of the Solar Cross. It is a symbol that is frequently encountered in ancient, runic inscriptions and only rarely found in heraldry.

Viking Sunwise Fylfot Cross

The Manji Cross I is a Buddhist icon that represents *dharma,* harmony and balance. It is one of the numerous variations of the Solar Cross and a variation of Widdershin Fylfot Cross. The Manji Cross I is a symbol that is frequently employed in Buddhist painting and sculpture.

Manji Cross I

Manji Cross II

The Manji Cross II is a Buddhist icon that represents strength and intelligence. It is one of the numerous variations of the Solar Cross and the Sunwise Fylfot Cross. It is a symbol that is frequently employed in Buddhist painting and sculpture.

Wavy Cross
aka Ondée Cross

The Wavy Cross is a variant of the Star Cross III. It consists of wavy elements proceeding from a centre point. It is a variation of the Greek Cross and a symbol that is employed in heraldry. It is also referred to as the Ondée Cross.

Lauburu Cross
aka Basque Cross, Crux Lauburu

The Lauburu Cross is found only in the Basque region of Northern Spain and South-western France. Its meaning is unknown, but right facing it is found over doorways and left facing on tombstones. It is one of the numerous variations of the Solar Cross and a symbol that is frequently employed in heraldry. It is also referred to as the Basque Cross and Crux Lauburu.

The Norse Solar Cross I is one of a number of runic symbols that is related to the fylfot cross. Its meaning is unknown, but left facing fylfot cannot necessarily be considered either feminine or associated with the moon. The Norse Solar Cross I is a magical/religious form and is not found in heraldry. It is also called as Odin's Cross and Woden's Cross.

Norse Solar Cross I
aka Odin's Cross, Woden's Cross

The Wolf Cross is related to the Sunwise Fylfot Cross. It is a cross form that is encountered in Norse runic design.

Wolf Cross

The Svastika (Nazi) is a symbol that is loathed by most free-thinking people. It is derived from the Sunwise Fylfot Cross and its design is based upon a grid of twenty-five squares. It appears only in heraldry. It is also referred to as the Sunwise Fylfot Cross, Crux Gammata, Crux Dissimulata, Crux Gammadion, Hooked Cross, Rebated Cross Potent, Bent Cross, Indian Cross and Cross Cramponned.

Svastika
aka Sunwise Fylfot Cross, Crux Gammata, Crux Dissimulata, Crux Gammadion, Hooked Cross, Rebated Cross Potent, Bent Cross, Indian Cross, Cross Cramponned

Barbée Cross II
aka Croix Tournée, Croix Cromponnée,
Arrow Cross

Like Barbée Cross I, Barbée Cross II is militaristic in its implication. The Barbée Cross II is a variation of the Barbée Cross I, and is also related to the Widdershins Fylfot Cross. It is a cross that is frequently employed in heraldry. It is also referred to as the Croix Tournée, Croix Cromponnée and Arrow Cross.

Zierscheiben Widdershin Fylfot Cross

The Zierscheiben Widdershins Fylfot Cross is connected, *en forme*, to the Kuna (aka: Cuna) Fylfot Cross and is encountered in the Late Iron Age in Germany. It is a cross form that is related to the Solar Cross, and a form that is decorative in application but may have had certain magical/spiritual significance.

Greek Crosses: Miscellaneous Variation

In addition to the variations of the Greek Cross as already discussed — i.e. Coptic Variations, Interlaced Variations, Boton/Pommé Variations, Annulated Variations, Pattée/Patonce Variations, Maltese Variations, Star Variations, Jerusalem Variations, Plant/Animal Variations, and Anchry, Milrine, Moline, Recercelée Variations — there are a number of other variations that do not fall within these categories. Virtually all of them are heraldic in genesis.

The Croissant Cross is composed of a Greek Cross with crescents at the ends of the arms. The moon or crescent moon is a symbol that is often associated with the Virgin Mary particularly in Spanish paintings of the seventeenth century. It is known in witchcraft as Lunate Cross. The Croissant Cross is a variation of the Greek Cross and is frequently employed in heraldry as well as ecclesiastical situations. It is also referred to as the Crescent Cross and the Lunate Cross.

Croissant Cross
aka Crescent Cross, Lunate Cross

The Verry Cross resembles the Capiteau Cross. However, essentially it is quite different as it is composed of four bell-forms. The Verry Cross is one of the numerous variations of the Greek Cross and a cross form that is frequently employed in heraldry. It is also referred to as the Vair-Bells Cross, Vairy Cross, Very Cross and Croix Vairé.

Verry Cross
aka Vair-Bells Cross, Vairy Cross, Very Cross, Croix Vairé

Osmorog Cross

The Osmorog Cross is a cross variation that appears almost exclusively in the arms of Poland. It, along with Rogacina Dwukrotnie Przekrzyzowana and Rogacina Przekrzyzowana crosses, is uniquely Polish in character and design. The Osmorog Cross is one of the numerous variations of the Greek Cross, and is a cross that is employed in Polish heraldry.

Rouchy Cross

The Roucy Cross is symbolic of faith. The three steps refer to the Trinity. The Roucy Cross is one of the numerous variations of the Greek Cross, and is a cross that is frequently employed in heraldry.

Aiguisée Cross II
aka Aiguise Cross, Urdée Cross, Verdy Cross,
Cross of Suffering, Passion Cross,
Pointed Cross, Humetty Pointed Cross

The Aiguisée Cross II is a variant of the Aiguisée Cross I. In this variant, the triangular terminations are separated from the crosspieces. The Aiguisée Cross II is one of the numerous variations of the Greek Cross and a symbol that is only employed in heraldry. It is also referred to as the Aiguise Cross, Urdée Cross, Verdy Cross, Cross of Suffering, Passion Cross, Pointed Cross and Humetty Pointed Cross.

The Lozengy Nowed Cross is a cross that is one of the numerous variations of the Greek Cross. In this instance, lozenges appear near the end of each crosspiece. The Lozengy Nowed Cross is a cross that is exclusively employed in heraldry. It is also referred to as the Nowy Lozengy Cross.

Lozengy Nowyed Cross
aka Nowy Lozengy Cross

The Quadrate Cross is a cross form that refers to the four Gospels and the dissemination of Christian teaching to the four quarters of the world. It is a variation of the Greek Cross and a symbol that is generally only employed in heraldry. It is also referred to as the Nowy Quadrate Cross.

Quadrate Cross
aka Nowy Quadrate Cross

The Clechée Cross I receives its name from the pointed ends or key-hole shaped. It is one of the numerous variations of the Greek Cross and a cross that is frequently employed in heraldry. It is also referred to as the Croix Vidée and is related to the Fusils Cross.

Clechée Cross I
aka Croix Vidée

Clechée Cross II
aka Croix Vidée

The Clechée Cross II is a variant of Clechée Cross I. It is one of the numerous variations of the Greek Cross and is frequently employed in heraldry as well as in ecclesiastical situations. It is also referred to as the Croix Vidée and is related to the Fusils Cross.

Masculy Cross II
aka Masclée Cross

The Masculy Cross II is so named for the five mascules — i.e. lozenges voided. These mascules are seen to represent the five wounds of the Christ at crucifixion. The Masculy Cross II is one of the numerous variations of the Greek Cross and a cross form that is frequently employed in heraldry. It is also referred to the Masclée Cross.

Coronated Cross

The Coronated Cross is so named because of the crown terminations. It is one of the numerous variations of the Greek Cross and a cross form that is frequently employed in heraldry.

The Capital Cross I is formed by four columns. The columns may refer to the column to which the Christ was traditionally tied when scourged. The column also symbolizes fortitude and constancy. The Capital Cross I is one of the numerous variations of the Greek Cross and a cross form that is frequently employed in heraldry. It is also called as the Croix Capiteau.

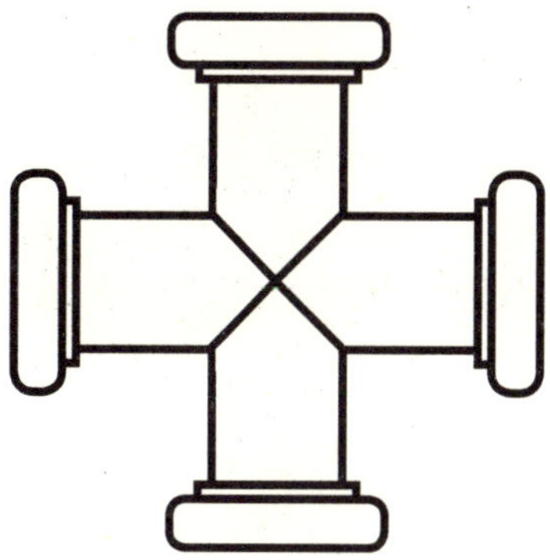

Capital Cross I
aka Croix Capiteau

The Teutonic Cross IV is found as part of the Coat of Arms of the Order of the Teutonic Knights. The Teutonic Knights were established to succour pilgrims who were travelling to the Holy Land. They were not essentially militaristic but established hospitals and hostels for the pilgrims, even though part of the cross is spear-like. In this instance, the militaristic implication is passive or protective rather than aggressive. The Teutonic Cross IV is exclusively found in heraldry. It is also known as the Teutonic Order Cross.

Teutonic Cross IV
aka Teutonic Order Cross

The composition of Double Potent Cross is made up of two crutches (potents), overlapping each termination. The Double Potent Cross is one of the numerous variations of the Greek Cross and a form that is frequently employed in heraldry. It is also referred to as the Cross Potent Crossed.

Double Potent Cross
aka Cross Potent Crossed

Dancetty Cross I
aka Croix Dancetté, Croix Emanchée

The Dancetty Cross I is an exaggerated variation of the Indented Cross. The term dancetty refers to a zig-zag form and is related to water. The Dancetty Cross I is one of the numerous variations of the Greek Cross and one in which the form of the crosspieces is rather elaborately treated. It is a cross form that is frequently employed in heraldry. It is also referred to as the Croix Dancetté and Croix Emanchée.

Double Claved Cross
aka Double Clavied Cross

The composition of Double Claved Cross is made up of two keys. However, it is apparent that three key-heads are here employed. It refers to the idea that the Faith unlocks doors, particularly to immortality. It is one of the numerous variations of the Greek Cross and a form that is employed in heraldry. It is also known as the Double Clavied Cross.

Lambeauxed Cross

The Lambeauxed Cross is a variation of the Lambeau Cross, a Latin Cross form. It is one of the numerous variations of the Greek Cross and a form that is employed in heraldry.

The Dancetty Cross II is a variation of the Dancetty Cross I. Predominating here is the zig-zag form. It is one of the numerous variations of the Greek Cross and one in which the form of the crosspieces is rather elaborately treated. It is a symbol that is often employed in heraldry. It is also referred to as the Croix Dancetté and Croix Emanchée.

Dancetty Cross II
aka Croix Dancetté, Croix Emanchée

The form of Indented Cross is related to the Dancetty Cross I, but with smaller notches or teeth and it is related to fire. The Indented Cross is one of the numerous variations of the Greek Cross and one in which the form of the crosspieces is rather elaborately treated. It is a cross form that is frequently employed in heraldry. It is also referred to as the Crux Denchée.

Indented Cross
aka Crux Denchée

The Invected Cross is a variation of the Engrailed Cross, but in opposition. It is one of the numerous variations of the Greek Cross and one in which the form of the crosspieces is rather elaborately treated and refers to the earth. The Invected Cross is a cross form that is generally employed only in heraldry. It is also referred to as the Crux Cannelée.

Invected Cross
aka Crux Cannelée

Branchy Cross
aka Ragulée Cross

The Branchy Cross is one of the numerous variations of the Greek Cross and one in which the form of the crosspieces is rather elaborately treated and it symbolizes the overcoming of difficulties. It is related to the Raguly Cross. The Branchy Cross is a symbol that is generally only employed in heraldry. It is also referred to as the Ragulée Cross.

Trianguly Cross

The Trianguly Cross is one of the numerous variations of the Greek Cross and one in which the form of the crosspieces is rather elaborately treated. The triangle has been the traditional symbol for the Trinity. The Trianguly Cross is a cross form that is generally employed only in heraldry.

Dovetail Cross
aka Lambeau Cross

The Dovetail Cross is a referent to the carpenter's trade and, therefore, is associated with St. Joseph and the Christ. It is one of the numerous variations of the Greek Cross and one in which the form of the crosspieces is rather elaborately treated. The lambeau normally refers to the first born son. The Dovetail Cross is a cross form that is generally employed only in heraldry. It is also referred to as the Lambeau Cross.

The Engrailed Cross is one of the numerous variations of the Greek Cross and one in which the form of the crosspieces is rather elaborately treated. The Engrailed Cross, *en dessein*, may refer to teeth. However, it seems to be a pure design element with no known referent to a toothed device. It is the opposite of Invected Cross, *en forme*. It is a cross that is generally employed only in heraldry. It is also referred to as the Croix Engrélée and Croix Engreslée.

Engrailed Cross
aka Croix Engrélée, Croix Engreslée

The Flory Engrailed Cross is a cross composed of Engrailed Cross and Flory crosses. It is one of the numerous variations of the Greek Cross and one in which the form of the crosspieces is rather elaborately treated. The Flory Engrailed Cross is a symbol that is generally employed only in heraldry. It is also referred to as the Croix Fleurée Engrélée.

Flory Engrailed Cross
aka Croix Fleurée Engrélée

The Cable Cross is one of the many crosses that is based upon common man-made objects — i.e. a cable or rope — and is related to the Rope Cross. It is one of the numerous variations of the Greek Cross and one in which the form of the crosspieces is rather elaborately treated. The Cable Cross is a cross form that is generally employed only in heraldry. It is also referred to as the Croix Cablée.

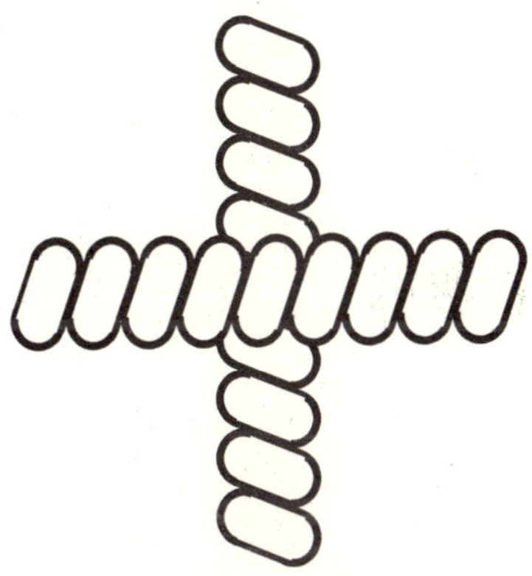

Cable Cross
aka Croix Cablée

Paternoster Cross

The Paternoster Cross refers to the beads in the rosary of the Roman Catholic faith. As such the origins of the form(s) are strictly ecclesiastical. The Paternoster Cross is one of the numerous variations of the Greek Cross and one in which the form of the crosspieces is rather elaborately treated. It is a symbol that is generally employed only in heraldry.

Nebulée Cross I
aka Nebuly Cross

The Nebulée Cross I may be depicted as here or with stepped forms as seen in Nebulée Cross II. The wavy lines refer to clouds and/or air. The Nebulée Cross I is one of the numerous variations of the Greek Cross and one in which the form of the crosspieces is rather elaborately treated. It is a symbol that is generally employed only in heraldry. It is also referred to as the Nebuly Cross.

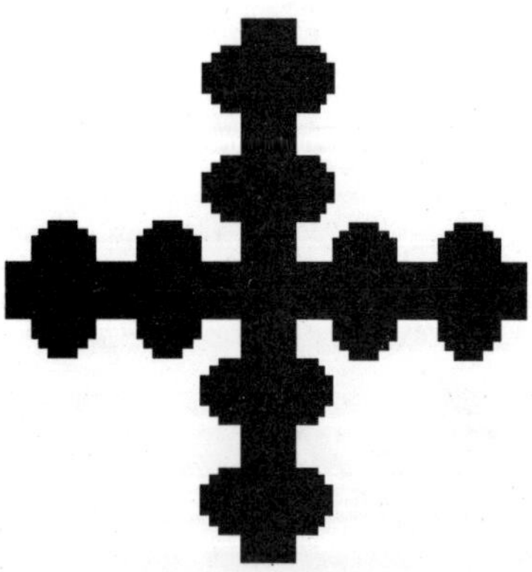

Nebulée Cross II
aka Nebuly Cross

The Nebulée Cross II is a variation on Nebulé Cross I and is one of the numerous variations of the Greek Cross and one in which the form of the crosspieces is rather elaborately treated. It is a cross form that is generally employed only in heraldry. It is also referred to as the Nebuly Cross.

The Saxon Cross II is one of the numerous cruciforms developed by the Saxons. In some forms it is related to the Celtic Cross. It is a variation of the Greek Cross and is employed in heraldry as well as in ecclesiastical situations. It is also referred to as the Hovingham Cross. It is related to the Saxon Cross I, III, IV and V.

Saxon Cross II
aka Hovingham Cross

The Cerdeña Cross is a cross of Spanish origin being used in the arms of Roderigo de Cerdeña. It is one of the numerous variations of the Greek Cross and a symbol that is frequently employed in heraldry as well as in isolated ecclesiastical situations.

Cerdeña Cross

The Savoy Cross is an elaboration of the traditional the Savoy Cross which is white on a red field. The central cross refers to that form. The Savoy Cross is one of the numerous variations of the Greek Cross and a symbol that is frequently employed in heraldry. It is also referred to as the Croix Savoie.

Savoy Cross
aka Croix Savoie

Moussué Cross II
aka Emousée Cross, Blunted Cross

The Moussué Cross is one of the numerous variations of the Greek Cross. It is a cross with blunted or rounded ends. The Moussué Cross is a cross form that is exclusively employed in heraldry. It is also referred to as the Emousée Cross and Blunted Cross.

Pendal Cross
aka Pandal Cross, Spindle Cross

The Pendal Cross is one of the numerous variations of the Greek Cross and a cross form that is solely employed in heraldry. It is also known as the Pandal Cross and Spindle Cross.

Potent Quadrate Cross

The Potent Quadrate Cross is derived from the Potent Cross and the Quadrate Cross. It is related also to St. Chad's Cross. The Potent Quadrate Cross is one of the numerous variations of the Greek Cross and a cross form that is only employed in heraldry.

The Crux Gemmata II is a cross in which exhibit thirteen gems. They refer to the Christ and the twelve disciples. The Crux Gemmata is a variation of the Greek Cross and a cross that is employed in heraldry and may appear as a necklace in an ecclesiastical situation. It is also referred to as the Jewelled Cross.

Crux Gemmata II
aka Jewelled Cross

The St. Thomas Cross II is a cross which is rather unique and found normally in and around the cultures of the Indian Ocean. It consists of a Greek Cross form surmounted by a dove and resting upon a lotus which in turn rests upon three steps. The lotus may represent the sacred flower found in India, one of the prime locales for the Nazrani (Christian) group. It is a cross that is employed in heraldry and may appear in isolated ecclesiastical situations. It is also referred to as the Nazrani Cross and Mar Thoma Cross.

St. Thomas Cross II
aka Nazrani Cross, Mar Thoma Cross

The Raguly Cross resembles a form with extensions, at an angle and cut close to the crosspiece. It is also referred to as a tree with the branches cut at a regular length and is symbolic of troubles encountered and overcome (*see* Burgundy Cross in St. Andrew's Cross section). The Raguly Cross is a variation of the Greek Cross and is employed in heraldry. It is also referred to as the Croix Ragulée, Ragulée Cross, Ragged Cross, Ragulated Cross and Croix Ecotée.

Raguly Cross
aka Croix Ragulée, Ragulée Cross, Ragged Cross, Ragulated Cross, Croix Ecotée

Demi Fleur-de-lys Cottised Cross

The Demi Fleur-de-lys Cottised Cross is a cross in which half *fleur-de-lys* form a border as well as a highly decorated pattern. The *fleur-de-lys* are traditionally symbolic of light and purity. The Demi Fleur-de-lys Cottised Cross is a variation of the Greek Cross and is employed in heraldry.

Demi Annuly Inverted Cross
aka Half Annulet Inverted Cross,
Anchory Cross

The Demi Annuly Inverted Cross is a cruciform that resembles an Anchor Cross, but in diminutive form. It is related to the Demi Annuly Cross as well as the Annulety Cross. The Demi Annuly Inverted Cross is a variation of the Greek Cross and a symbol that is exclusively heraldic in nature. It is otherwise known as the Half Annulet Inverted Cross and Anchory Cross.

Demi Annuly Cross
aka Half Annulet Cross

The Demi Annuly Cross is a cruciform that is related to the Demi the Annuly Inverted Cross as well as the Annulety Cross. In addition, it is a variation of the Greek Cross and a symbol that is exclusively heraldic in nature. It is also referred to as the Half Annulet Cross.

The Double Parted Fleury Cross is a cruciform that is rarely encountered. It is made up of four bow-shaped or crescent-shaped elements giving it a decidedly menacing appearance. It is a variation of the Greek Cross and a symbol that is exclusively heraldic in nature.

Double Parted Fleury Cross

Solar Crosses

The term Solar Cross, or Sun Cross, refers to any cross in which there is a major circular element or disc — i.e. solar disc — that is part of the whole. The Solar Cross or a cross within a circle is truly an ancient symbol, predating Christianity and encountered in the earliest manifestations of primitive societies throughout the world. Like the fylfot, it is not geographically isolated nor restricted to a specific time period. In ancient times the solar disc along with the moon's forms was most often venerated and appear to have had certain spiritual significance.

Solar Cross
aka Gnostic Cross, Odin's Cross, Woden's Cross, Sun Wheel Cross, Taranis Wheel Cross

The Solar Cross is an ancient symbol which consists of the sun disc and the Greek Cross. It is a symbol that is found in Neolithic Europe (e.g. Swiss Solar Cross), Pre-Columbian America (e.g. Caddo Solar Cross), dynastic China and pre-Christianized Scandinavian (e.g. Odin's Cross). The Solar Cross is one of the numerous variations and a cross form that is employed in heraldry as well as frequently found in ecclesiastical situations. It is also referred to as the Gnostic Cross, Odin's Cross, Woden's Cross, Sun Wheel Cross and Taranis Wheel Cross.

Celtic Cross I
aka High Cross, Solar Cross, St. John's Cross, Irish Cross, Iona Cross

The Celtic Cross I is one of the numerous variations of the Solar Cross. The Celts who inhabited Ireland and other British islands are associated with this cross. It is also referred to as a Solar or Sun Cross because of the circle which may be solid. It is felt by some that the circular element was included to strengthen the stone crosspieces and was essentially structural in nature. It is a cross form that is employed in heraldry but more frequently it is found in ecclesiastical situations. It is also known to as the High Cross, Solar Cross, St. John's Cross, Irish Cross and Iona Cross.

The Celtic Cross II is a variation of Celtic Cross I and is one of the numerous variations of the Solar Cross. It is a cross form that is employed in heraldry but more frequently it is found in ecclesiastical situations.

Celtic Cross II

The Atlantis Cross is a variation of the Solar Cross and is also allied to the Celtic Cross. This cross is related to esoteric societies who claim descent from Atlantis. The three circles refer to Plato's description of the Atlantean capitol. It is employed exclusively in heraldry.

Atlantis Cross

The Ionic Cross is so named as St. Columba took Christianity to Ionia. This cross is a combination of the Celtic or Solar Cross and the Byzantine Cross. Ionia was made up, in part of what was Byzantium. The Ionic Cross is one of the numerous variations of Solar Cross and a cross form that is employed in heraldry as well as frequently found in ecclesiastical situations. It is also referred to as the St. Columba's Cross.

Ionic Cross
aka St. Columba's Cross

Cleves Cross II

The Cleves Cross II is composed of a Sun Cross and a Croix Fleur-de-lys with the addition of twelve small circles. It is a Solar Cross variation of the Cleves Cross I. The Cleves Cross II is one of the numerous variations of Solar Cross and a cross form that is frequently employed in heraldry.

Alisée Cross
aka Crois Paté Convexed

The Alisée Cross is related to the Crux Pattée or Cross Formée as well as the Solar Cross. The term *alisée* comes from the French "reamed" and may refer to its shape. The Alisée Cross is one of the numerous variations of the Solar Cross and is frequently employed in heraldry. It is also called as the Crois Paté Convexed.

Jerusalem Cross III
aka Knights of Jerusalem Cross, Franciscan Custody of the Holy Land Cross, Fivefold Cross

The Jerusalem Cross III is a variation of Jerusalem Cross I and II. It is one of the numerous variations of the Solar Cross and a cruciform symbol that is employed in heraldry but is more prevalent in ecclesiastical situations. It is also referred to as the Knights of Jerusalem Cross, Franciscan Custody of the Holy Land Cross and Fivefold Cross.

The Chi Rho Cross III is a variant of Chi Rho Cross I and II. It is one of the numerous variations of the Solar Cross and a cross form that is frequently employed in heraldry but is more prevalent in ecclesiastical situations. It is also referred to as the Labarum, Constantine's Cross and Chrismon.

Chi Rho Cross III
aka Labarum, Constantine's Cross, Chrismon

The Nowy Cross I refers to a form in the middle of a cross that may be round or square and is sometimes described as a knot or node or bump. It is related to the Celtic Cross. The Nowy Cross I is one of the numerous variations of the Solar Cross and a symbol that is frequently employed in heraldry.

Nowy Cross I

The Nowy Cross II is a variation of the Nowy Cross I and is related to the Celtic Cross. It one of the numerous variations of the Solar Cross and is frequently employed in heraldry.

Nowy Cross II

Basque Cross Rosary

The Basque Cross Rosary is related to the Solar Cross. It is slipped on the finger and the rosary is recited. The Basque Cross Rosary is one of the numerous variations of the Solar Cross and a form that is frequently employed in ecclesiastical situations.

Ogressy Cross
aka Bezant Cross, Bezanty Cross, Golpy Cross, Platy Cross, Torty Cross

The Ogressy Cross is one of a number of crosses that are of the same size and shape. Only their colours differ — e.g. Bezanty Cross is yellow; Golpy cross is pink or rose in colour; Platy Cross is white; Torty Cross is red and Ogressy Cross is black. The Ogressy Cross is one of the numerous variations of the Solar Cross and a form that is frequently employed in heraldry. It is also referred to as the Bezant Cross, Bezanty Cross, Golpy Cross, Platy Cross and Torty Cross.

Globus Cruciger I
aka Triumphant Cross, Orb Cross

The Globus Cruciger I represents the triumph of Christianity over the world, the Christ dominance over death and the dominance of an earthly ruler over his/her realm. It is one of the numerous variations of the Solar Cross and a cross form that is frequently employed in ecclesiastical situations as well as in heraldry from time to time. The Globus Cruciger I is also referred to as the Triumphant Cross, and Orb Cross.

The Globus Cruciger II is a variation of Globus Cruciger I. It is one of the numerous variations of the Solar Cross and a cross form that is frequently employed in ecclesiastical situations as well as in heraldry from time to time. The Globus Cruciger II is also referred to as the Triumphant Cross and the Orb Cross.

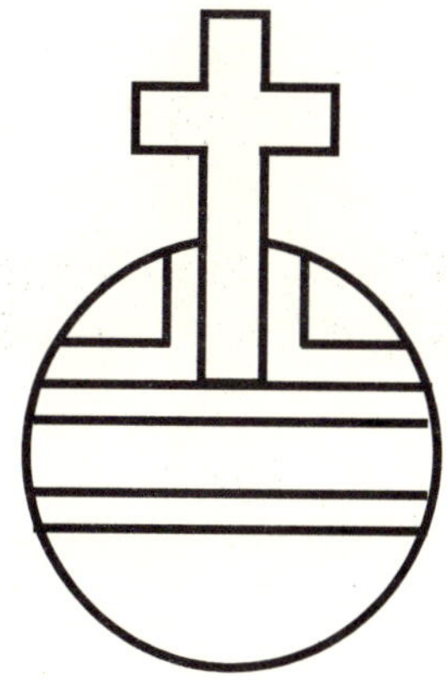

Globus Cruciger II
aka Triumphant Cross, Orb Cross

The Ansated Cross is related to the Ankh and Celtic Cross. It is composed of the Solar and Tau crosses. The Ansated Cross is one of the numerous variations of the Solar Cross and is employed in heraldry as well as in ecclesiastical situations.

Ansated Cross

The Presbyterian Cross is a cross form that has been adopted as the standard for the Presbyterian denomination. It is related to both the Celtic Cross and Gothic Cross. The Presbyterian Cross is one of the numerous variations of the Solar Cross and a cross form that is frequently employed in ecclesiastical situations.

Presbyterian Cross

Manx Cross II
aka Celtic Cross III

The Manx Cross II is one of a number of variations on a theme. The Isle of Man was an important site of Celtic culture. The Manx Cross II is related to the Manx Cross I and a form of the Celtic Cross — i.e. a Latin Cross with circular voids at the crossing. It is a variation of the Sun Cross and a cross that is employed in ecclesiastical situations. It is also referred to as the Celtic Cross III.

Manx Cross III
aka Celtic Cross IV

The Manx Cross III is one of a number of variations on a theme. The Manx Cross III is related to Manx Cross I and II, and a form of the Celtic Cross — i.e. a Latin Cross with circular voids at the crossing. It is a variation of the Sun Cross and a cross that is employed in ecclesiastical situations. It is also referred to as Celtic Cross IV.

Manx Cross IV
aka Joalf's Cross, Celtic Cross V

The Manx Cross IV is one of a number of variations on a theme. The Manx Cross IV is related to the Manx Cross I, II and III, and a form of the Celtic Cross — i.e. a Latin Cross with circular voids at the crossing. It is a variation of the Sun Cross and a cross that is employed in ecclesiastical situations. It is also referred to as the Joalf' Cross and Celtic Cross V.

The Manx Cross V is one of a number of variations on a theme. It is related to Manx Cross I, II, III and IV and a form of the Celtic Cross — i.e. a Latin Cross with circular voids at the crossing. It is a variation of the Sun Cross and a cross that is employed in ecclesiastical situations. It is also referred to as the Thurith's Cross and Celtic Cross VI.

Manx Cross V
aka Thurith's Cross, Celtic Cross VI

The Caddo Solar Cross is associated with Native American cultures, particularly of the south-western United States. It is a symbol of both sun and fire. It is one of the numerous variations of the Solar Cross and a symbol that is sometimes employed in ecclesiastical situations. It is also referred to as the Sun Cross.

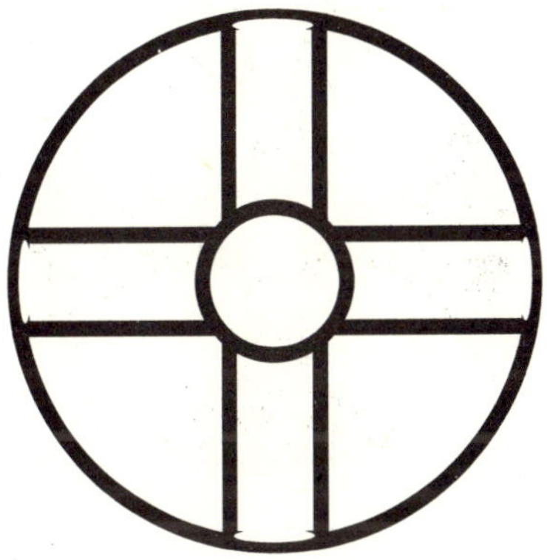

Caddo Solar Cross
aka Sun Cross

The Buddha Solar Cross is related to the Swarog Circle Cross, *en forme*, and a variation on Dharma Wheel. It is a form that may occasionally be seen in heraldry, but is more often encountered in Buddhist ecclesiastical situations.

Buddha Solar Cross

The Tarnis Cross represents the Tarnis Wheel. Tarnis was a Celtic god of thunder, related to Thor and the symbol was assumed by the Celtic Christians. The eight-spoked wheel is also sacred to the Buddhists. It is a variation of the the Solar Cross, and is a cross that is frequently employed in heraldry. It is also referred to as Taranis Wheel Cross and Dharma Wheel.

Tarnis Cross
aka Taranis Wheel Cross,
Dharma Wheel

The Saxon Cross III is one of a number of distinctive early cross forms found in Great Britain. It is one of the numerous variations of the Solar Cross and a cross form that is employed in heraldry but is more frequently seen in ecclesiastical situations. It is related to the Saxon Cross I, II, IV, and V, also known as Paté Convexed Cross, Paté Globical Cross and Paté Circuled Cross.

Saxon Cross III
aka Paté Convexed Cross,
Paté Globical Cross,
Paté Circuled Cross

The Saxon Cross IV is one of a number of distinctive early cross forms found in Great Britain. The Saltire cross interwoven with four circles may be seen to represent the four gospels or the taking of the Word to the four corners of the earth. It is a variation of the Solar Cross and a cross form that is employed in heraldry but is more frequently seen in ecclesiastical situations. It is related to the Saxon Cross I-V.

Saxon Cross IV

The Saxon Cross V is one of a number of distinctive early cross forms found in Great Britain. It is one of the numerous variations of the Solar Cross and a cross form that is employed in heraldry but is more frequently seen in ecclesiastical situations. It is related to the Saxon Cross I-IV.

Saxon Cross V

The Saxon Cross VI is one of a number of distinctive early cross forms found in Great Britain. It is one of the numerous variations of Solar Cross and a cross form that is employed in heraldry but is more frequently seen in ecclesiastical situations. It is related to Saxon Cross I-V and VII. It is also referred to as the Wheel Cross and Rolleston-on-Dove Cross.

Saxon Cross VI
aka Wheel Cross, Rolleston-on-Dove Cross

The Golgatha Cross is related to the Nowy Cross II and the Coptic Cross II. It is a variation of the Solar Cross and is also related to the Coptic Cross II. The four nails in the quarters refer to the nails of the crucifixion. It is one of the numerous variations of the Solar Cross and is frequently employed in heraldry, but rarely encountered in ecclesiastical situations.

Golgatha Cross

Norse Solar Cross II
aka Odin's Cross, Woden's Cross

The Norse Solar Cross II is related to the Saxon Cross IV in the use of intertwining form(s). A number of cruciforms of the Scandinavian countries and the British islands employed this elaborate, interweaving in many of their forms. It is one of the numerous variations of the Solar Cross seen to have had magical/spiritual significance. It is also referred to as the Odin's Cross and Woden's Cross.

Swiss Solar Cross I

The Swiss Solar Cross I is one of a number of small, solar cross forms unearthed in Switzerland. They date to the second millennium BCE. It is one of the numerous variations of the Solar Cross that is seen to have had magical/spiritual significance.

Swiss Solar Cross II

The Swiss Solar Cross II is one of a number of small, solar cross forms unearthed in Switzerland. They date to the second millennium BCE. It is one of the numerous variations of the Solar Cross that is seen to have had magical/spiritual significance.

The Swiss Solar Cross III is one of a number of small, solar cross forms unearthed in Switzerland. They date to the second millennium BCE. The four circles in the quadrants may refer to the four stages of the moon. It is one of the numerous variations of the Solar Cross that is seen to have had magical/spiritual significance.

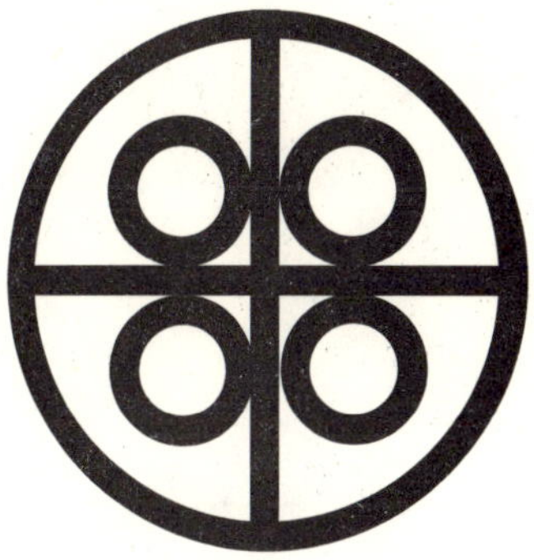

Swiss Solar Cross III

The Canterbury Cross I is an old Saxon cross form found near the Canterbury Cathedral. It may be seen as a Solar Cross. It consists essentially of a Quadrate Cross with a voided square laid over a Pattée Cross, similarly voided. The three small rounded forms in each arm are seen to refer to the Holy Trinity. Together they may refer to the twelve apostles or the months of the year. The Canterbury Cross I is a variation of the Greek Cross and a symbol that is found in heraldry as well as in ecclesiastical situations.

Canterbury Cross I

The Canterbury Cross II is a variation of the Canterbury Cross I. It is derive either from the Solar Cross or from the Greek Cross and is frequently employed in ecclesiastical situations.

Canterbury Cross II

The Templar Cross is a variation of the Knights of Christ's crosses. It is a form of Solar the Cross and appears in heraldry. The Templar Cross is also related, *en forme*, to the Alisée Cross and the Saxon Cross III. It is also known as the Paté Convexed Cross, Paté Globical Cross, Paté Circuled Cross, Saxon Cross III, Alisée Cross and Crois Paté Convexed.

Templar Cross
aka Paté Convexed Cross, Paté Globical Cross, Paté Circuled Cross, Saxon Cross III, Alisée Cross, Crois Paté Convexed

The Swarog Circle Cross is an ancient Slavic symbol which holds certain magical/spiritual significance. It is a not a heraldic or Christian ecclesiastical device. It is also called a Sun Cross.

Swarog Circle Cross
aka Sun Cross

The Lazarus' Cross II is related to Lazarus' Cross I and an example of one of the various Solar crosses. It is a heraldic device and may occasionally be encountered in ecclesiastical situations.

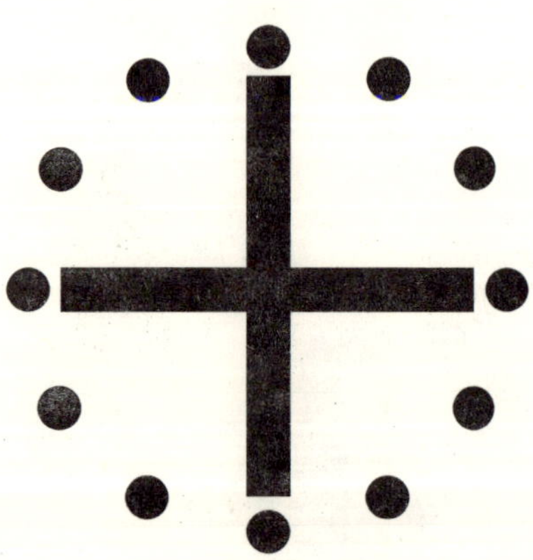

Lazarus' Cross II

The Capital Cross II is a variation of the Capital Cross I and is an example of one of the various Solar crosses. It is a heraldic device and never seen in ecclesiastical situations. It is also referred to as Croix Capiteau.

Capital Cross II
aka Croix Capiteau

Solar Crosses: Militaristic Variation

By the end of the crusades the appearance of the circular shield as opposed to the rectilinear shield (**Figure 8**) became less prevalent. Similarly, the employment of the Solar Cross variations as a heraldic, militaristic device became also less prevalent.

Celtic Cross VII
aka Third Positionist Cross, White Nationalist Cross, Occident Cross, Groupe Union Droit Cross, Breton Nationalism Cross

The Celtic Cross VII is one of the numerous variations of the Solar Cross which has the militaristic implications — i.e. associated with a militaristic order or group. Numerous groups have adopted this form as a symbol. The Celtic Cross VII is a symbol that is generally only employed in heraldry. It is also referred to as the Third Positionist Cross, White Nationalist Cross, Occident Cross, Groupe Union Droit Cross and Breton Nationalism Cross.

Taranis Cross

The Taranis Cross is related to the Thor's Cross. It is one of the variations of the Solar Cross which has militaristic implications — i.e. associated with a militaristic order — and specifically employed upon a round shield. It is a (cross form symbol) that is generally employed only in heraldry.

St. Cuthbert's Cross
aka Thor's Cross

The St. Cuthbert's Cross is related to the Nowy Cross I. It is one of the numerous variations of the Solar Cross which has militaristic implications — i.e. associated with a militaristic order. In this case the St. Cuthbert's Cross is a cruciform that was adapted to a round shield. It is a cross form that is generally employed only in heraldry. It is also referred to as the Thor's Cross.

Saltire Crosses

The Saltire Cross is one of the most popular crosses although its frequency is over-shadowed by the Greek Cross in heraldry. Saltire comes from the old French *saultoir*, meaning a stile. As a stile, its form is understood. Traditionally, St. Andrew is said to have been crucified on an "X"-shaped cross. Like St. Peter, it is said that he requested not to be executed on a cross similar in form to the cross of the Christ's crucifixion, hence it symbolizes a modest, unassuming character. The Saltire Cross also is iconic for man's faith. Hence the name St. Andrew's Cross is often applied to the Saltire Cross. This cruciform often appears in flags — e.g. the flag of Scotland, the flag of Great Britain, the flag of Russia (eighteenth century), the flag of Burgundy, the flag of the Spanish Military, the flag of St. Patrick and the flag of Jamaica. In addition, numerous Greek Cross forms are often rotated 45° to form a Saltire Cross — e.g. the Bretesse Cross Saltire, the Moline Saltire Cross and the Vairy Cross Saltire.

The St. Andrew's Cross I is so named because St. Andrew, feeling unworthy to be crucified in the same manner as the Christ, requested a different cross form. Essentially, it is a Greek Cross rotated 45°. It is associated with humility. The St. Andrew's Cross I is a cross form that is employed in heraldry as well as in ecclesiastical situations. It is also referred to as the Crux Decussata, Saltire Cross and Boundary Cross.

St. Andrew's Cross I
aka Crux Decussata, Saltire Cross, Boundary Cross

The St. Andrew's Cross II is a variation on St. Andrew's Cross I. It is seen in the form of an "X" — i.e. the crosspieces are not 90° to each other. It is a cross form that is employed in heraldry as well as in ecclesiastical situations. The St. Andrew's Cross II is also referred to as the Crux Decussata, Saltire Cross and Boundary Cross.

St. Andrew's Cross II
aka Saltire Cross, Crux Decussata, Boundary Cross

St. Andrew's Cross III
aka Saltire Cross, Crux Decussata

The St. Andrew's Cross III is a variation on St. Andrew's Cross I except that the crosspieces are thicker in dimension. It is a cross form that is employed in heraldry as well as in ecclesiastical situations. The St. Andrew's Cross II is also referred to as the Crux Decussata and Saltire Cross.

St. Julian Cross
aka Missionary Cross, Cross Crosslet

St. Julian Cross is a variation on St. Andrew's Cross. The crosslets point to the four corners of the world as St. Julian is one of the Patron Saints of travellers. It is a cross form that is employed in heraldry. The St. Julian Cross is also referred to as Missionary Cross and Cross Crosslet (rotated 45°).

Gugnir Cross
aka Spear of Odin, Sword of Odin

The Gugnir Cross is a variation of the Saltire Cross and associated with the Norse mythology. It was a magical weapon given to Odin which always hit its mark and then returned to the one who threw it. Therefore, as it is sometimes employed in Christian heraldry, it refers to the dominance and history of Christianity. It is also referred to as the Spear of Odin and Sword of Odin.

The Jumis Cross is related to the Norse/Baltic deity of the harvest, Jumis. It is said that it represents crossed corn stalks. It is seldom, if ever, seen in heraldry and found only in ancient runic inscriptions.

Jumis Cross

The Chi Rho Cross IV is one of the many forms of Chi Rho Cross I. It may also be seen as one of the numerous variations of the Saltire Cross and a symbol that is employed in heraldry as well as often encountered in ecclesiastical situations. It is also referred to as the Labarum, Constantine's Cross and Chrismon.

Chi Rho Cross IV
aka Labarum, Constantine's Cross, Chrismon

The Chi Rho Cross V is one of the many forms of Chi Rho Cross I, referring to the Greek letter *chi* (χ) and *rho* (ρ), which in turn refers to *Christus Rex* or Christ the King. It may also be seen as one of the numerous variations of the Saltire Cross and a symbol that is employed in heraldry as well as often encountered in ecclesiastical situations. The Chi Rho Cross V is also referred to as the Labarum, Constantine's Cross and Chrismon.

Chi Rho Cross V
aka Labarum, Constantine's Cross, Chrismon

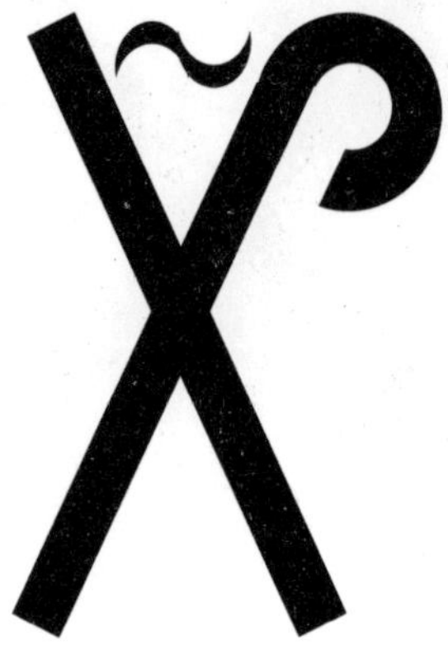

Chi Rho Cross VI
aka Labarum, Constantine's Cross, Chrismon

The Chi Rho Cross VI is one of the many forms of the Chi Rho Cross I, referring to the Greek letter *chi* (χ) and *rho* (ρ). It may also be seen as one of the numerous variations of the Saltire Cross and a symbol that is employed in heraldry as well as often encountered in ecclesiastical situations. The Chi Rho Cross VI is also referred to as the Labarum, Constantine's Cross and Chrismon.

Episcopal Saltire Cross

The Episcopal Saltire Cross is across that is made up of nine Cross Crosslet Crosses, diagonally arranged. It is part of the heraldry for Episcopal Church and is an ecclesiastical cross that has limited use. It is one of the numerous variations of the Saltire Cross and a cross form that is frequently employed in ecclesiastical heraldry.

Vatican Papal Cross

The Vatican Papal Cross is composed of crossed keys. The keys refer to the keys to heaven. It is an ecclesiastical cross that has limited use as it is reserved for papal coat of arms. Vatican Papal Cross is one of the numerous variations of Saltire Cross and a symbol that is frequently employed in ecclesiastical heraldry.

The Burgundy Cross is formed by two ragulated arms. It was early employed by the Dukes of Burgundy in their coat of arms. The Burgundy Cross is one of the numerous variations of the Saltire Cross and a symbol that is frequently employed in heraldry. It is also referred to as the Saltire Raguly Cross.

Burgundy Cross
aka Saltire Raguly Cross

The Bowen Cross is related to the Masculy Cross. It is formed by a Bowen knot turned 45°, an ancient symbol. It is one of the numerous variations of the Saltire Cross and a symbol that is frequently employed in heraldry. It is also referred to as the Croix Frettée and Fretty Cross.

Bowen Cross
aka Croix Frettée, Fretty Cross

The Crosslet Flory Saltire Cross is a variation of the Cross Crosslet and Fleurette Cross rotated to the Saltire configuration. It is one of the numerous variations of the Saltire Cross and a symbol that is employed exclusively in heraldry.

Crosslet Flory Saltire Cross

Bone Cross

The Bone Cross is generally only depicted in paintings and then found at the base of the cross, often along with a skull. It symbolizes physical death. It is one of the numerous variations of the Saltire Cross and a symbol that is employed in heraldry as well as in ecclesiastical representations.

Cramponned Cross

The Cramponned Cross is related to the Barby Cross. It is one of the numerous variations of the Saltire Cross and a symbol that is frequently employed in heraldry, particularly of the Neo-Nazi groups. It is also referred to as Croix Cramponée.

Saxon Cross VII
aka Toisa's Cross, Exeter Cross

The Saxon Cross VII is one of a number of distinctive early cross forms found in Great Britain. It resembles the interlaced design so popular in Saxon and Celtic cultures. It is one of the numerous variations of the Saltire Cross and a cross form that is employed in heraldry but is more frequently seen in ecclesiastical situations. It is related to Saxon Cross I-VI. It is also referred to as the Toisa's Cross, and Exeter Cross.

The Recercely Saltire Cross is the Saltire variation of the Recercely Cross and a cross that is only employed in heraldry. *See* the Recercely Cross for further details.

Recercely Saltire Cross

The Engrailed Saltire Cross is the Saltire variation of the Engrailed Cross. It is a cross that is generally employed only in heraldry. It is also referred to as the Croix Engrélée Saltire. *See* the Engrailed Cross for further details.

Engrailed Saltire Cross
aka Croix Engrélée Saltire

The Fleur-de-lys Saltire Cross is the Saltire variation of the Fleur-de-lys Cross. It is a cross that is generally employed only in heraldry. *See* the Fleur-de-lys Cross for further details.

Fleur-de-lys Saltire Cross

Moline Saltire Cross

The Moline Saltire Cross is the Saltire variation of the Moline Cross. It is a cross that is generally employed only in heraldry. *See* the Moline Saltire Cross for further details.

Ermine Cross Saltire

The Ermine Saltire Cross is the Saltire variation of the Ermine Cross. It is a cross that is generally employed only in heraldry. *See* the Ermine Cross for further details.

Vairy Cross Saltire

The Vairy Cross Saltire is the Saltire variation of the Vairy Cross. It is a cross that is generally employed only in heraldry. *See* the Vairy Cross for further details.

The Bretesse Cross Saltire is the Saltire variation of the Bretesse Cross. It is a cross that is generally employed only in heraldry. *See* the Bretesse Cross for further details.

Bretesse Cross Saltire

The Compony-Counter-Compony Saltire Cross is the Saltire variation of the Compony Cross. It is a cross that is generally employed only in heraldry. *See* the Compony Cross for further details.

Compony-Counter-Compony Saltire Cross

The Cheky Saltire Cross is the Saltire variation of the Cheky Cross. It is a cross that is generally employed only in heraldry. It is also known as the Chequy Saltire Cross. *See* the Cheky Cross for further details.

Checky Saltire Cross
aka Chequy Saltire Cross

Solomon's Knot II

The Solomon's Knot II is the Saltire variation of the Solomon's Knot I. It refers to the Old Testament King who, through his wisdom, was able to maintain a peaceful balance in difficult situations. The Solomon's Knot II is a variation of the Saltire Cross and a form that is employed in heraldry almost exclusively.

Saltire Counter Embattled Cross

The Saltire Counter Embattled Cross is the Saltire variation of the Bretesse Cross. It is a cross that is generally employed only in heraldry. *See* the Bretesse Cross for further details.

Saltire Crosses: Baptismal Variation

The Saltire Cross, Baptismal Variation consists of the combination of a Saltire Cross and a Greek Cross overlaid. Not only is this cruciform applicable to the rite of baptism, it is also seen to have been a form or reinforcement, particularly on a circular shield — e.g. the Escarbouche Cross.

The Baptismal Cross I is essentially composed of the Greek Cross and St. Andrew's Cross, or the Greek Cross and the "Chi" of Chi Rho Cross. It symbolizes the age of baptism (eight years) and the eight days between the Christ's entry into Jerusalem and resurrection. Earlier, this cross was used by Egyptians to symbolize the chaos of the eight gods before the creation of the sun. The Baptismal Cross is one of the numerous variations of the Saltire Cross and a symbol that is frequently employed in heraldry.

Baptismal Cross I

The Baptismal Cross II is a variation of the Baptismal Cross I. In this variation, the Saltire element is traditionally thinner than Greek the Cross component. The Baptismal Cross II is one of the numerous variations of the Saltire Cross and a symbol that is frequently employed in heraldry.

Baptismal Cross II

The Lothringian Cross is a variation of the Baptismal Cross. It is named after Lothair I, Holy Roman Emperor, and ruler of Lothari Regnum and was encountered as an iconic element in the heraldry of that emperor. The Lothringian Cross is one of the numerous variations of the Saltire Cross and a symbol that is frequently employed in heraldry.

Lothringian Cross

Cleves Cross III

The Cleves Cross III is a variation of the Cleves Cross I and related to the Escarbouche Cross. It is one of the numerous variations of the Saltire Cross and a symbol that is frequently employed in heraldry. *See* the Cleves Cross I for further details.

Escarbouche Cross
aka Mandeville Cross

The Escarbouche Cross is one of the numerous forms of Baptismal Cross. It is suggested that an *escarbouche* is a device found on shields to strengthen them — i.e. crossed metal straps that would give the wooden shield greater strength. The Escarbouche Cross is a variation of the Saltire Cross and a symbol that is frequently employed in heraldry. It is also referred to as the Mandeville Cross.

Miscellaneous Crosses

Most cruciforms fall within the five forms noted above — i.e. Tau, Latin, Greek, Solar and Saltire. However, for every rule, there is generally an exception. There are a few crosses which do not fall within these five categories.

The Coptic Cross XII is one of a number of miscellaneous crosses that do not easily fall into the five types noted — i.e. neither Tau, Latin, Greek, Solar nor Saltire. A number of Coptic crosses are of similar design — i.e. a long vertical and a shorter horizontal crosspiece, generally centred along the vertical axis. It is a cross form that is generally seen in ecclesiastical situations and in smaller form, worn about the neck.

Coptic Cross XII

The Coptic Cross XIII, as the Coptic Cross XII possesses a long vertical and a shorter horizontal crosspiece. However, the centre section is clearly a Greek Cross, *en forme*. This cross form was carved into the wall of the Temple of Isis, Egypt.

Coptic Cross XIII

The St. Hans Cross is one of a number of miscellaneous crosses that do not easily fall into the five types noted. "Hans" is the diminutive of "Johannes" and refers to St. John the Baptist. It is a cross form that is generally employed only in heraldry. It is also referred to as the Bowen Cross.

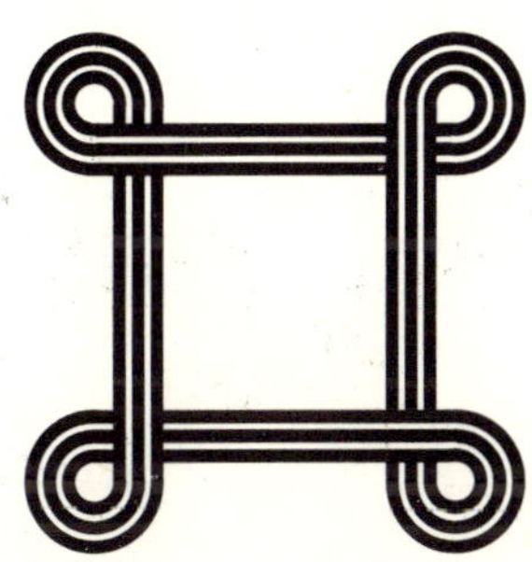

St. Hans Cross
aka Bowen Cross

Scandinavian Cross
aka Nordic Cross, Danneborg Cross, Off-centred Cross

The Scandinavian Cross is one of a number of miscellaneous crosses that do not easily fall into the five types noted. It is specifically a cross that is found in the flags of Sweden and Denmark. The Scandinavian Cross is a cross form that is generally employed only in heraldry. It is also referred to as the Nordic Cross, Danneborg Cross and Off-centred Cross.

Horizontal Cross
aka Flag Cross, Order of St. Lazarus of Jerusalem Cross III

The Horizontal Cross is one of a number of miscellaneous crosses that do not easily fall into the five types noted. It is specifically a cross that is found in the flags of England and Savoy. It is a cross form that is generally only employed in heraldry. It is also referred to as the Flag Cross and Order of St. Lazarus of Jerusalem Cross III.

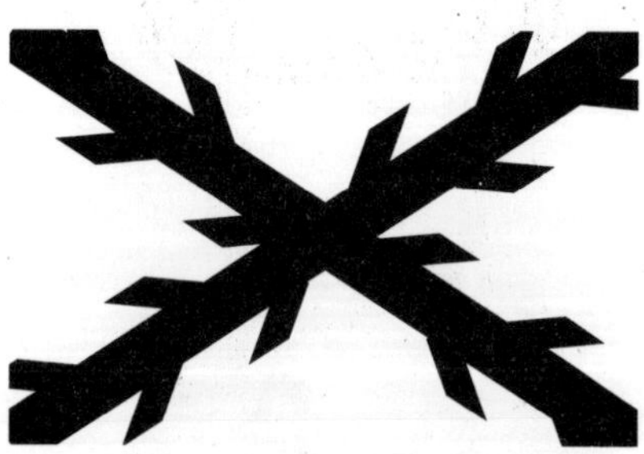

Spanish Military Cross

The Spanish Military Cross is a variation of the Burgundy Cross. It is one of a number of miscellaneous crosses that do not easily fall into the five types noted. Spanish Military Cross is a cross form symbol that is generally employed only in heraldry. Its application as a military cross places it amongst those crosses which have militaristic implications.

The Wahl Cross is one of a number of miscellaneous crosses that do not easily fall into the five types noted. Its form suggests a relationship to the fylfot crosses. It is a symbol that is generally employed only in heraldry. It is also referred to as the Delfity Cross and Croix Delphitée.

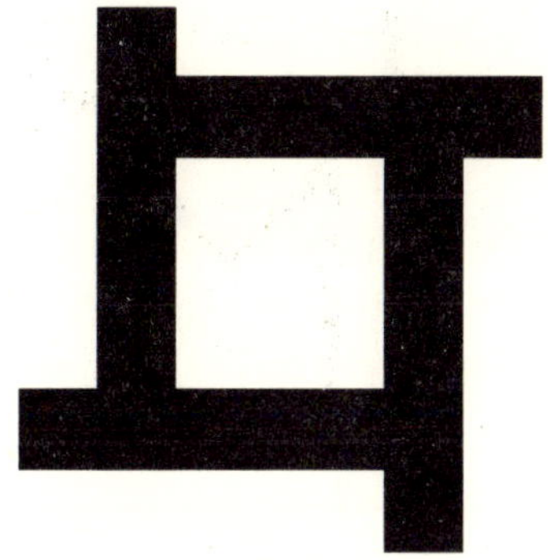

Wahl Cross
aka Delfity Cross, Croix Delphitée

The Star Cross V is essentially the imposition of a Latin Cross within a Star of David. It is one of a number of miscellaneous crosses that do not easily fall into the five types noted. It is a symbol that is generally employed only in heraldry. It is also referred to as the Crux Mogen Dovid.

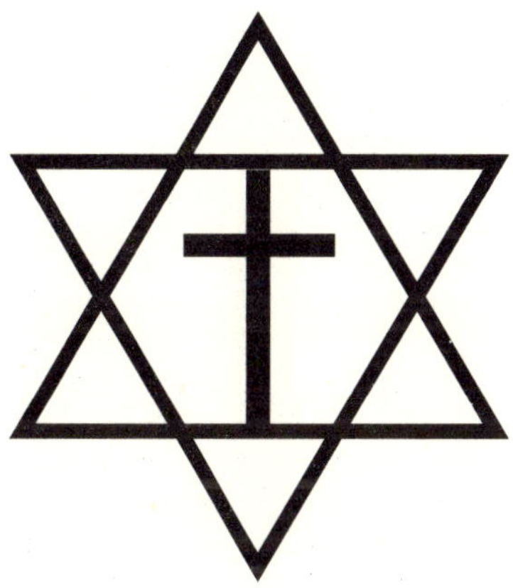

Star Cross V
aka Crux Mogen Dovid

The Croix à cinq bras is a rare cruciform. It is one of a number of miscellaneous crosses that do not easily fall into the five types noted. It is a cross form that is employed only in heraldry. It is also known as the Five Armed Cross.

Croix à cinq bras
aka Five Armed Cross

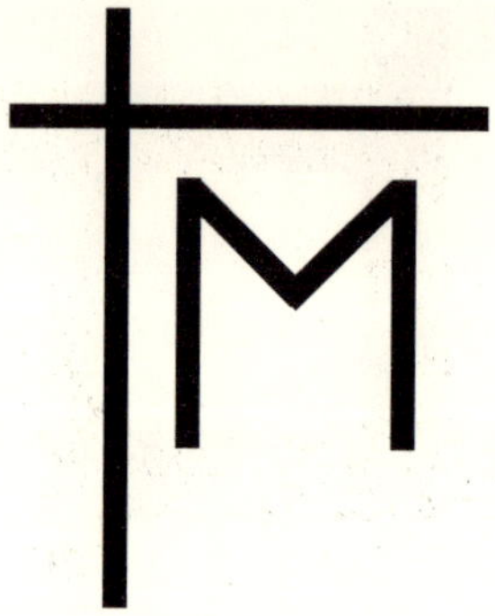

Marian Cross II

The Marian Cross II is one of a number of miscellaneous crosses that do not easily fall into the five types noted. Specifically, it is the element employed by Pope John Paul II. It is a cross form that is generally employed only in heraldry or in ecclesiastical literature.

Lebanese Forces Cross

The Lebenese Forces Cross is a relatively recent addition. It is one of a number of miscellaneous crosses that do not easily fall into the five types noted. It is a cross form that is generally employed only in heraldry.

Palm Cross

The Palm Cross is one of a number of miscellaneous crosses that do not easily fall into the five types noted. It is a cross form that is generally employed only in heraldry or in ecclesiastical literature.

The Pompeiian Cross is unique as it was an item of graffiti found in Pompeii. It is palindrome that is said to mean: "He who holds and sets the wheel of things in motion" or "The sower of Arepo works with help of a wheel". Many see this as applying to the Christ. It is also referred to as the Sator Cross.

Pompeiian Cross
aka Sator Cross

Coloured Crosses

Crosses not only appear in different shapes and variations, they appear in various colours too. Some of them are listed below:

White: Saltire on blue field = Scotland
Horizontal Cross on red field = Savoy
Scandinavian Cross on red field = Denmark
Greek Cross on red field = Switzerland
Horizontal Cross on black field = Cornwall

Black: Greek Cross on white field = Brittany

Red: Flory Fitchy Footed = St. James
Saltire Raguly Cross = Burgundy Cross and/or Spanish Military Cross
Saltire Cross = St. Patrick's Cross
Horizontal Cross = St. George's Cross (England)
Greek Cross = Black Death Cross
Lebanese Forces Cross
Cross of Lorraine = Honour Kack (France)

Orange: Greek Cross = Northern Ireland Cross, Ulster Cross
Horizontal Cross = King William of Orange

Yellow: Greek = Pope John Paul II
Saltire = Jamaica Cross
Horizontal Cross on blue field = Sweden Cross
Horizontal Cross on black field = St. David's Cross (Wales)

Green: Greek Cross = St. Lazarus Cross
Maltese Cross = St. Lazarus Cross

Blue: Saltire Cross on white field = Russia (eighteenth century)

Purple: Greek Cross = royalty

Resources

As noted in the Preface, the images herein were gleaned primarily from the Internet. This, in part, was due to the paucity of printed material in the various libraries where I had taken residence and the availability of purchasing prime resources. The cruciforms in common use presented no problem. However, there were myriad examples that were most unusual. These were included in this compilation after cross referencing them with other Internet sources. Every effort was made to verify these "unusual" cross forms.

Internet

http://altreligion.about.com/library/glossary/blsymbols.htm
http://altreligion.about.com/library/glossary/symbols/bldefsswastika.htm
http://artexchangeafrica.com/shop/index.php?cPath=68_81
http://commons.wikimedia.org/wiki/Category:Cross_Fleurie
http://commons.wikimedia.org/wiki/Category:Lithuanian_heraldic_dictionary
http://commons.wikimedia.org/wiki/Category:Saltier
http://commons.wikipedia.org/wiki/image.Religious_symbols.svg
http://commons.wikimedia.org/wiki/Swastika
http://en.wikipedia.org/wiki/Cross
http://en.wikipedia.org/wiki/cross.html
http://en.wikipedia.org/wiki/Image:TeutonicCoA.png
http://en.wikipedia.org/wiki/Irminsul
http://en.wikipedia.org/wiki/Solar_symbol
http://en.wikipedia.org/wiki/Swastika
http://flagspot.net/flags/rel-chor.html#dominic
http://helena-schrader.com/wktsymbols.html
http://heraldry.lordkyl.net/index.html
http://heraldry.lordkyl.net/glossary/glossary_co. html
http://heralds.westkingdom.org/Templates/Crosses/index.html
http://historymedren.about.com/od/pimbley_c_5.html
http://historymedren.about.com/od/pimbley/a/pim_c_5.htm
http://images.google.com.my/images?hl=en&lr=lang_en&resnum=0&q= processional%20 cross&um=1&ie=UTF-8&sa=N&tab=wi
http://museums.ncl.ac.uk/archive/old_fotm/old_fotm96
http://museums.ncl.ac.uk/archive/old_fotm/old_fotmo96
http://perso.numericable.fr/~briantimms/era/early%20of%20arms.html
http://perso.numericable.fr/~briantimms/era/early%20rolls%20of%20arms.htm
http://picasaweb.google.com/rowijopicasa/islandOfPhilae#5053783799980807298.html
http://stpaulhavre-zionchinook.com/Welcome!_files/The%20Crosses.html
http://tmg110.tripod.com/lexicon2.html
http://web.ukonline.co.uk/cj.yolley/ctm/ctm-base-england.html
http://www.allstates-flag.com/fotw/flags/vxt-hrld.html
http://www.altreligiou.about.com/library/glossary/symbols/bldefsjumis.htm
http://www.americancollegeofheraldty.org/crosses.html
http://www.angelfire.com/empire/medievalheraldry
http://www.bartleby.com/81/4373.html

http://www.bluffton.edu/~sullivanm/highcrosses/intro.html
http://www.burkes-peerage.net/sites/common/sitepages/heindex.asp.html
http://www.cavemanart.com/osroene/orthodox,htm
http://www.chivalricorders.org/orders/spanish/alcantar.htm
http://www.conspiracycafe.net/forum/index.php?showtopic=11678
http://www.crosscrucifix.com/glossaryhome.html
http://www.crosses.org/history.html
http://www.crwflags.com/fotw/flags/gr_byz.html
http://www.designboom.com/history/cross.html
http://www.designboom.com/history/cross_2.html
http://www.dictionaryofheraldry.com/blasonfront.html
http://www.digiserve.com/heraldry/pimbley.htm
http://www.duffergeek.com/archive/2006_02_01_archive.htm
http://www.en.wikipedia.org/wiki/Boreyko_coat_of_arms
http://www.en.wikipedia.org/wiki/serbian_crosss
http://www.exeter.gov.uk/timetrail/05_saxon/object_detail.asp?photoref=501.html
http://www.factophile.com
http://www.fleurdelis.com/crosses.html
http://www.fleurdelis.com/meanings.html
http://www.geocities.com/Heartland/Estates/5126/EOHS_ARMS.html
http://www.goedjn.com/wishford/burkes/h15-glss.htm
http://www.guidetosymbols.com
http://www.heraldrica.org/topics/glossary/atlas. htm
http://www.heraldryclipart.com/heraldry-dictionary.html
http://www.heraldryclipart.com/dk.html
http://www.heraldryclipart.com/heraldry-symbolism.html
http://www.heralds.net/saitou/parker/jpglossa.html
http://www.heraldsnet.org/saitou/parker/Jpglossa.htm
http://www.hugenotcross.com.html
http://www.iacmusic.com/symbolspage
http://www.intelinet.org/swastika/swasti09.htm
http://www.isle-of-man.com/interests/crosses/index.html
http://www.languedoc-france.info/1901_cross.htm#heraldry.html
http://www.levity.com/alchemy/hermahera.html
http://www.library.nd.edu/rarebooks/digital_projects/heraldry/charges/crosses.shtml
http://www.midcoast.com/~martucci/flags/designs/crosses.html
http://www.middle-ages.org.uk/medieval-shields.htm
http://www.midwesternepigraphic.org/swastika01.html
http://www.newadvennt.org/cathen/c.html
http://www.northvegr.org/lore/swastika/064.php
http://www.nyrond.org/university/heraldry/www.demon.co.uk/apl385/gilling/hcross.html
http://www.nyrond.org/university/heraldry/www.demon.co.uk/apl385/gilling/hlist.html
http://www.nyrond.org/university/heraldry/www.demon.co.uk/apl385/gilling/hlist.htm#P
http://www.orderstjohn.org/osj/cross.htm
http://www.ragweedforge.com/cat-cross.html
http://www.rarebooks.nd.edu/digital/heraldry/cadency.html
http://www.rarebooks.nd.edu/digital/heraldry/charges/crosses.html
http://www.rarebooks.nd.edu/digital/heraldry/charges/ordinaries.html
http://www.riotacts.com/fire/maltesecross.html

http://www.sca.org/heraldry/laurel/precedents/daud2/armory5.html
http://www.seiyaku.com/customs/crosses/
http://www.seiyaku.com/customs/crosses/index.html
http://www.seiyaku.com/customs/crosses/index-all.html
http://www.seiyaku.com/customs/crosses/index-other.html
http://www.stpetersknanaya.org/history.htm
http://www.szlachta.org/heraldry.html
http://www.thewebsite.com/heraldry/charges_crosses.html
http://www.unexplained_mysteries.com/forum/index.php
http://www.world-enlightment.com/Circle-Symbols
http://www.1911encyclopedia.org/Heraldry
http://www2.prestel.co.uk/church/oosj/cross.html

Printed Material

Brooke-Little, John, *An Heraldic Alphabet*, London, 1973.

———, *Boutell's Heraldry*, London, 1973.

Burke, John Bernard, *The General Armory of England, Scotland, Ireland and Wales; Comprising a Registry of Armorial Bearings from the Earliest to the Present Time*, London, 1884; Baltimore, 1967.

Dennys, Rodney, *The Heraldic Imagination*, New York, 1975.

Elvins, Mark Turnham, *Cardinals and Heraldry*, London, 1988.

Fairbairn, James, *Fairbairn's Crests of the Families of Great Britain & Ireland*, 2nd rev. edn., New York, 1911.

Fox-Davies, Arthur, *A Complete Guide to Heraldry*, New York, 1993.

Friar, Stephen, ed., *A Dictionary of Heraldry*, New York, 1987.

Friar, Stephen and John Ferguson, *Basic Heraldry*, New York, 1993.

Gwynn-Jones, Peter, *The Art of Heraldry*, London, 1998.

Humphery-Smith, Cecil, *Edited and Augmented General Armory Two*, London, 1973.

Innes of Learney, Sir Thomas, *Scots Heraldry*, 2nd edn., Edinburgh and London, 1956.

Le Févre, Jean, *A European Armorial: An Armorial of Knights of the Golden Fleece and 15th Century Europe*, London, 1971.

Louda, Jiri and Michael Maclagan, *Heraldry of the Royal Families of Europe*, New York, 1981.

Moncrieffe , Ian and Don Pottinger, *Simple Heraldry, Cheerfully Illustrated*, London, 1953.

Neubecker, Ottfried, *Heraldry: Sources, Symbols, and Meaning*, London, 1997.

Parker, James, *A Glossary of Terms Used in Heraldry*, Oxford: James Parker & Co., 1894 (Newton Abbot: David & Charles, 1970).

Paul, James Balfour, *An Ordinary of Arms Contained in the Public Register of All Arms and Bearings in Scotland*, Edinburgh, 1903.

Platts, Beryl, *Origins of Heraldry*, London, 1980.

Rietstap, Johannes B., *Armorial General*, The Hague, 1904-26; Baltimore, 1967.

Siebmacher, Johann J., *Siebmacher's Grosses und Allgemeines Wappenbuch Vermehrten Auglage*, Nürnberg, 1890–1901.

Slater, Stephen, *The Complete Book of Heraldry*, New York, 2003.

Volborth, Carl-Alexander von, *Heraldry: Customs, Rules, and Styles*, Dorset, 1981.

Wagner, Sir Anthony R., *Heralds of England: A History of the Office and College of Arms*, London, 1967.

Whitmore, William, *The Elements of Heraldry*, New York, 1968.
Williamson, David, *Debrett's Guide to Heraldry and Regalia*, London, 1992.
Woodcock, Thomas and John Martin Robinson, *The Oxford Guide to Heraldry*, New York, 1988.

Cross Index

Advent Cross 20, 23
Aiguise Cross 51, 162
Aiguisée Cross I 51
Aiguisée Cross II 162
Alaisé Cross 109
Alisée Cross 109, 178, 188
Alpha & Omega Cross I 47
Alpha & Omega Cross II 47
Altar Cross 27, 85
Anchor Cross I 65
Anchor Cross II 66
Anchor Cross II 123
Anchor Cross III 123
Anchor Cross IV 124
Anchor Double Parted Cross 127
Anchory Cross 124, 174
Anchry Cross 123-24
Ankh 30
Ankh Cross 30
Annulets Braced Cross 51
Annuletted Cross 105
Annuletted Rebated Cross 105
Annulety Cross I 104
Annulety Cross II 105
Annulety Cross III 105
Annulety Fretted Cross 105
Ansata Cross I 30-31
Ansata Cross II 30
Ansata Cross III 31
Ansata Cross IV 31
Ansated Cross 181
Anserated Cross 69, 152
Anticipatory Cross 19
Archepiscopal Cross 60
Armenian Cross I 44
Armenian Cross II 44
Arrow Cross 132, 160
Asatru Cross 22
Atlantis Cross 177
Avellane Cross I 119
Avellane Cross II 119
Avellan Cross 119
Avellane Doubled Cross 120
Avellan Doubled Cross 120
Avellane Invected Cross 120
Avellan Invected Cross 120
Avellane Pommelled Cross 119
Avellan Pommelled Cross 119

Baptismal Cross I 201
Baptismal Cross II 201
Barbée Cross I 132
Barbée Cross II 160
Basque Cross 158
Basque Cross Rosary 180
Batonée Cross 121
Bent Cross 20, 151, 159
Bethlehem Star Cross 49
Bezant Cross 102, 180
Bezanty Cross 180
Biparted Cross 97
Bishop's Cross 101, 134
Blessing Cross 35
Blunted Cross 26, 172
Book of Silk Flyfot Cross 155
Bordered Urdé Cross 141
Bone Cross 196
Boreyko Flyfot Cross 153
Bosnia Flyfot Cross 154
Botonny Cross 34, 101
Botonny Fitchy Cross 80
Boundary Cross 191
Bouttonnée Cross I 34
Bouttonnée Cross II 101
Bouttonnée Fichée Cross 80
Bouttonnée Processional Cross 57
Bowen Cross 98, 195, 203
Branchy Cross 168
Bretesse Cross I 129
Bretesse Cross II 130
Bretesse Cross Saltier 199
Breton Nationalism Cross 190
Broken Cross 28
Budded Cross 34, 101
Budded Fitchy Cross 80
Buddha Solar Cross 183
Burgundy Cross 195
Burre Cross 134
Byzantine Cross I 37
Byzantine Cross II 37
Byzantine Cross III 38
Byzantine Processional Cross 58

Cable Cross 169
Caddo Solar Cross 183
Calvary Cross I 27
Calvary Cross II 43
Camargue Cross 43
Canterbury Cross I 187
Canterbury Cross II 187
Capital Cross I 165
Capital Cross II 189
Caravaca Cross 65
Celtic Cross I 176
Celtic Cross II 177
Celtic Cross III 182
Celtic Cross IV 182
Celtic Cross V 182
Celtic Cross VI 183
Celtic Cross VII 190
Cercelée Cross 124
Cercely Cross 102
Cerdeńa Cross 171
Chain Cross 51
Champaine Cross 131, 140
Checky Cross 87
Checky Saltier Cross 199
Chi Rho Cross I 31
Chi Rho Cross II 32
Chi Rho Cross III 179
Chi Rho Cross IV 193
Chi Rho Cross V 193
Chi Rho Cross VI 194
Chrismon 31-32, 179, 193-94
Clechée Cross I 163
Clechée Cross II 164
Cleves Cross I 74
Cleves' Cross II 178
Cleves Cross III 202
Compony Cross 86
Compony-Counter-Compony Saltier Cross 199
Conjoined Cross 85
Conqueror's Cross 85

Constantine's Cross 31-32, 179, 193-94
Constantine's Labarum 179
Coptic Cross 30-31
Coptic Cross I 38
Coptic Cross II 39
Coptic Cross III 39
Coptic Cross IV 39
Coptic Cross V 92
Coptic Cross VI 92
Coptic Cross VI 93
Coptic Cross VIII 93
Coptic Cross IX 93
Coptic Cross X 94
Coptic Cross XI 94
Coptic Cross XII 203
Coptic Cross XIII 203
Coptic Processional Cross 56
Coronated Cross 164
Coronel Cross 138
Cossack Cross 108
Cottised Cross 100
Couped Fitchy Fusil Cross 81
Cowherder's Cross 43
Cramponned Cross 196
Crenel Cross 129
Crescent Cross 50, 161
Croissant Cross 161
Croix Aiguisée 131, 140
Croix Ancre 123-24
Croix Anillée 41
Croix à cinq bras 205
Croix Botonnée 34
Croix Bourdonnée 101, 134
Croix Cablée 169
Croix Capiteau 165, 189
Croix Cercelée 102
Croix Commissée 19
Crois Paté Convexed 188
Croix Croisée 89
Croix Croissant 50
Croix Cromponnée 132, 160
Croix Coticée 100
Croix Dancetté 166-67
Croix Delphitée 205
Croix de Fourchette 134
Croix Demembré 84
Croix du Chevaliers du Saint-Esprit 147
Croix Echequetée 87
Croix Ecotée 173
Croix Emanchée 166-67
Croix Engrélée 169
Croix Engrélée Saltier 197
Croix Engreslée 169
Croix Equipollée 84
Croix Erminée 122
Croix Estoilée 112-13
Croix Fer-de-moline 41
Croix Fiché 80
Croix Fleur-de-lys 136
Croix Fleurée 74
Croix Fleurée Engrélée 169
Croix Fouché 134
Croix Fourché 42
Croix Frettée 195
Croix Fruitagée 120
Croix Gringolée 118
Croix Guivrée 118
Croix Gyronnée 86
Crux Militia Jesus Christi 136
Croix Molinée 41
Crois Paté Convexed 178
Croix Patté Fichée 79
Croix Pheonée 129
Croix Pommée 33, 101
Croix Ragulée 173
Croix Recercelée 102, 124
Croix Recercellée 41-42, 102, 124
Croix Recercellé 41-42, 102
Croix Sarcellée 34
Croix Savoie 171
Croix Tau Fitchée 23
Croix Tournée 132, 160
Croix Trèfle 121
Croix Trépflée 34, 101
Croix Tréfflée Fichée 80
Croix Vairé 87
Croix Vidée 163
Cronel Cross 138
Cross Cramponned 151, 159
Cross Crosslet 89, 192
Cross Crosslet Double Fitched of all Four Rebated 130
Cross Crosslet Crossed I 72, 91
Cross Crosslet Crossed II 91
Cross Crosslet Crossly 91
Cross Crosslet Double Crossed 91
Cross Crosslet Humilis 40
Cross Damaḍon 132
Cross Double Crossed 91
Cross Enhendee 110
Cross of Pheons 129
Cross of Suffering 51
Cross of Suffering 162
Cross of the Fathers 71
Cross Patonce 110
Cross Pattee Fleuron 110
Cross Potent Cross 130
Cross Potent Crossed 165
Crosslet Fitchy Cross I 80
Crosslet Fitchy Cross II 80
Crosslet Flory Saltier Cross 195
Crown and Cross 49
Crusader's Cross 115-17
Crusader Kingdom of Jerusalem Cross 115-16
Crux Cannelée 167
Crux Capitata 25
Crux Commissa 20, 23
Crux Decussata 191-92
Crux Denchée 167
Crux Dissimulata 151, 159
Crux Flamant 113-14
Crux Gemina 60, 63-64, 67
Crux Gammadion 151, 159
Crux Gemina Fitchée 69
Crux Gammata 159
Crux Gemmata I 52, 151
Crux Gemmata II 173
Crux Hasta 56
Crux Humilis 25
Crux Immissa 25

Crux Immissa Quadrata 83
Crux Invertere 26
Crux Invincta 57
Crux Lauburu 158
Crux Mogen Dovid 205
Crux Ordinaria 26
Crux Simplex 19
Crux Stellata 113
Crux Sublimis 25
Crux Suppedaneum 61, 71
Crux Taumata 19

Damascus Cross 132
Dancetty Cross I 166
Dancetty Cross II 167
Danneborg Cross 204
de Gaulle Cross 63-64
Delfity Cross 205
Demi Annuly Cross 174
Demi Annuly Inverted Cross 174
Demi Fleur-de-lys Cottised Cross 174
Demisarcel Cross 133
Dharma Wheel 184
Dismas Cross 20-21
Dismembered Cross 84
Dolphin Cross 51
Double Avellaney Cross 120
Double Claved Cross 166
Double Clavied Cross 166
Double Fruitage Cross 120
Double Fitch Cross I 139
Double Fiché Cross 139
Double Fichée Cross II 139
Double Fichée Cross III 139
Double Fitched and Rebated Cross 133
Double Fitchy Quartered Cross 140
Double Parted Fleury Cross 175
Double Potent Cross 129, 165
Double-span Cross 29
Dovetail Cross 168
Dymock Cross 133

Earth Cross 83
Eastern Cross 71
Eastern Orthodox Cross I 71
Eastern Orthodox Cross II 71
Egyptian Cross 20, 23
Eight-point Cross 145-46
Embattled Cross 130
Emousée Cross 26, 172
ṃmoussé Patriarchal Cross 62
Empty Cross 49
Endented Cross 143
Engrailed Cross 169
Engrailed Saltier Cross 197
Enhendée Cross I 69
Enhendée Cross II 75
Entrailed Cross 104
Episcopal Saltier Cross 194
Ermine Cross 122
Ermine Cross Saltier 198
Escarbouche Cross 202
Eternal Cross 48
Ethipoian Cross 38, 92-93
Ethiopean Processional Cross 59
Everlasting Cross 55
Exeter Cross 196

Fimbriated Cross 25, 99
Finnish Liberty Cross 156
Fishtail Cross 145-46
Fitchy at All Points Cross 112, 141
Fitchy at All Points & Quartered Cross 142
Fitchy at All Points & Quarter Pierced Cross 142
Fitchy-foote Cross 77
Fitchy-Footed Cross 77
Fitchy Foot at All Points Cross 142
Fitchy of Four Cross 138
Five Armed Cross 205
Fivefold Cross 115-16, 178
Fixed Cross 77
Flag Cross 204
Flaming Cross I 113
Flaming Cross II 114
Fleur-de-lys Cross 75
Fleur-de-lys Saltier Cross 197
Fleurette Cross 75
Fleuronny Cross 74
Fleury Cross 74
Fleury Fitchée 144
Floretty Cross 74
Flory Cross 74
Flory Engrailed Cross 169
Flory Fitch Cross 78
Forked Cross 42, 126
Formée Cross 108-09
Fouchy Cross 134
Fourché Cross I 126
Fourché Cross II 126
Fourchette Cross 37
Fourchy Cross 42
Fracted Cross 83
Franciscan Custody of the Holy Land Cross 115-16, 178
Free French Cross 63-64
Fretty Cross 195
Fruitagee Cross 120
Furka Cross 20
Fusils Cross I 130
Fusils Cross II 131
Fylfot Cross 99-100

Gamma Cross 100
Gammadia Cross 99-100
Gammadia Cross I 99
Georgia's Cross 117
Globus Cruciger I 180
Globus Cruciger II 181
Glory Cross 49
Gnostic Cross 176
Gobony Cross 83, 86
Golden Dawn Rose Cross 50
Golgatha Cross 185
Golpy Cross 180
Goshavank Cross 44
Graded Cross 27, 85
Gradey Cross 85
Greek Cross 83
Greek Cross Fichy 140

Greek Flyfot Cross 154
Gringolee Cross 118
Groupe Union Droit Cross 190
Gungnir Cross 192
Gurgity Cross 152
Gyronny Cross 86

Half Annulet Cross 174
Half Annulet Inverted Cross 174
Hameḍon Cross 126
Hammer Cross 21
Hand Held Cross 35
Handled Cross 30
Hasta Cross 56
Heytesbury Cross 43
High Cross 176
Hirosaki Flyfot Cross 155
Holy Cross 27
Holy Rood 25
Hooked Cross 151, 159
Horizontal Cross 204
Hovingham Cross 171
Huguenot Cross 146
Humetty Cross Ringed 104-05
Humetty Pointed Cross 162

IHS Cross 48
Iberian Cross 136
Indented Cross 167
Indian Cross 151, 159
Infinity Cross 55
Interlaced Cross 96
Invected Cross 167
Iona Cross 176
Ionic Cross 177
Irish Cross 176
Irminsu Cross 22
Iron Cross 109

Jerusalem Cross I 115
Jerusalem Cross II 115
Jerusalem Cross III 116, 178
Jeweled Cross 173
Joalf's Cross 182
Jumis Cross 193

Khachkar Cross 44
Knights Hospitalier Cross 145-46
Knights of Christ's Cross I 131
Knights of Christ's Cross II 132
Knights of Jerusalem Cross 115-16, 178
Knights of the Grand Cross 69
Knights Templar Cross 109
Knotted Cross 95
Kuna Flyfot Cross 153

Labarum 31-32, 179, 193-94
Lambeau Cross 27, 168
Lambeauxed Cross 166
Lamen Cross 50
Languedoc Cross 45, 107
Languedoc Cross I 106
Languedoc Cross II 106
Languedoc Cross III 106
Latin Cross 25
Latin Cross Flory 74
Latin Cross Potent 40
Latin Cross Voided 25
Lauburu Cross 158
Lazarus' Cross I 103
Lazarus' Cross II 103, 188
Lebanese Forces Cross 206
Leo XIII Processional Cross 58
Lietuvis Kryzius 29
Lithuanian Cross 29, 127
Long Cross Felloe 66
Looped Cross 96
Looped Tau Cross 30-31
Lorraine Cross 61
Lorraine Cross I 63
Lorraine Cross II 63
Lorraine Cross III 63
Lorraine Cross IV 64
Lorraine Cross V 64
Lorraine Cross VI 73
Lorraine Cross (with hook) 66
Lothringian Cross 63, 201
Lozengy Cross 130-31
Lozengy Nowyed Cross 163
Lunate Cross 50, 161

Maltese Cross 108
Maltese Cross I 145
Maltese Cross II 145
Maltese Cross III 146
Maltese Cross IV 146
Maltese Cross V 149
Maltese Knight's of Bath Cross 147
Mandeville Cross 202
Manichean Cross 43
Manji Cross I 157
Manji Cross II 158
Manx Cross I 38
Manx Cross II 182
Manx Cross III 182
Manx Cross IV 182
Manx Cross V, 183
Marian Cross 89
Marian Cross I 48
Marian Cross II 206
Mariner's Cross 65
Maronite's Cross 70-71
Mar Thoma Cross 43, 173
Martin Luther Cross 52
Masclée Cross 98, 164
Masculy Cross I 98
Masculy Cross II 164
Masculy Interlaced Cross 98
Masonic Teutonic Cross 90
Midsommarstang Cross 53
Military Order of St. James of the Sword 78-79
Miller Rebated Cross 42
Miller's Cross 42, 125
Miller Rebated Cross 126
Mill-iron Cross 125
Millrind Cross 125
Milrine Cross 41
Milrine Cross I 125
Milrine Cross II 125
Milrine Cross III 125
Missionary Cross 192
Moline Cross 41, 125
Moline Nowy Masculy Cross 128

Moline Pierced Lozengy Cross 128
Moline Saltier Cross 198
Moline Voided Cross 41
Moon Cross 50
Moussué Cross I 26
Moussué Cross II 172

Narbonne Cross 61
Natal Cross 49
Nativity Cross 49
Nazrani Cross 43, 173
Nebulée Cross I 170
Nebulée Cross II 170
Nebuly Cross 170
Neronic Cross 28, 48
Nero's Cross 28
Nestorian Cross 121
Nordic Cross 204
Norse Solar Cross I 159
Norse Solar Cross II 186
Nowy Cross I 179
Nowy Cross II 179
Nowy Lozengy Cross 163
Nowy Masculy Cross 96
Nowy Quadrate Cross 163

Obelus Cross I 53
Obelus Cross II 54
Obelus Fitchy Cross I 82
Obelus Fitchy Cross II 82
Occident Cross 190
Occitan Cross I 106
Occitan Cross II 106
Occitan Cross III 106
Occitan Cross IV 45, 107
Odin's Cross 159, 176, 181
Off-centred Cross 204
Ogressy Cross 180
Old Testament Cross 19
Ondée Cross 158
Orb Cross 180-81
Orden de Santiago de Espada Cross 78-79
Order of Alcantara Cross I 135
Order of Alcantara Cross II 135
Order of Avis' Cross 136
Order of Calatrava's Cross I 136
Order of Calatrava's Cross II 137
Order of Christ Cross 131
Orden de Milica Cross 136
Order of Montessa Cross 137
Orden Nova Cross 136
Order of St. James Cross I 78
Order of St. James Cross II 78
Order of St. James Cross III 78
Order of St. James Cross IV 79
Order of St. John of Jerusalem of Rhodes and of Malta Cross 145-46
Order of St. Lazarus of Jerusalem Cross I 148
Order of St. Lazarus of Jerusalem Cross II 148
Order of St. Lazarus of Jerusalem Cross III 204
Order of Santo Domingo's Cross 136
Order of Sint Jacob Cross 77
Order of the Cross of Liberty 156
Order of the Holy Sepulchre Cross 80
Order of the Holy Spirit Cross 147
Osmorog Cross 162

Pall Cross 22, 126
Palm Cross 206
Pandal Cross 172
Papal Cross I 70
Papal Cross II 70
Papal Cross III 71
Passion Cross 51, 162
Paternoster Cross 170
Patriarchal Charged and Voided Cross 68
Patriarchal Cross I 60
Patriarchal Cross II 61
Patriarchal Cross III 61
Patriarchal Cross IV 61
Patriarchal Cross V 67
Patriarchal Cross Fitchy 69
Patriarchal Paté Cross 67
Patriarchal Paté Conjoined & Annulated Cross 68
Patriarchal Paté Fleury Cross 67
Patriarchal Pommeté Cross 68
Patriarch Cross 70-71
Partée Double Cross 97
Partée Double and Fretted Cross 97
Pate Cross 108-09
Paté Cross 108-09
Paté Circuled Cross 184, 188
Paté Convexed Cross 184, 188
Paté Fitchy Cross 143
Paté Globical Cross 184, 188
Patee Cross 108-09
Patée Cross 108-09
Patonce Pattée Cross I 110
Patonce Pattée Cross II 110
Patonce Pattée Cross III 110
Pattee Cross 108-09
Pattée Cross I 108
Pattée Cross II 108
Pattée Cross III 109
Pattée Cross IV 109
Pattée Double Fitchée Cross 81
Pattée Fitchée Cross I 79
Pattée Fitchée Cross II 79
Pattée Fitchée Rebated Cross 81
Pattée Fitchy Foot Cross 79
Pattée Fitchy Disjointed Cross 143
Pattée Notched Cross 133
Pattée Patriarch Cross 62
Pattée Quadrate Cross 111
Paty Cross 108-09
Paty Fitchy Foot Rebated Cross 81
Pendal Cross 172
Penal Cross 54
Perkons Cross 154
Peronnée Cross 85
Persian Cross 55
Pheon Cross 129
Platy Cross 180
Point in Point Cross 88

Pointed Cross 51, 162
Polish Medieval Processional Cross 58
Pommelly Cross 101, 134
Pommée Cross 134
Pommée Cross I 33
Pommée Cross II 33
Pommée Cross III 101
Pommée Cross IV 102
Pommelly Cross 101
Pompeiian Cross 207
Pomy Cross 33
Pope's Cross 28
Portale Cross 26, 54
Portate Cross 26, 54
Portate Patriarchal Cross 67
Potency Cross 87
Potent Cross 87, 89
Potent Cross Humilis 40
Potent Quadrate Cross 172
Potent Rebated Cross 152
Potent-repotent Cross 152
Potent-repotent in Four points Cross 152
Potent Sunwise Flyfot 152
Potency Cross 87
Potenty Cross 87
Presbyterian Cross 181
Protestant Cross 25

Quad Fitchy Cross 138
Quadrate Cross 163
Quatrefoil Cross 122
Quarter Cross 86
Quarter Pierced Cross I 84
Quarter Pierced Cross II 84
Quarter-voided Cross 84
Quatrefoil Cross 122
Quad Fitchy Cross 138

Ragged Tau Cross 22
Ragulée Cross 168
Rouchy Cross 162
Raguly Cross 173
Raguly Tau Cross 22
Ragulated Cross 173
Ragulated Tau Cross 22
Ragulée Cross 168
Rebated Cross Potent 151, 159
Rebated Lambeau Cross 66
Recercele Cross 42, 124
Recercely Cross 124
Recersile Cross 102
Regeneration Cross 108
Resarcelled Cross 102
Recercelée Cross 42, 102
Recercelée Cross I 42
Recercelée Cross II 42
Recercely Cross 42
Recercely Saltier Cross 197
Recersile Cross 102
Regeneration Cross 145-46
Rhodes Flyfot Cross 153
Rogacina Cross 21
Rogacina Dwukrotnie Przekrzyzowana Cross 72
Rogacina Przekrzyzowana Cross 64
Rogacina Przekrzyzowana i Rozdarta Cross 72
Rolleston-on-Dove Cross 185
Roman Cross 48
Roman Sacred Cross 98
Rood Cross I 34
Rood Cross II 40
Rope Cross I 46
Rope Cross II 46
Rope Cross III 46
Rose Cross 35
Rose Cross 52
Rosicrucian Cross 50
Rosicrucian Cross I 35
Rosicrucian Cross II 52
Rousset Cross 140
Rune Cross 91
Russian Cross 71
Russian Grand Priory of the Knights of St. John of Jerusalem Cross 149
Russian Knights of St. John of Jerusalem Cross 147
Russian Orthodox Cross 35

Sacrifice Cross 76
St. Andrew's Cross I 191
St. Andrew's Cross II 191
St. Andrew's Cross III 192
St. Anthony's Cross 20, 23
St. Boniface Cross 48
St Brendon's Cross 51
St. Bride's Cross 95
St. Bridgit's Cross 95
St. Brighid's Cross 95
St. Chad's Cross I 90
St. Chad's Cross II 116
St. Chad's Cross III 116
St. Clement's Cross 65
St. Columba's Cross 177
St. Cuthbert's Cross 190
St. George's Cross 83
St. Gilbert's Cross I 26
St. Gilbert's Cross II 54
St. Hans Cross 203
St. James Cross 78, 144
St. John of Jerusalem's Cross 145-46
St. John's Cross 108, 145, 176
St. Lazarus Cross 83
St. Nicholas Cross, 62
St. Nino Cross 27
St. Olga's Cross 62
St. Peter's Cross 26
St. Thomas Cross I 43
St. Thomas Cross II 173
Saltier Cross 191-92
Saltier Counter Embattled Cross 200
Saltier Raguly Cross 195
Saltiered Cross 85
Sarcelée Cross III 102
Sarcellee Cross 34
Sarcelly Cross 34, 102, 124
Sarcelly Disjointed Cross 99
Sator Cross 207
Savoy Cross 171

Saxon Cross 33
Saxon Cross II 171
Saxon Cross III 184, 188
Saxon Cross IV 184
Saxon Cross V 185
Saxon Cross VI 185
Saxon Cross VII 196
Scandinavian Cross 204
Serbian Cross 102
Serbian Processional Cross 57
Shepherd's Cross 32
Shrouded Cross 49
Siroun Cross 44
Sixteen-point Cross 138
Skull & Crossbones with Cross 50
Slavic Cross 71
Slavonic Cross 35
Slipped Cross 118
Snowflake Cross I 53
Snowflake Cross II 90
Solar Cross 176-77
Solomon's Knot I 95
Solomon's Knot II 200
Spanish Military Cross 204
Spear of Odin 192
Spindle Cross 172
Square-pierced Cross 84
Star Cross 141
Star Cross I 112
Star Cross II 112
Star Cross III 113
Star Cross IV 113
Star Cross V 205
Stepped Cross 27, 85
Sun Cross 183, 188
Sundolf's Cross 38
Sun Wheel Cross 176
Sunwise Fylfot Cross 151, 159
Sunwise Fylfot Solar Cross 157
Swallow Tail Cross 122
Swarog Circle Cross, 188
Svastika 159
Swiss Solar Cross I 186
Swiss Solar Cross II 186
Swiss Solar Cross III 187
Sword of Odin 192

Taranis Cross 184, 190
Taranis Wheel Cross 176, 184
Tau Cross I 19
Tau Cross II 20
Tau Cross Fitchy 23
Templars' Cross 132, 188
Teutonic Cross I 40
Teutonic Cross II 89
Teutonic Cross III 89
Teutonic Cross IV 165
Teutonic Order Cross 165
Thieves' Cross I 20
Thieves' Cross II 20
Thieves' Cross III 21
Thieves' Cross IV 28
Third Positionist Cross 190
Thor's Cross 76, 190
Thor's Hammer 76
Thunder Cross 154
Thurith's Cross 183
Titulus Cross 60
Toisa's Cross 196
Torty Cross 180
Toulouse Cross 45, 107
Toulouse Cross I 106
Toulouse Cross II 106
Trefly Cross 121
Trefoil Cross 101
Trefoil Fitchy Cross 80
Trianguly Cross 168
Triple Fitch Cross 93, 138
Triple Parted Cross 97
Triple Parted and Fretted Cross 98
Triumphant Cross 180
Tronconnée Cross 84
Tursaansydan Cross I 155
Tursaansydan Cross II 156

Ukraine Cross 71
Ukranian Kyiv (Kiev) Cross 53, 90
Urdée Cross 51, 162
Urdée Cross I 131
Urdée Cross II 140
Urdy Cross 131, 140

Vair-Bells Cross 161
Vairy Cross 87, 161
Vairy Cross Saltier 198
Valencia Cross 136-37
Vatican Papal Cross 194
Venerable Order of St. John Cross 149
Verdy Cross 131, 140, 162
Very Cross 87, 161
Victor's Cross 85
Victory Cross 57
Viking Sunwise Fylfot Cross 157
Voided Cross 99
Voided & Disjointed Milrine Cross 127
Voided Champaine Cross 141
Voided Milrine Cross 127
Voided or Bordered Maltese Cross 148
Voided Urdé Cross 141
Voided Urdy Cross 141
Voided Verdy Cross 141

Wahl Cross 205
Wavy Cross 158
Western Cross 25
Wheel Cross 185
White Cross 25
White Nationalist Cross 190
Wind Cross 83
Widdershins Fylfot Cross 151
Widdershins Fylfot Solar Cross 156
Woden's Cross 159, 176, 186
Wolf Cross 159

"Y" Cross 20

Zierscheiben Widdershin Flyfot Cross 160
Zurich Cross 65

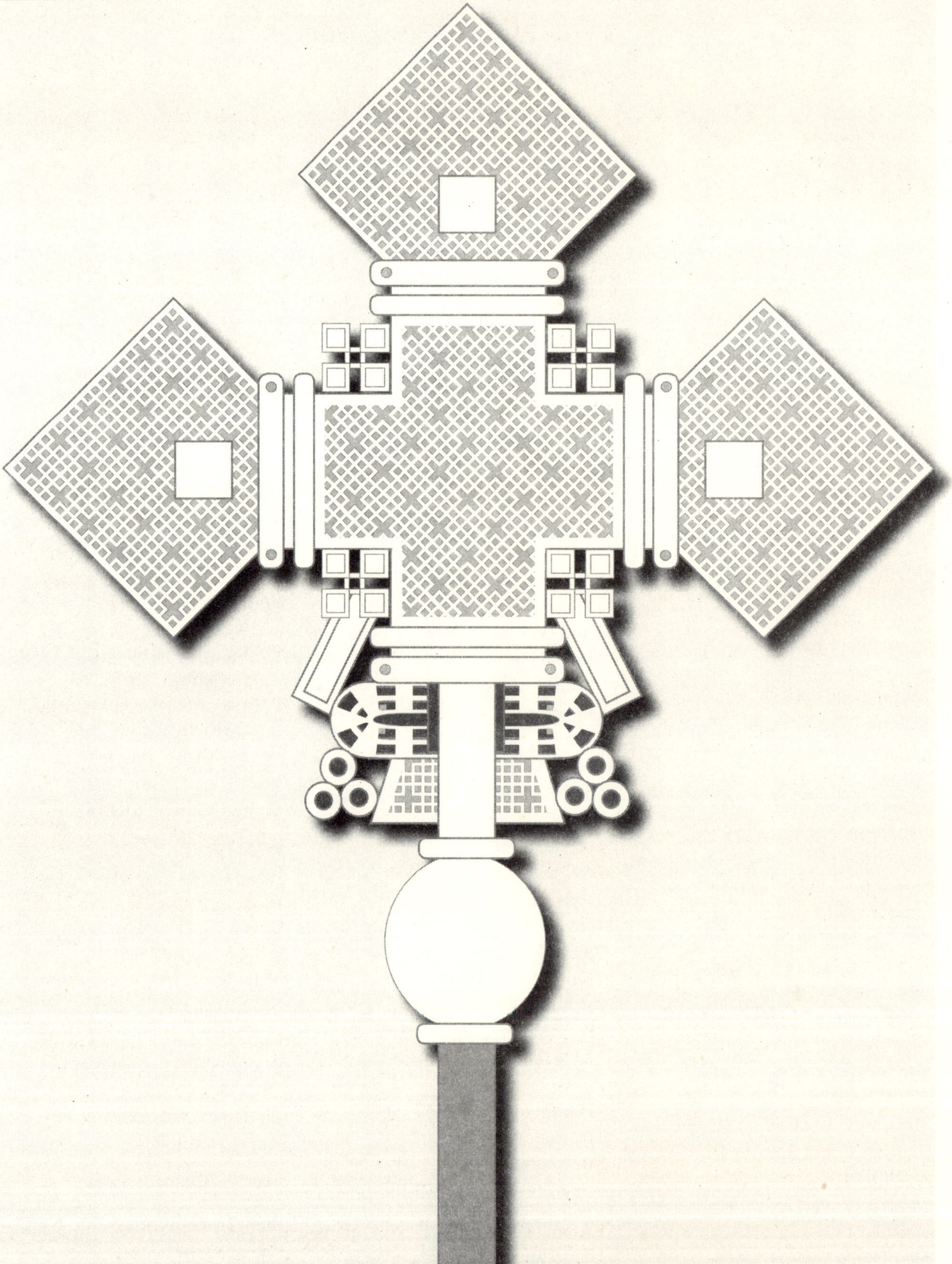

Note: The cruciform that appears above and throughout this work is an example of an elaborate, filigree, processional Coptic Cross from Ethiopia.